MW01012950

STREETWISE

RELATIONSHIP MARKETING ON THE INTERNET

STREETWISE

RELATIONSHIP MARKETING ON THE INTERNET

Create One on One
Bonds with Prospects
and Customers and
Keep Them Forever

by Roger C. Parker

Adams Media Corporation
Holbrook, Massachusetts

Acknowledgments

Although an an author's name appears alone on the cover of a book, books are really the result of team efforts.

Major players deserving recognition for their heroic efforts in this book include Jere Calmes, Acquisitions Editor at Adams Media who never lost faith and was a constant source of motivation and inspiration, his assistant Dawn Thompson who helped (this is you, Dawn), pull together so many of the pieces, John Knapp of www.howzone.com who's knowledge of the technical aspects of the web contributed so much to this book, and, as usual, my loyal and supportive wife Betsy.

All authors are also indebted to their agent who helps assemble and coordinate the team, in my case Margot Maley Hutchinson of Waterside Productions.

Published by Adams Media Corporation
260 Center Street, Holbrook, MA 02343. U.S.A.
www.adamsmedia.com

ISBN: 1-58062-255-0

Printed in the United States of America.

J I H G F E D C B A

Library of Congress Cataloging-in-Publication data
available upon request from publisher.

This publication is designed to provide accurate and authoritative information with regard to the subject matter covered. It is sold with the understanding that the publisher is not engaged in rendering legal, accounting, or other professional advice. If legal advice or other expert assistance is required, the services of a competent professional person should be sought.
— From a *Declaration of Principles* jointly adopted by a Committee of the American Bar Association and a Committee of Publishers and Associations

Cover illustration by Eric Mueller.

This book is available at quantity discounts for bulk purchases.
For information, call 1-800-872-5627.

Visit our exciting small business Web site: www.businesstown.com

CONTENTS

SECTION I: AN INTRODUCTION TO BUSINESS ON THE WEB

SECTION II: FIVE STEPS TO A SUCCESSFUL RELATIONSHIP MARKETING INITIATIVE

SECTION III: BUILDING A RELATIONSHIP-ORIENTED WEB SITE

FOREWORD

The Web is a unique communication tool, using it skillfully will directly affect the future of your business. Roger Parker tells you how to effectively make your business profitable online using a step-by-step Customer Development Cycle™ of Introduction, Comparison, Transaction, Reinforcement and Advocacy. You can build lasting alliances with your customers by incorporating this five-stage relationship marketing program into your online business development plan. It will give you the framework you need to personalize your Web site, basing it on your customers' relationship with your business.

As a business professional, you need to know how the Web fits into your business to meet your customers' needs and expectations. This book can show you the way. Whether you're building the site yourself or getting help from an outside consultant, you'll be prepared with the knowledge you need to make intelligent decisions about your online business.

The idea of creating information premiums is a prefect example of how Parker integrates seasoned marketing concepts and Web technology, explaining how to generate a perception of 'value' for the information you offer on your site. He offers a method for figuring out what information is important and why. He also includes a worksheet that helps you determine your information incentives and then he tells you how to electronically distribute those incentives.

This book is chock full of ideas and tools that can help you use the Web to its fullest capacity in your business. But the most important thing that you'll learn is how crucial meeting your customers' needs and expectations really is to the success of your site. This is clearly evident in the chapter *"Determining your market's information needs,"* where you'll learn the significance of meaningful content.

> ". . . Information forms the heart and soul of Web site success. To succeed, you must provide, and continue to provide, meaningful content—information that will help turn prospects into customers, customers into repeat customers and repeat customers into ambassadors. . . ."

It really all boils down to finding the perfect fit between information your target market wants or needs and information that supports your business' marketing goals. Taking an information-driven view of Web site design guarantees that the information on your site will be meaningful to your customers.

This book describes several approaches you might take in figuring out how to provide meaningful content on your site: Intuition, Historical, Goal-driven, Competitor, Analytical, and Partnership. These approaches can help you determine your customers' information needs, your marketing goals, what your competition is doing, the amount of traffic on your site and what your customers think about your site.

After you figure out how to give your customers meaningful content, Parker explains how to separate *information* from *design*. Information development demands a systematic approach at each stage of your relationship marketing program within the Customer Development Cycle™. Case studies demonstrate how this is done.

Along with case studies, you'll find information on how to put the ideas in this book to work. This is one of the most valuable elements in Roger Parker's book. Parker actually shows you how to implement his ideas in the real world.

Roger Parker has skillfully woven his years of business experience, entrepreneurial savvy and knowledge of the Web into a no-nonsense approach for success on the Web.

Lynne Duddy
Senior Information Architect
Agency.Com
Portland, Oregon
March 2000

Why do most Web sites fail? I'll tell you why. Because the people behind have swallowed the hype hook, line and sinker. Because people believe that Web sites are static billboards for your company, instead of realizing that the interactivity of the Web is what makes them special. Because your CEO believes your company is so special that people will find you, instead of you having to go out and actually drag people in. Because the siren song of splashy marketing is so much more appealing than the hard and dusty work of building relationships one at a time.

In this brilliantly simple book, Roger Parker has taken the guesswork out of figuring out what to do next. He's painstakingly outlined all the steps (and some of them look SO simple) that you probably skipped the first or second or third time you built that expensive, flashy site of yours.

I don't think there's a company online, from Yahoo! to Buzz Gantry's Bait Shop, that can't benefit from the advice in this book. No matter what you sell, no matter why you are online, there's a big pile of great ideas inside this book, just waiting for you.

So here, in your hands, if you want it, is the secret to succeeding online. And of course, if you don't have the time to do it right, when are you going to find the time to do it over?

Seth Godin
Author
Permission Marketing
free@permission.com

Introduction

It's hard to pick up a newspaper, turn on a televised news program, or listen to the financial news on the radio without hearing about the latest overnight Internet success stories. Hardly a day goes by without a headline story describing the latest overnight millionaires created by an initial public offering of a new Internet stock, creating a category of product or service that was unknown a day earlier.

The nation's news media has been so fixated on overnight Internet and e-commerce success stores that it has ignored coverage of what's realistic for most businesses. This emphasis on the success of Amazon, eBay, and various "business-to-consumer" (delivery of gardening supplies, groceries, and pharmaceuticals) and "do-it-yourself" investment Web sites that it has had the unfortunate effect of blinding most businesses to the relatively unglamorous, but far more realistic and attainable, ways the Web can be used to help most businesses improve their profitability.

The "Web Success Stories of the Day" typically ignore the following realities that characterize most existing businesses:

- Most businesses serve a geographically limited, often face-to-face market. Their market consists of customers and prospects who either visit their office or store or meet only occasionally at client offices.
- The budgetary, time, and talent resources of most existing businesses are often limited compared to business start-ups funded by millions of dollars of investment capital.
- Most existing businesses are established and profitable—or they wouldn't be in business. This is in contrast to most Web start-ups, which are cash-flush from public and private investors but are rarely profitable the first years. Overnight success stories are the exception rather than the rule.

What This Book Is and Isn't

This is a "bridge" book. The goal is to bridge the gap between the latest relationship marketing theories and short-term and long-term strategies for the Web. This book will also detail the specific steps you can take to develop and implement a successful five-step Web initiative. It's one thing to read and get excited about theories like one-to-one marketing that are often written from the perspective of multimillion dollar firms with multimillion dollar Web budgets; it's another to apply the lessons and philosophies to your own business.

Case Studies

This book uses the case study approach to show how the techniques of relationship marketing can be applied to your business. The case studies also illustrate a successful Web initiative. The goal is to drive home the importance of identifying the information needs of your market at each stage of the relationship cycle and satisfying these needs. The case studies include:

- whale watch operator
- professional practice (oral surgeon)
- French restaurant
- outdoor clothing retailer
- electronics distributor
- accountant
- financial planner
- art gallery
- day care center
- realtor
- graphic designer

Most Web Sites Fail

The short-term goal is to help you avoid the mistakes that others have made when producing a Web site. The long-term goal is to help you take a realistic look at ways the Web might transform your business.

My goal is to provide a realistic perspective on the Web that is difficult to achieve because of the media's preoccupation with Web matters. It's hard to maintain a realistic perspective when just about every day the morning newspaper profiles another twenty-year-old Web millionaire, and the prices of Web stocks appear in ticker-tape fashion along the bottom of the television screens on every health club exercise room in America.

Yes, the Web continues to occupy an exponentially growing role in CD (customer direct) and B-to-B (business to business) marketing; Web stocks are hot, and every day the Web creates a new cadre of millionaires whose companies have never earned a cent of profit. And it is entirely conceivable that, in five years, your business may be completely different.

Yet, before you can jump to the future you have to succeed in the present. And that's what this book is all about: planning a Web initiative that will satisfy both short-term and long-term objectives.

A Web initiative is more than a just Web site. Your Web site is just part of the equation. A successful Web initiative is based on information. Success comes from identifying your market's information needs and satisfying them on an ongoing basis—with the emphasis on "ongoing." This requires addressing sticky issues, like "Who's going to prepare and package the information?" and "How's it going to be distributed in a timely fashion?"

A successful Web initiative involves more than hiring a design firm or purchasing the latest software program and doing the work yourself. A successful Web initiative involves technology issues like database management and e-mail. You need to establish a database that—in the short term—permits you to keep Web site visitors "in the loop" and—in the long term—integrates Web site visitors with customers and prospects you deal with on a face-to-face basis.

E-mail is an essential part of a successful Web initiative. E-mail to qualified prospects, Web site visitors who have asked to be kept informed, is both free and highly effective. E-mail maintains your firm's visibility (or mindshare) and can drive visitors to your Web site. But to succeed, e-mail requires information (as contrasted to brag-and-boast advertising claims).

The most exciting part of this whole process is that creating a successful Web initiative forces you back to basics. It forces you to take a new look at your business, your customers, and the products or services that you provide. A Web initiative, in short, forces you back to marketing. Not "Java," not "cool" or "killer designs," but back to the basic questions:

- What business are we in?
- Who are our customers?
- What do they want that we can profitably provide?
- What information do they require?

You may have initially purchased this book because you need to create an effective Web site. But, one year or two years down the road, you may end up finding that this book has helped you smoothly transform your business into something totally different. You may be in the same business, but operating far more efficiently and profitably. Or, you may have painlessly expanded into new areas without jeopardizing or sacrificing your core expertise.

Welcome to the new world—where the latest technology is used, not for its own sake, but to help you satisfy more customers more efficiently than ever before. The Web is not magic. The Web simply represents marketing taken to a new level of efficiency.

A Sensible Alternative

Rather than focusing entirely on new opportunities, most businesses would be better off to address the following challenges:

- Existing businesses should focus on ways they can use the Web to maximize the efficiency and profitability of their existing markets, products, and services—those customers and prospects that, ultimately, depend on face-to-face contact. Businesses should first explore how the Web can enhance the efficiency of their current marketing and promotional efforts before exploring new terrain.
- Instead of borrowing millions of dollars, or risk losing control of their company in order to attract investments necessary to develop and promote new Web-based ventures—in

effect starting new businesses from scratch—existing businesses should strive for efficiency, using the Web to build on what they already have at the lowest possible cost. Most businesses should be able to self-fund their Web initiatives by saving money that would otherwise be spent less efficiently or by making additional investments as they reap the benefits of their initial Web efforts.

• Existing profitability should not be sacrificed to develop new Web-based business ventures that may pay off in the future. Businesses should adopt the Web rather than have the Web adopt them.

This is not to say that the Web is not going to transform most businesses. My goal, however, is to inject a note of realism. The Web should be treated as a technology rather than as a magic bullet that can make you rich overnight.

Business Transformation

The Web is going to change your business. That's a given. But that change, if it is going to be a healthy change, has to take place over time. In most cases, it has to take place while existing products and services are being sold and existing markets are being served.

Equally important, in most cases, healthy business transformation has to be self-funded. Self-funded business transformation avoids "robbing Peter to pay Paul," or, in worst cast scenarios, losing control of your business to outside investors. Self-funding also avoids financial overextension that can result in reduced customer service, which inevitably results in lost customers because of poor service. Self-funding also frees the future of your business from the ups and downs of interest rates and the financial markets, which are way beyond your control.

Yes, it may be fun to read about the overnight millionaires of Silicon Valley. But, in the coming months, it will be far more challenging, rewarding, and fun to learn from the Silicon Valley start-ups while using the tools of relationship marketing to build your existing business without taking unnecessary risks or investing the huge amounts of capital it takes to drive visitors to the Web sites of new Internet businesses.

A year or two from now your business may be completely different, or it may be just two-thirds different. But by taking the steps incrementally rather than suddenly, you can enjoy success without risking what you have in order to emulate something others may have.

Relationship Marketing

Relationship marketing is the key. Learn from what others are doing but maintain your focus on how you can use the Web to build closer bonds with your existing customers and prospects. The Web may be a new technology, but that doesn't mean you can't use it as a classic marketing tool to build close, loyal, relationships with your existing customers.

Relationship marketing, as described in this book, involves leveraging your future off of your existing customers and prospects. It begins small, but, like a pebble thrown into the middle of a pond, its ripples reach all the shores.

This book is based on the idea that "one size does not fit all"—all visitors are not alike. Instead, there are five stages, or levels, in the relationship between a business and each of its customers and prospects. These stages usually take place face to face, although the five stages are designed to provide a structure for creating an effective Web site. These stages include:

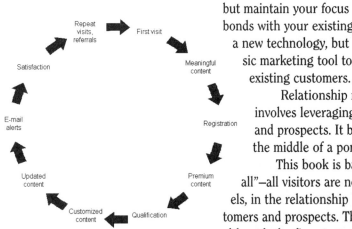

1. *Introduction,* where the business and individual Web site visitors introduce themselves to each other. Ideally, the business explains its products, services, and philosophies, as well as explains the benefits of its offerings.
2. *Comparison* takes place when Web site visitors are closer to a purchase. The comparison stage is where the business attempts to communicate a unique competitive advantage over others selling its products and services. The mutual

exchange of information between business and visitor should continue at this stage as more and more detailed information is exchanged. As visitors qualify themselves by providing information about the products or services they're looking for, the business should be able to provide increasingly detailed information.

3. *Transaction* logically follows comparison, if (and only if) the business has provided the right information. Often, businesses will provide customized or personalized incentives to motivate visitors at the comparison stage to make the commitment to purchase the firm's product or service.

4. *Reinforcement* is the stage that spells the difference between long-term success or failure. At the reinforcement stage, businesses endeavor to create a loyal, repeat customer out of a one-shot transaction. Reselling past customers has long been the secret to the success of most profitable businesses. Businesses should use the Web to reward past customers and encourage them to buy again.

5. *Advocacy* is the final stage, when a business provides customers with the incentives and tools they can use to refer the business to their friends. This creates an ever expanding community of loyal customers.

Who Should Read This Book?

This book is intended for the business owner or manager who is concerned that he or she is being left behind by the Internet revolution and who may be confused by the many books and articles that stress the design and technological aspects of Web site creation. It is for those who want to harness the Web to serve their existing business rather than quitting their job or selling their current business and starting a new business from scratch.

The principles behind *Relationship Marketing on the Internet* are equally valid for business-to-business marketing as well as business-to-consumer marketing. In each case, customer and prospect relationships take place in five steps .

Remember, success is simply a combination of skills, attitudes, and knowledge.

After reading Section 1
you should have a better
idea of what Web
marketing involves and
perhaps be able to identify
some of the reasons your
Web site isn't as productive
as you had hoped.

How This Book Is Organized

This book is divided into six sections:

Section 1: An Introduction to Business on the Web

Chapter 1 provides an overview of how the Web is transforming business and the importance of addressing the Internet, no matter how successful your current business is. Chapter 2 looks at the trends occurring in the Web and outlines some of the additional ways you can incorporate the latest technologies into your Web site. Chapter 3 describes some of the reasons that many businesses have not experienced the Web success they anticipated when they first put up their Web site.

After reading Section 1 you should have a better idea of what Web marketing involves and perhaps be able to identify some of the reasons your Web site isn't as productive as you had hoped.

Section 2: Five Steps to a Successful Relationship Marketing Initiative

Chapter 4 provides an overview of the five stages of the customer development cycle. It also introduces the concepts of open versus premium content and the importance of developing information-based incentives that can be distributed for free via the Web to advance customers along the customer development cycle.

Chapters 5 through 9 describe the five stages of the customer development cycle in detail, outlining what should occur at each stage.

Section 3: Building a Relationship-Oriented Web Site

The chapters in Section 3 are devoted to the tasks needed to implement a five stage relationship marketing program. Chapter 10 emphasizes the importance of viewing your relationship marketing Web site initiative as a process rather than an event. Success will not come overnight. It's important not to attempt too much at once.

Chapters 11 and 12 focus on identifying your market's information needs so you provide the meaningful content that your customers and prospects want when they visit your Web site.

Chapters 13 and 14 are devoted to functional areas like preparing effective e-mail to "drive" customers from level to level of the customer development cycle and promoting your Web site. Chapter 15 is devoted to technical issues that you should be familiar with in order to optimize your Web site's performance, and Chapter 16 reviews the basics of effective Web site design.

Chapter 17 is devoted to scheduling your efforts in establishing a relationship marketing program, with definite objectives for each quarter. This chapter also describes what your business may look like after you've harnessed the Web appropriately using relationship marketing strategies.

Conclusion

After reading this book you will have gained the information you need to create a Web-based relationship marketing program that can, over time, transform your Web site and your business. This book will help you replace the typical "one way" Web site with one that offers customized content for visitors at different stages of the customer development cycle. This book will help you save time and money by optimizing the advantages of color and other technical features that the Web offers.

By following the ideas in this book, you will be able to save money by reducing your marketing expenses. Instead of putting up the costs and delays of producing, printing, and mailing postcards and newsletters, you'll learn how to replace them with e-mail. More important, in the long run, as you concentrate on developing incentives, you'll undoubtedly uncover additional profit opportunities that you can use.

At the end of a year, your existing core business will not only be more profitable, achieved by reducing your marketing costs and doing a better job of customer retention, but you'll be able to identify and begin exploring new profit opportunities, often involving cross-marketing with other, non-competing,

> By following the ideas in this book, you will be able to save money by reducing your marketing expenses.

An Introduction to Business on the Web

Overview of Section I

How the Web is transforming business.
How to incorporate the latest technologies into your Web site.
Why businesses may not experience the Web success they anticipated.

The Web and the Future of Your Business

Always remember that this whole thing was started by a mouse.

—WALT DISNEY

Invented in 1989 as a way for scientists to share research information, the World Wide Web has evolved, almost overnight, to become an indispensable business tool, marketing vehicle, and shopping and entertainment medium all rolled into one. It spans the globe and touches the lives of millions of people every day. It seems everyone you talk to has their own idea of what the Web is good for. Most businesspeople agree that a Web site is a "must have" for their business. The Web is no longer optional. But insofar as the expectations of a business Web site, there is little overall agreement, and since the technology is so new, there is little history to turn to for the answer.

Relationship marketing has emerged, beside the Web, as one of the great buzzwords of our time. The benefits of relationship marketing have been widely chronicled, and many businesses today are working hard to implement the concepts. But relationship marketing, too, is often poorly understood, and it is, understandably, challenging to really know how to implement relationship marketing concepts within the context of ones own business. This book seeks to tie the two grand concepts of the Web and relationship marketing together and to spell out an approach that will be viable for any small business with a product or a service to sell to customers. This book provides the insight that you, the small business owner, will need to harness the Web appropriately, implementing relationship marketing strategies within your business.

> The Web is emerging as an indispensable marketing tool.

The Web is emerging as an indispensable marketing tool. Although traditional forms of marketing and sales will continue to be important parts of our lives for the foreseeable future, the Web will become an increasingly important marketing tool into the new millennium.

Yes, the Web has often been oversold. The media is filled with new overnight millionaires' created by the Web, and Web success stories abound. At times, skepticism can, indeed, be healthy. Yet just because the Web has occasionally been oversold is no reason for you to dismiss its very real advantages.

The Web is likely to have a major impact on your business. The purpose of this book is to provide a framework for you to adopt the Web and adapt your business to the challenges and opportunities the Web offers you—*because things will never be the same again!*

What the Web Offers You

There are three important benefits the Web offers you:

1. **Superior communications**. The Web enhances customers and prospect communications by permitting you to communicate *more information* at *less cost* than ever before possible. More important, this exchange of information can, and—as I constantly emphasize throughout this book—in order to succeed *has to* flow in both directions, i.e., from business to prospect and from prospect to business. Prospect-to-business communications, based on forms and e-mail, are as important as business-to-prospect messages in the form of e-mail and customized content. The Web, in short, replaces monologue with dialog. It's the first media since the face-to-face meeting and telephone call that permits interactive marketing.

2. **Reduced costs**. Not only does the Web permit you to communicate with customers and prospects better than ever before, it eliminates many of the costs that have traditionally been associated with distributing your message. The Web frees you from media, i.e., newspaper and magazine ad costs, as well as the printing and postage costs associated with newsletters and direct mail. The Web also eliminates the expensive production and re-press charges associated with color photographs. *Web production is definitely not free, but your money buys a lot more*. In addition to helping you communicate better, the Web can reduce your costs of doing business—permitting you to be more price competitive. The

> Web transactions cost a fraction of conventional transactions. According to a study released by eMarketer (http://www.emarketer.com), the cost of processing an airline ticket the traditional way is $8.00, on the Web it is $1.00.

Web can help you reduce your costs of producing as well as distributing your products and services

3. **New opportunities**. Superior communications combined with reduced costs offers new opportunities that may transform the way you do business. As you begin to use the Web for more and more purposes, you may find your initial business plan changing as unexpected opportunities present themselves to you. Today, for example, you may own a small store selling fishing supplies to a local market. Tomorrow, you may be find yourself also booking fishing trips to distant locations or selling specialized fishing books, apparel, and artwork to fishing aficionados around the country—*and enjoying your business more than ever before!* In addition, the process of analyzing your business from a Web point of view offers you an opportunity to improve your business by rethinking your current customer communications and relationships.

* Sales at the Barnes & Noble Web site *(http://www.barnesandnoble.com)* are expected to grow from $14 million in 1997 to $100 million during 1998, according to industry analysts.
* A study by Chilton Research Services in October of 1997 indicated that nearly one in four adults uses an online service or navigates the Web. Other studies cite figures approaching 50 percent.
* Growth of Web sales in products like airline tickets has been exponential, growing from 500,000 purchasers to over 2 million people making reservations in 1998.

Because these three advantages are central to all that follows, let's take a closer look at each one.

Superior communications

Start by asking yourself, "What does it take to convince a prospect to buy?" (You'll be asking yourself this question over and

---

How Important Is the Web?

Here are just a few examples of how the Web is transforming the way business is conducted. The growth, in many cases, is exponential.

over again as you prepare your Web site.) Chances are the Web (and e-mail) offers you a better way to convince prospects than any communications medium ever before available. Here are eight ways the Web permits you to do a better job of communicating and convincing.

Color

Color sells because it communicates better. Advertisements that contain color are noticed by more people, read by more people, and remembered by more people. Audiences rate presenters using colored visuals, i.e. slides and overheads, as more convincing and more organized. Color enhances the communicating power of all types of documents by permitting selective emphasis and doing a better job of organizing document contents. Color also does a better job of projecting a marketing image than black and white.

Although advancing technology is reducing the costs associated with printed color, color continues to significantly increase the cost of ads, brochures, and newsletters. Color printing continues to offer an excellent example of economies of scale; the more you print, the less you pay per copy. But, you still have to print a lot of copies to take advantages of per-copy savings.

Color is free, however, on the Web! It costs no more to communicate in color than it does in black and white. This means you can do a better job of communicating and convincing without raising costs.

Photographs

Color photographs do a better job of communicating and convincing than black and white photographs. The disadvantage, however, is that four-color photographs require four-color printing. In addition, prepress production costs of readying four-color photographs for printing can significantly increase your printing costs.

On the Web, however, color photographs are free. Yes, you or the individual creating your Web site have to pay special attention to certain technical limitations, but the added time it takes to prepare color photographs for the Web is insignificant compared to the previous necessity to utilize four-color printing for your document. In addition, color photographs can be as large as desired without

For an ongoing look at the way the Web is changing the way business is conducted, visit sites like http://www.tipworld.com and subscribe to the Internet Business News of the Day e-mail newsletter.

incurring extra costs—although, as noted before, there is a trade-off in the time it takes to download and display the photograph on the visitor's computer.

Space

The Web offers you as much space as you need to communicate your message. There are no arbitrary limitations. Unlike 30-second radio spots, which can only extend 30-seconds, or four-page newsletters that must not become four-and-a-quarter page newsletters, you can include as much information as desired on your Web site. If it takes 10 and pages to describe your latest product or service, you can use 10 pages to describe it.

Flexibility

Once your catalog, newsletter, or price list is printed, it's carved in stone. It's extremely difficult to add or delete products, update prices, or change your recommendations. Any changes make your stock of already-printed copies completely obsolete. Worse, it can take months to prepare, print, and distribute updated information.

The Web replaces inflexibility with flexibility. It takes just seconds to update a Web site. If you run out of your featured product at 5:00 P.M. on a Sunday afternoon, you can update your Web site and substitute a new product by 5:15 P.M.

Movement

Print communications are static. The images do not change. Yet we live in a world of moving images. We're brought up on television and movies. We're used to seeing logos rotate into position, text superimposed over photographs, and multiple images on a television screen (like stock market quotations underneath displays of the current temperature). Print is positively *boring* when compared to the local news broadcasts of even the most provincial television station.

The Web permits you to add movement to your online communication. If it serves an appropriate purpose, you can show how the parts of your product fit together, or the sequence of events that your proposed service can set into motion.

> Print communications are static. The images do not change. Yet we live in a world of moving images.

Sound

You can also add sound and video to your Web site when sound and video will help you do a better job of communicating and convincing. Visitors can listen to your narration as they watch a series of illustrations highlighting your product's superior construction, or you can even include a video film clip showing your product in use.

Around-the-clock access

Not only are banker's hours a thing of the past, our society is turning into a seven-day/twenty-four-hour-a-day society. The Web permits you to interact with customers and prospects whenever they may contact you. Already, many online retailers are finding that the greatest number of their sales occurs late at night, after their stores are closed.

Your Web site permits you to be present, even when you're at home or on vacation.

Interactivity

"Interactive" is a popular buzzword. *What does interactivity mean?*

Interactive refers to the way that the Web responds to the visitor's requests for information as well as the way the Web encourages the creation of a dialog between visitor and advertiser. Let's start by considering two aspects of the Web: sequence and customization.

- *Sequence*. Traditionally, advertising and marketing "broadcasts" identical messages to all magazine readers, radio listeners, or television viewers. Everybody passively encounters the same message in the same sequence. The Web is different, however. The Web is an active media. Visitors to your Web site can go directly to the information they want, avoiding information they're not interested in.
- *Customization*. The Web permits you to create a customizable experience for every visitor. You do this by permitting visitors to pre-qualify themselves by indicating their areas of interest, previous experience, or geographic area and offering

> Interactive refers to the way that the Web responds to the visitor's requests for information as well as the way the Web encourages the creation of a dialog between visitor and advertiser.

every visitor a different experience based on their response. *It's like being able to send a personalized direct-mail catalog to every one of your customers and prospects.* For example, if your firm sells tools and building supplies, on the first page you can ask visitors if they are professional contractors or homeowners. If they respond "homeowner," you can ask them if they are interested in building fine cabinetry as a hobby or are interested in adding a shed to their garage. The Web pages that would then appear would be totally different in each case.

- *Follow-up.* This is another key advantage of interactivity. The Web encourages prospects to quickly and easily contact you, requesting further information or asking questions. Registration forms are an essential part of most Web sites. Registration forms make it easy to create a database of prospect names, postal and e-mail addresses, and other buying information. Information can be automatically added to your prospect database, making it easy to respond to their queries and contact customers in the future.

Low fixed costs

Internet service providers, firms that host Web sites for other businesses, usually have a minimum monthly hosting fee. In most cases, your Web site has to grow extremely large before costs significantly increase.

This is in contrast to print communications. The cost of advertising in print media like magazines is based on the popularity of the publication. The more readers the publication has, the more it will cost you to advertise in it. Likewise, printing, postage, and addressing costs increase as you mail more copies of your catalog or newsletter. It costs more to send 10,001 copies of a newsletter than 10,000 copies. Each additional copy costs more.

On the Web, however, costs are fixed. Once your Web site is up and running, whether it is accessed 10 times a day or 10 times a minute, your costs are likely to remain the same.

> In most cases, your Web site has to grow extremely large before costs significantly increase.

Attention

One of the major ways Web marketing differs from conventional advertising is that visitors to your Web site are there because they want to be. *Your message is the reason visitors are at your Web site,* unlike radio and television advertising, for example, where your message is an interruption to the ballgame or their favorite sitcom. Your message is also more likely to be read and remembered because your Web site visitor's attention is monopolized by the computer monitor—unlike what happens with radio advertising, for example, which is typically encountered while listeners are doing something else—i.e., driving, talking, napping, working, etc. Like a book or magazine article, the Web dominates your prospect's attention.

One of the major ways Web marketing differs from conventional advertising is that visitors to your Web site are there because they want to be.

Popularity

The Web is the result of the proliferation of personal computers in our lives. So complete has this proliferation become that the Web has become a mass media, successfully competing with television—the mass media that best symbolized the era gone by. As the number of people on the Web has increased, the number of people watching television has dropped.

Reduced costs

In addition to reducing communications costs while improving the quality of customer and prospect communications, the Web can help you become more competitive by reducing your cost of doing business. Reducing your cost of doing business, of course, permits you to reduce your selling price and, hence, become more competitive. Here are some of the ways businesses that embrace the Web can reduce costs without sacrificing customer service:

Electronic delivery

More categories of products can be delivered directly over the Internet. This is particularly true if your product involves distributing information. E-mail costs nothing and various technologies permit you to sell information electronically—such as by offering access to password-protected files—rather than printing the information on paper and shipping it. Web-based sales are revolutionizing the airline and banking industries, and more computer software is being sold this way.

A significant amount of music is already distributed over the Web instead of being sold in local music stores. Books will soon follow, either read on screen or printed out. A new category of electronic book, a specialized computer with a built-in display that is the size of a traditional printed book, can be comfortably held in the hand and read in bed, on an airplane, or in your favorite easy chair. The contents of the "book" will be purchased and downloaded through a Web site, bypassing traditional bookstores entirely.

Customer support

Post-sales telephone calls can be a major expense for firms selling sophisticated products. Customer support costs and frustrations can be reduced by posting answers to frequently asked questions on your Web site. Both buyer and seller benefit; sellers benefit from reduced costs and buyers benefit from immediate and twenty-four-hour-a-day access to desired information without telephone tag.

Focused selling

> By permitting prospects to presell and prequalify themselves, sales professionals like Realtors can spend their time more effectively.

By permitting prospects to presell and prequalify themselves, sales professionals like Realtors can spend their time more effectively. Rather than wasting time and gasoline driving customers around to a variety of houses, many of which turn out to be unacceptable, Realtors can focus their time on showing fewer, more appropriate homes. The Web sites of many real estate agents, for example, permit prospects to prequalify the homes they view, depending on their financial resources, avoiding the wasted time of looking at homes out of their price range.

Vendor relationships

As businesses get connected and begin to sell increasing amounts of products over the Web, it becomes a relatively simple step to involve vendors in each transaction. Rather than waiting until the next inventory period to reorder, vendors can be immediately notified when a sale occurs, automatically reordering the product. This reduces administrative costs and saves time–eliminating out-of-stock situations–and permits the business owner to spend more time selling, less time on routine ordering.

New opportunities

Failure to embrace the Web means failure to adapt your business not only to a changed environment but also a failure to utilize the latest technology. This change does not have to happen overnight, but you should be aware of the potential advantages that changed markets and technology can offer. For example, automating more and more operations–such as replacing personally typed correspondence with automated e-mail responses–means that you can spend more time on those things that you do best.

The Web also offers you an opportunity to re-examine and remodel your business. You may identify new, unserved business opportunities. Equally important, you may discover areas where you are wasting time, competing in arenas where you cannot possibly win.

Analyzing your business from the Web point of view may not only uncover numerous areas where you can do a better job of serving your customers and prospects, you may also uncover new opportunities to put your existing enthusiasms and expertise to work. For example, you may be able to repackage information that you already possess and use it to either develop new products and services or use the information to develop long-term customer relationships.

> Failure to embrace the Web means failure to adapt your business, not only to a changed environment, but also a failure to utilize the latest technology.

Web Challenges

Although powerful, it's important to also note that the Web is not perfect. It presents its own set of challenges.

Lack of tangibility

Your message immediately disappears when your visitor's computer is turned off or they return to their word processing program.

Although you can encourage visitors to print out relevant pages of your Web site, many won't—and even fewer will be able to print your Web site out in color.

This, of course, is a major difference between the Web and print communications. Print communications can last for decades (as my basement proves).

Not everyone is connected

Although the number of connected households increases daily, Web access is readily available in libraries, and there are numerous devices that can display Web pages on a television, the Web remains far from a universal media.

Before you embark on a serious Web program, you should make sure that members of your market are connected.

Bandwidth

Although technology is constantly improving, access to the Web may be slow in some areas. There may not be sufficient bandwidth to accommodate everyone who wants to go online at a given time. Limited bandwidth means that it will take time for the text and graphics that make up your Web site to arrive on a visitor's computer.

The speed of your visitors' computer and telephone connections may also be a factor. If they are using an older, slower, computer and an older, slower modem (the device that connects a computer to the telephone), they may find your Web site frustratingly slow.

These problems, of course, should not dissuade you from joining the Web revolution. But being forewarned is being forearmed.

Will they find you?

Success comes from more than just creating an attractive and information-rich Web site. You have to make sure that visitors will find your Web site. You have to constantly promote your Web site in order to make it easy for prospects to locate you.

> Success comes from more than just creating an attractive and information-rich Web site. You have to make sure that visitors will find your Web site.

New technology

Like learning to ride a bicycle, the Web involves a learning curve. Whether you do the work yourself or hire others to help you, the Web still involves making an investment in mastering a new technology and a new vocabulary. Once you have mastered the Web by creating a successful site and have created a process for responding to prospects and constantly promoting and upgrading its content, you'll wonder how you ever did without it. But, in the meantime, you are likely to encounter some frustrating experiences both within and beyond your organization.

Depersonalization

As you begin to take advantage of the many opportunities the Web offers to save you money, such as automated sales and customer support, you have to make sure that you don't sacrifice your firm's essential humanity and personality. Automation can, indeed, cut costs and improve service, but your presence as a living, breathing business owner should never disappear. Even when saving money, your customers and prospects appreciate and look for a human touch.

Putting the Web to Work for You

Web success is based on information. The success of your Web endeavors will be directly proportional to the amount and quality of information your Web site gathers and distributes. Over time, the information generated *by* and distributed *from* your Web site is likely to have a major impact on the way you do business.

This change, of course, does not have to be disruptive. Change can be introduced as rapidly or as slowly as desired. In most cases, moderation is a virtue. Your firm's transition to a Web and information-based business can take place gradually, without serious dislocation.

Let's start by taking a brief look at the Web's twin roles as an information collector and distributor.

> Automation can, indeed, cut costs and improve service, but your presence as a living, breathing business owner should never disappear.

The Web as information collector

As a *collector* of information, the Web makes it easy for you to sell more efficiently, fine-tune your product and/or service offerings, and do a better job of supporting your customers—which will lead to repeat sales and word-of-mouth recommendations. The Web does this by facilitating communication and dialog. Figure 1-1 illustrates the six key functions a Web site offers your business.

FIGURE 1-1 THE SIX KEY FUNCTIONS AND TYPES OF INFORMATION A WEB SITE CAN PROVIDE YOUR BUSINESS.

1. **Sales**. If your business is set up to accept credit cards and if your product or service can be shipped, orders can flow directly into your Web site for immediate fulfillment. In many cases, however, sales will continue to involve face-to-face encounters: visits to your store or your client's place of business, telephone calls, and/or personal encounters.

2. **Leads**. Most businesses grow one prospect at a time. By making it easy for customers to identify themselves—by registering—a properly promoted Web site can create a constantly growing reservoir of new business leads for you and your sales staff to follow-up in person or via e-mail. In addition to basic name, address, position, and area of interest information, your Web site can be set up to provide you with increasingly sophisticated data about your market and its intentions.

3. **Questions**. The Web offers prospects a nonthreatening, noncommittal way to ask questions without committing themselves to a face-to-face meeting. Two things happen when you encourage Web site visitors to ask you questions. First, by engaging them in dialog, your credibility increases and the customer begins to feel comfortable dealing with you. Second, by keeping track of the questions that customers ask, patterns will emerge that you can use to improve your Web site in the future.

4. **Referrals**. To the extent that your Web site offers genuinely helpful advice—or meaningful content—visitors to your Web site will refer it to their friends and coworkers. More important, your registration form can directly generate referrals by

inviting visitors to submit the names of others who are likely to be interested in the information your Web site contains.

5. **Suggestions**. No business is perfect. Every business can learn from its customers and prospects. The Web makes it easy for prospects as well as customers to provide real-world feedback at no cost. Since nobody knows your customers better than they do, and nobody knows how well your products perform in the field than your customers do, your best source of market intelligence may be contained in the next customer Suggestion Box feedback form submitted to your Web site.

6. **Complaints**. All too often, dissatisfied customers are more likely to complain about poor treatment or unsatisfactory performance to their friends rather than to the business itself. By offering free and easy communication, the Web provides an easy way to find out where your business needs fine-tuning.

The above six benefits of a Web site, of course, are based on the creation of a Web site that is more than just an "electronic brochure," a derogatory term used to describe a Web site that simply provides a one-way exchange of information. Successful Web sites involve a two-way exchange of information. The visitor must be able to choose the information they want to view and the sequence in which they encounter it. Visitors must also be encouraged to submit their e-mail and postal addresses, as well as other pertinent information, so you can involve visitors in the five-step customer loyalty cycle described later in this chapter.

The Web as information distributor

Your Web site will succeed to the extent it distributes the right type of information to the right prospects at the right time. There are eight basic types of information your Web site should distribute.

1. **Offerings**. At the very least, your Web site should describe the products or services your firm offers. The Web is ideally suited to these descriptions because, as David Ogilvy wrote

One-Way Versus Two-Way Web Sites

Understanding the difference between one-way and two-way Web sites is crucial to your ability to put the Web to work. The goal is to use the Web to create two-way Web sites. The visitor must be involved in the exchange of information.

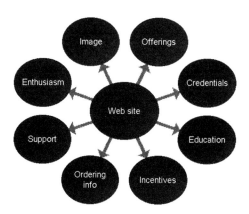

FIGURE 1-2 YOUR WEB SITE SHOULD DISTRIBUTE EIGHT TYPES OF INFORMATION.

A billboard by the side of the highway or a printed brochure "broadcasts" information to a passive reader. The exchange of information flows in only one direction. The reader has no control over the information that appears on the billboard or in the brochure.

in his *Confessions of an Advertising Man* over twenty years ago, "the more you tell, the more you sell." As we'll see later in this chapter, the Web offers you space to communicate as much information as needed to arouse desire for your product or service.

2. **Credentials**. "Why should prospects buy from you?" Second in order of importance to describing your product and service is the importance of explaining what makes you the best place to buy. Is it your location, your selection, your experience, your warehouse pricing, or what?

3. **Education**. Ultimate success comes from not only offering the right products and services at the right prices, but also educating your market. Web sites with a strong educational component expand the market by attracting new buyers to your product or service. Adding an education component to your Web site also allows you to step your prospects up to higher-quality products by explaining to them the advantages they will enjoy if they purchase a higher-quality product. Education also enhances your credibility because it proves that you possess unusual expertise. If customers do not understand the benefits of buying what you're selling, or don't know how to identify quality when they encounter it, they're unlikely to buy on more than the basis of price.

4. **Incentives**. You can close a higher percentage of sales by offering incentives for immediate purchase, such as discounts or premiums. More important, you can use the Web as a promotional medium, inviting prospects to special events or offering visitors to your Web site special discounts or premiums.

5. **Ordering information**. If your firm is set up to process credit cards, you can often close the sale right then and there on the Web site using a ordering form. In other cases, you'll want to include ordering information such as delivery and set-up charges, shipping information, directions to your office or store, and mailing or telephone information.

6. **Support**. Products are no better than the support the seller offers the buyer. A computer software program that doesn't

load or a color printer that doesn't print frustrates the buyer—often trying to set it up in the middle of the night—and can cost the seller hundreds of dollars in support costs as well as negative word-of-mouth. By providing answers to frequently asked questions twenty-four hours a day, Web sites can simultaneously reduce customer support costs and create happier customers. Customer support often involves replacing time-consuming telephone calls with e-mail; for example, many car dealers offer customers the ability to schedule maintenance on the Web.

7. **Enthusiasm**. Experienced salespeople know that the initial sale is just the first step; the easiest and most profitable sales come from repeat customers. The Web offers excellent opportunities for maintaining customer enthusiasm by showing customers not only how to make the most of their purchase but by suggesting additional purchases that can augment the pleasure they receive. Web sites can maintain enthusiasm by showing how others enjoy their purchase as well as by rewarding customers by offering them specialized content not available to those who haven't purchased yet. For example, car dealers can describe weekend drives and provide recommended restaurants and favorable reviews of the cars their customers have just purchased.

8. **Image**. The above information, plus the colors, layout, and typeface designs used to communicate it, together create an image of the company. Image operates on a nonverbal, emotional level. Image creates feelings of like or dislike towards the firm. Your Web site should project an accurate image of your firm, communicating feelings like youthful, conservative, expensive, high-tech, anti-establishment, or academic.

> Visitors are not only allowed to choose the information they want to access, they are invited to participate by asking questions and by submitting comments.

Information and the Web wars

Web wars are divided into three types of battles: presale battles, point-of-sale battles, and post-sale battles. The information that flows into and out of your Web site should change based on the particular marketing battle that your Web site is involved in with any given customer at any particular point in time. Winning these three types of battles requires different types of information flowing into and out of your Web site.

- **Presale battles** include the battle to be noticed and the battle to arouse desire. Success is unlikely to occur if prospects don't visit your Web site, or if your Web site does not provide compelling information.
- **Point-of-sale battles** involve competition, providing compelling reasons why your product or service is superior to those offered by your competitors. How does your firm differ from the competition? What makes your products or services different from the competition?
- **Post-sale battles** involve the battle to resell past customers and the battle to generate word-of-mouth referrals and recommendations. How can you convince customers to buy again? What additional products or services are they likely to need? How can you encourage them to recommend your firm to their friends?

The Web wars are won one battle at a time, and the battles that make them up must be fought in the right order. Before you can engage in point-of-sale battles, for example, you first have to win presale battles. And before you can engage in post-sale battles, you have to win point-of-sale battles.

> Web sites should be viewed as an investment in your firm's survival.

When Should You Start?

Web sites should be viewed as an investment in your firm's survival. To avoid the Web is to hobble your firm's future. Yes, you can probably continue in business without a Web site. The lack of a Web site, in itself, is as unlikely to put your out of business as the presence of a Web site, by itself, is unlikely to create immediate wealth.

Nevertheless, there are several compelling reasons to begin working now on your Web site.

The Web and the Future of Your Business

- **Success builds on success.** No matter how much time or money you invest in your first Web site, it's unlikely to be perfect. Improvement is always possible—but not without a first attempt. The sooner you get started, the sooner you can begin to make meaningful improvements in your Web site. Success will come to the extent that you become comfortable and experienced working with both the marketing and technical aspects of the Web.

- **Your competitors may already be there.** The sooner you establish a Web site presence, the sooner you can begin to compete. The longer you wait, the more chance there is that prospects who would otherwise buy from you will purchase from one of your competitors and move along *their* customer bonding cycle. Additional problems involve acquiring a Web site address, or URL. The longer you wait to register your desired address, the greater the chance that someone else will choose the URL you desired.

- **Accommodating change.** Although your initial Web activities may begin slowly, they will likely pick up as new profit opportunities occur to you. Ideas for new products and services will likely soon become available. If you procrastinate getting started, you're not only sacrificing business that's available today, but you'll be less likely to be able to take advantage of opportunities for reduced costs, improved customer service, or even totally new product or service offerings that the Web makes possible.

> The sooner you establish a Web site presence, the sooner you can begin to compete.

The Web is not a silver bullet that can save a dying business or create instant wealth. Few businesses have experienced the success that the Amazon.com's and Dell Computer's of the world have enjoyed. In the next chapter we'll explore some of the trends and technologies affecting your business as you move to the Web.

For more information on this topic, visit our Web site at www.businesstown.com

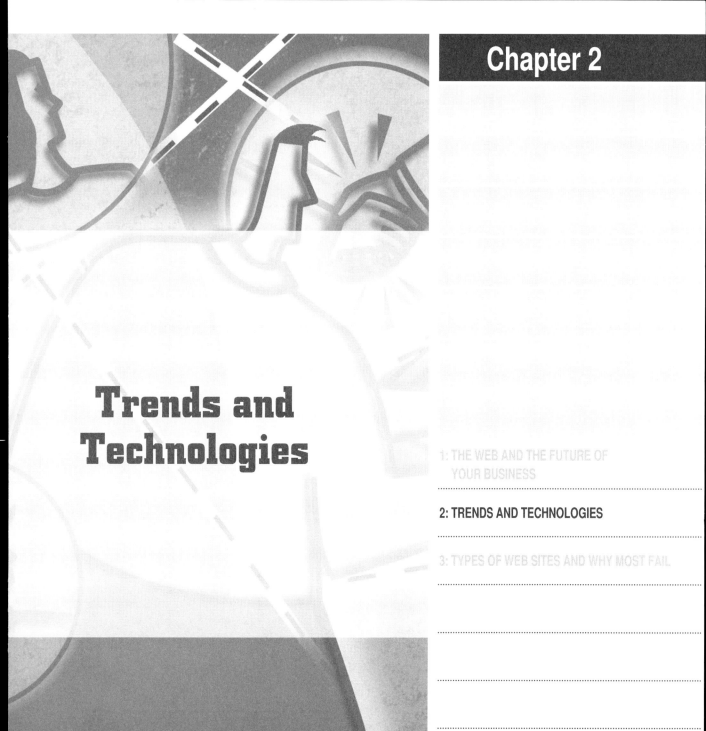

Trends and Technologies

The thing is to be able to outlast the trends.

—PAUL ANKA

There are good reasons people call the front edges of advanced technology the bleeding edge: most advanced hardware or software tools lack convenience, are hard to use, crash a lot, and cost an arm and a leg. One must be very dedicated, or enthusiastic, to suffer these challenges in order to be the first on the block to adopt the latest hardware or software. In advanced Web technologies the bleeding edge is defined by using protocols and technologies on your Web site that can only be viewed over high-speed Internet connections or the fastest workstation with the latest Web browser. In other words, you are limiting your audience of site visitors to a small part of the population. In business, particularly with your relationship marketing Web site and e-mail initiative, it is usually prudent to adopt a more conservative approach.

Still, as technology advances, a time will definitely come when you should adopt new techniques, new technologies, and new strategies. That time is when the technologies are entering the mainstream and the majority of your customers are able to take advantage of them. You need to stay in touch with technology and with the capabilities of your customers and their Internet connections or be left behind.

With the Web improving and changing daily, nobody can ever be fully caught up with the advancing technology. The following observations, however, might help you gain a better perspective of the business and technology trends that are occurring and their potential impact on your business.

Technology Trends

Technology is evolving at breakneck speed. The cost of hardware, software, and Internet access continues to drop and the capabilities offered continue to advance. The size of the Web population continues to grow, and it's demographic mirrors society as a whole. The numbers of places people are when they access the Web is increasing as well.

> With the Web improving and changing daily, nobody can ever be fully caught up with the advancing technology.

The ubiquity of the Web

Lower prices for computers and Internet access means that the number of people who can visit your Web site continues to grow. Millions of new users each year join the 60–80 million current Web users. This means that more of your customers and prospects can visit your Web site more frequently. This is in conjunction with several other ongoing trends.

People are also getting more in the habit of going to the Web site for their news. The major newspapers have Web sites that contain updates of their print articles and late breaking news. Instead of being tied to on-the-hour or quarter-hour news broadcasts, you can visit your favorite television station's Web site for late breaking news. When you want to find out the five day weather forecast in virtually any town throughout the United States, you can locate it on the Web.

The Web is no longer a novelty. For many, it is not even exciting. It is simply a universal communications tool, as accepted as the television or telephone, to help people locate information on demand. The implication is that your customers and prospects are likely to turn to your Web site before calling you on the phone or visiting your place of business. If your Web site does not project an accurate image of your firm's offerings and attitudes, you will not get a second chance for their business. Soon, Web-based video conferencing will reduce the amount of business travel as people in distant offices will be able to communicate without leaving their home towns—or their homes.

Increased bandwidth and speed

Increased bandwidth—permitting much faster information delivery and the delivery of richer information—is quickly becoming commonplace. Modems are being retired by home users and replaced with technologies like cable modems and digital subscriber lines. The number of service providers clamoring to provide access to the home will assure this trend continues and competition will keep costs low. Web usage in the office is becoming universal and businesses are adding high-speed Internet connectivity to their local area networks.

> The Web is no longer a novelty. For many, it is not even exciting. It is simply a universal communications tool, as accepted as the television or telephone, to help people locate information on demand.

These fast and convenient Internet connections take much of the frustration out of the Web and make it possible for you to incorporate advanced media to communicate sound and video on your Web site.

> These fast and convenient Internet connections take much of the frustration out of the Web and make it possible for you to incorporate advanced media to communicate sound and video on your Web site.

The Web is a global phenomenon

The tools of the Web–modems and other types of connections along with Web-ready hardware and software–are in use throughout the world. This removes the geographic boundaries of your business, which is made all the more realistic by the near-universal use of credit cards that automatically compute currency changes from country to country.

The Web browser is the universal platform for business

In the past, many software programs for specific markets, such as legal billing, used proprietary software that was both expensive to acquire and difficult to learn. Databases were accessed through proprietary, custom-made front ends. These applications and many others, from inventory to accounting to point-of-sale, are being reprogrammed to be browser compliant.

The Web eliminates the need for you to purchase or develop custom software. This universal acceptance of Web standards means that your will continue to grow and you can easily customize your Web site for customers without starting from scratch.

Wireless handheld browsing and wireless e-mail

People will be able to access your Web site information from more places. At the same time, you will be able to contact them when they are nearby, perhaps sending them an e-mail containing a special offer when they happen to be within a few miles of your business location. Perhaps you'll offer them the ability to click a button asking you to contact their nearby friends for an impromptu get together at your café. Handheld devices with wireless access are making this possible.

Cellular telephones and handheld personal information managers are becoming indistinguishable and can connect to the Internet through wireless connections. Many new models feature micro Web browsers that allow limited Web browsing. They rely on unique pages that are formatted differently than your regular Web pages. A protocol called WAP, or Wireless Application Protocol, is broadly accepted as the platform for this. Wireless e-mail is another related technology that is becoming increasingly commonplace. Most current cellular PCS networks let you send short e-mail messages to cellular telephones. It is the ability of cellular networks to identify the location of the handset that opens the door to the fascinating relationship marketing ideas listed above.

Currently, the speed of wireless data connections to handheld devices is slow and the screens are small. New developments will certainly change this over the next few years. At the same time, these technologies rely on sophisticated technologies within the network of the carriers. These technologies are currently only available in limited areas, but the carriers are expanding their wireless networks as quickly as they can and adding data and Internet capabilities.

Advanced media becoming practical

A picture is worth a thousand words. This is not only true in the richness of what it can communicate, but in the case of moving pictures—streaming video—it is true regarding the size of the data and the speed of access and downloading.

Advanced media consisting of live or prerecorded audio and video, animation using technologies like Macromedia Flash and Apple QuickTime 3D, and VRML (Virtual Reality Modeling Language) is becoming increasingly practical. While impossibly slow using dial-up modem connections, the fact that high-speed Internet connections are becoming more common make it a reality for more people.

This makes it possible to communicate information in new ways and to personalize your visitor's experience. Your voice can communicate nuances through expression and tone that help visitors get to know you better before they even met you.

> A picture is worth a thousand words. This is not only true in the richness of what it can communicate, but in the case of moving pictures—streaming video—it is true regarding the size of the data and the speed of access and downloading.

More important, if you have complicated information to communicate, the Web permits you to show procedures or the process of creating as effectively as the best PBS television program. Animation permits you to "assemble" a whole out of a group of individual parts and, unlike television, if the message isn't perfectly understood the first time, the segment can be immediately replayed.

Sound, movement, and video must be used with restraint. Like any technological breakthrough, they can easily be overused, obscuring your message rather than enhancing it. Blinking messages and moving text often attract attention to one part of your Web site at the expense of other parts.

E-commerce becomes commonplace

Most Web users shop online. While they may ultimately make their purchase in your store, more and more are actually carrying out the final transaction using credit cards on Web sites. The majority of users, in fact, have already made purchases online. More users are realizing that their credit card number is perhaps more likely to be stolen from a receipt in the dumpster behind the restaurant than off of the Web. All of these things have contributed to the explosion of e-commerce. Whether you sell small products or expensive services, you should be familiar with e-commerce.

Adding e-commerce capabilities can be as simple as using one of the free services from companies like Yahoo.com or as complicated as buying, programming, and installing an e-commerce application suite on your own servers that is integrated with your own warehouse and shipping operations. In any case, the basic components are the same:

- A way to present products, hopefully selected from a database and presented based on the interests of the visitor
- A way for visitors to select and order the product (usually called a shopping cart application)
- A way to accept credit card payments and calculate tax and shipping charges

> Adding e-commerce capabilities can be as simple as using one of the free services from companies like Yahoo.com or as complicated as buying, programming, and installing an e-commerce application suite on your own servers that is integrated with your own warehouse and shipping operations.

- A way to send that order to the people who will put the gadget in the box and apply a shipping label to it.
- And of course, a way to notify the customer that it was shipped, provide the shipper's tracking number (with a link to the shipper's tracking Web site), and offer a 30-day discount coupon for accessories, which you present on a personalized Web page with their name at the top.

Business Trends

Although technology advances with increasing speed, the following marketing trends are also apparent.

Reduced profit margin

More products are being discounted to the extent where they are sold at a loss in order to build traffic to various Web sites. The hope is that customers who visit once and purchase a loss leader will come back and purchase other, more expensive, products. The cost of customer acquisition is high in terms of both the media advertising necessary to drive visitors to new Web sites as well as the low prices necessary to attract purchases.

There is an unhealthy side effect to this corrosive price competition: customer service is often lacking. When products don't arrive on time, there is often no one to call and e-mail queries are not answered. It is up to you, implementing the strategies in this book, to counteract this trend. It is on this basis that you will be able to beat your competition and develop that almost lost but priceless thing: customer loyalty.

> The price of admission for newcomers to the Web is going up and up. Ever increasing amounts of money are being spent in traditional media to attract visitors to Web sites.

Increased price of admission

The price of admission for newcomers to the Web is going up and up. Ever increasing amounts of money are being spent in traditional media to attract visitors to Web sites. Hundreds of millions of dollars are being spent in local and national newspapers, on radio, television, and on national, regional, and local cable networks promoting Web sites. The goal of attracting new visitors is blinding companies to the need to run a profitable business.

The value of relevant information

The one constant in this constantly changing landscape is the importance of relevant information delivered to the right person at the right time. Relevant content delivered at the right time is as important today as it was 10 or 20 years ago. It is becoming even more of a way to stand out from your competition.

When people are new to a field—whether they are buying their first home, exploring the world of high-performance sailboats, looking for information about vacation destinations, or looking for the cheapest airline ticket to Newark—relevant information delivered at the right time is the key to success.

Although technology is advancing, the need for relevant, timely information remains constant. Make information the cornerstone of your Web initiative. Use technology as appropriate, but don't take your eyes off the ball and forget to provide the appropriate content to your customers and prospects at the right time.

Embracing New Technologies

There are dozens of ways you can employ technology to improve the performance of your Web site. When appropriate, you can take advantage of improved bandwidth and browser compatibilities by incorporating a variety of advanced technologies.

Calculators

One of the easiest ways you can improve your competitive advantage is to include an online calculator. Realtors and automobile dealers frequently use online calculators to allow visitors to calculate monthly purchase or lease payments. Visitors can play with down payment and length of term until they come up with a financing or leasing arrangement that works for them. This, obviously, saves the sales staff a lot of time and can show visitors that they can actually afford a larger home than they might otherwise have thought.

Return on investment calculators are a variation on this. A consultant or a secretarial service, for example, could use a return on investment calculator to help clients see for themselves how much money they can save by outsourcing certain activities rather than hiring new employees and incurring long-term commitment for overhead and benefits.

Creating these is quite simple and most often consists of a few lines of JavaScript code embedded within the page. JavaScript calculators are convenient in that they impose no additional demands on your server hardware. The actual calculations are performed by the visitor's computer.

> Relevant content delivered at the right time is as important today as it was 10 or 20 years ago. It is becoming even more of a way to stand out from your competition.

Audio

Sound can be easily added to a Web site. Many radio stations are broadcasting on the Web, which allows them to keep in contact with students and business travelers away from home. Many Realtors include audio directions that explain how to locate a specific home listing.

Audio can be delivered as a file or it can be a continuously downloaded stream. The advantage of delivering audio as a file is that it can be replayed and shared with others. The advantage of streaming audio is that it begins to play almost immediately, before the entire file has downloaded. Streaming audio also supports live broadcasts such as radio stations and seminars.

Take the case of a consultant who, as part of his services, presents seminars or serves as a meeting facilitator. Since the consultant's voice is such an important part of the value he brings to his client, he can add a great deal of selling power to his Web site by including audio clips taken from previous presentations. These clips should be short and, ideally, include audience laughter or applause. Even better, the consultant could include audio clips containing comments from previous seminar participants. Spoken endorsements are much more powerful than written endorsements, greatly enhancing the consultant's ability to sell himself through his Web site.

Video

If a picture equals a thousand words, a moving picture equals a million words. If a consultant or seminar presenter wanted a way of thoroughly convincing prospective clients that he is an excellent presenter, he could include video clips of past presentations on his Web site.

Online video would, in the long run, cost less and be more effective than duplicating copies of videocassettes and sending them via overnight express delivery to prospective clients. The consultant's costs would be lower and the client would receive immediate information. Although video clips take a few minutes to download, clients seriously considering hiring the consultant would willingly wait the time in order to be able to immediately preview a performance.

Since video clips, once posted on a Web site, do not increase site costs regardless of the number of people who view them, whale watch operators could post video clips of previous cruises, or a bed and breakfast could direct past customers to a page containing downloadable clips of the town decorated for Christmas.

Streaming video (and streaming audio for that matter) places bandwidth demands on the server in proportion to the number of people receiving the stream concurrently. It takes 10 times the bandwidth to deliver streaming audio or video to 10 people at once as it does to one. Advanced techniques like IP Multicast are often employed for large presentations of thousands of simultaneous viewers and actually employ a number of servers located around the country. The stream is served to the viewer from the nearest server.

Web cams

Web cams are similar to video in that they show by picture rather than tell using words. Web cams can be used to establish a feeling of community as well as communicate the desirability of visiting a location. Unlike video, Web cams do not show constant action. Instead, they show "slices" of action updated at 15-minute (or whatever amount of time is appropriate) intervals.

Web cams are excellent for maintaining a sense of community. I return to *www.komotv.com* to check out the weather in Seattle because KOMO-TV has a camera on their broadcast tower overlook-

> If a picture equals
> a thousand words, a
> moving picture equals a
> million words.

ing downtown Seattle. I frequently visit it when I am homesick. I also check the Washington State Department of Transportation's Web cams located along Seattle's freeways to see how the traffic is doing.

A Web cam pointed at the front door of a bed and breakfast, showing the changing seasons, can help visitors remember the good time they had when they visited.

Animated text and graphics

Animated text can be extremely distracting. It is hard to read a paragraph of text when, right next to it, other text is blinking "Free!" or "Click here!" or there's a rotating logo on the same page. However, there are times when animated text and graphics make sense.

Animated text, when it is the primary focus on a Web page, can focus the visitor's attention on new ideas as they are introduced. In a manner similar to presentations, new ideas can be introduced one idea at a time. This controls the visitor's reading speed and emphasizes each new idea as it is introduced.

In a similar way, animated graphics can be extremely powerful. A chart or graph can "grow" to prove a point. Or, on a medical site, the direction of radiating lines can show visitors how to identify the true signs of a heart attack and differentiate it from indigestion.

Animated graphics make sense if you want to illustrate a procedure, a timeline, or the steps necessary to complete a job. MacroMedia Flash is the leading technology for animation on the Web.

> There are times when animated text and graphics make sense.

Shopping cart

If you are going to supplement your current business with online selling, you'll want to add shopping cart capability to your Web site. A shopping cart fills out an order form, one step at a time, so visitors don't have to constantly move back and forth between catalog pages. By clicking on an item on a catalog page and indicating a quantity, the item(s) are automatically added to the order form.

Shopping carts greatly facilitate buying. If the visitor has previously submitted a credit card or purchase order information, all the visitor has to do to place an order is to click the "submit" button of the order form and the order is on its way!

Question and answer forums

One of the best ways you can learn about your customers' and prospects' real needs is to make it easy for them to ask questions. Authors and radio personalities often use question and answer forums to identify topics to address in future books. Question and answer forums also help firms discover weaknesses in their product's instructions or documentation. If the same questions keep coming up time and time again, it shows that the procedure or topic is not adequately treated in their instructions or documentation.

Questions and answer forums require the active participation of the sponsoring firm. Visitors submitting questions expect (and have a right to) a reasonably fast response. Whenever possible, the response should be personalized, though there are software programs available that will automatically reference a database containing answers to frequently asked questions.

The ideal scenario, of course, is for the response to be personalized as much as possible. Even if the majority of the response is from a database, the response can be personalized in a few seconds if someone has been given time and resources to respond to questions.

Question and answer forums are ideal for building a sense of community among those interested in a field or activity. Some Web sites, such as *www.photo.net,* are highly advanced. Responses to questions are automatically sent via e-mail to the individual who submitted the question as well as posted on the question and answer forum for visitors to learn from.

Discussion groups

One of the best ways businesses can learn from their customers is to sit back and listen to what they have to say about their products and services. Discussion groups involve visitors posting questions and comments that everyone who visits the Web site can access. Discussion groups are either moderated or unmoderated. When discussion groups are moderated, someone is responsible to maintain certain levels of decorum and censor defamatory statements.

Unmoderated discussion groups resemble free for alls in that there is no control or censorship and anything posted is instantly

> Questions and answer forums require the active participation of the sponsoring firm. Visitors submitting questions expect (and have a right to) a reasonably fast response.

available to all visitors. Like question and answer forums, discussion groups are great for building a sense of community among purchasers of a product or service. They provide the business owner or manager with a unequalled way of learning from their customers and prospects. Forums and discussion groups are like real world focus groups. Only, instead of gathering 10 or 15 "typical" buyers of a product or service into a room and asking them questions, participation is far more democratic and there is less opportunity for a few extroverts to dominate the forum or discussion.

Chat

Chat is a real time version of a discussion group. Chat software permits visitors to a Web site to immediately communicate with each other on the screen of their computer.

Although often associated with adult sites, scheduled chat sessions could be extremely valuable by permitting individuals involved with a project to communicate. For example, a building contractor could schedule a chat session each Monday morning with the client and those working on a new shopping mall. The chat session could include the building's architects, the client, subcontractors, suppliers, and—if necessary—building inspectors and others whose approval needs to be involved. The contractor could provide a video showing progress on the project and invite everyone's input.

> An Internet site is a Web site posted on the World Wide Web. Anyone with a Web browser can access it.

Intranets and extranets

An *Internet* site is a Web site posted on the World Wide Web. Anyone with a Web browser can access it. An *Intranet*, however, is a specialized version of a Web site. It is a password-protected site that is only accessible to employees of a firm on their internal local area network. Although intranets are typically used to communicate company news, e-mail addresses, and telephone extensions, they also typically contain information about vacation policies and other benefits.

An *extranet* is yet a third type of Web site. An extranet is a special controlled-access Web site, typically password-protected, that can be shared by those within and outside of the company to connect with internal databases like inventory and order processing. A building contractor could set up an extranet containing project specifications, blueprints, and schedules that could be shared from offices and mobile computers by everyone associated with the project. This sharing of information could become a significant competitive advantage to the builder by keeping everyone informed and avoiding communications problems.

Virtual reality modeling

As products become more expensive and sophisticated, visitors will willingly put up with long downloading times in order to encounter the information they're interested in. Virtual reality modeling can put Web visitors in the driver's seat. Instead of being forced to see what the camera saw when it took a static picture, virtual reality modeling allows the user to control the image they view. Using either their computer mouse or the up/down, left/right cursor control keys, they can look to the left, right, up, down, or zoom in for a closer look or zoom out for a more distant look. This is accomplished using a seamless series of photographs stitched together to form a 360-degree view, or it can employ computer-generated scenes through which the viewer can navigate. Virtual reality is the closest thing to being there, and when the product or service being sold warrants, it can provide a most convincing sales argument.

> There's virtually no limit to what the Web can communicate. The only limiting factor, of course, is appropriateness.

Conclusion

There's virtually no limit to what the Web can communicate. The only limiting factor, of course, is appropriateness. All of the above involve an additional initial investment in Web site development—but this is not the issue. The real issue of whether an investment in advanced Web technology is appropriate depends solely on whether it helps communicate the firm's message or is simply employing technology for technology's sake.

Technology for technology's sake rarely pays for itself. Technology used to convincingly communicate marketing messages can, however, make the difference between a sale or a lost sale's opportunity. In the next chapter we'll look at some of the reasons that why Web sites fail to generate major profits—and how you can avoid making the same mistakes.

For more information on this topic, visit our Web site at **www.businesstown.com**

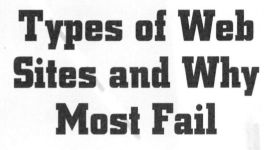

Types of Web Sites and Why Most Fail

Failure is success if we learn from it!

—MALCOLM FORBES

Most companies with Web sites are still trying to figure out what they want the Web to do for their business. As they seek an answer to that question, they experiment. They try out some ideas developed over lunch and, seemingly overnight, erect a Web site for all the world to see. Unfortunately, many of these Web sites that appear on the World Wide Web look exactly like the experiments they are. Moreover, the typical lack of foresight, ongoing examination, refinement, and follow through surrounding these sites indicates a future that doesn't look too bright.

One easy solution to this is to conclude that the Web has no value for your business, dismiss it altogether, and simply carry on without it. While this head-in-the-sand approach may actually work for a while, it doesn't really help to evolve and grow the business. In fact, it probably renders the business increasingly vulnerable to competition and without any real defense to the Web savvy firm who is wisely leveraging the Web for all it's worth. Another solution, the one we are pursuing here, is to gain an understanding of the Web and implement a proven approach to harness it as a tool to increase sales, increase profits, reduce operating costs, and develop a lasting relationship with our customers—one that can spark new growth. The first step is to have a close look at what other companies are doing with the Web then learn from and build upon their experiments.

Competition requires a new approach to Web design and content. The increasing number of Web sites, the failure of search engines to keep up-to-date, and the increasing bombardment of traditional mass media advertising with advertisements intended to drive traffic to large, well-funded Web sites forces a new approach to Web sites—one firmly based on the needs of your firm's customers and prospects.

Old formulas are no longer valid. A new approach to Web content is required, one that places more emphasis on the information needs of your customers at each stage of their relationship to your business. Instead of the typical one-dimensional "brochure" Web site

> The first step is to have a close look at what other companies are doing with the Web then learn from and build upon their experiments.

or the price-oriented, high-visibility "transaction" Web sites like Amazon.com or E*Trade.com that dominate the media's attention, there is a need for a new approach to Web site development, one based on relationship marketing and the five-step customer development cycle described in this book.

How Design and Content Contribute to Web Site Failure

There are several reasons most Web sites fail, most common reasons include:

- **Slow loading**. Web sites fail when they take too long to load. Visitors are in a hurry. Ten seconds watching an hourglass seems like an eternity when you're in a hurry. The problem is that Web design has been in the hands of designers whose income often increases in direct proportion to the complexity of the Web site. As a result, large graphics and special effects often unnecessarily slow down Web site performance to the extent that visitors leave, rather than wait for a large logo to appear.
- **Difficult to read**. Color often hinders more than it enhances. Colored backgrounds and texture effects often reduce readability. Black type against a white background is easy to read—but lacks the "drama" designers often build into a site in order to gain client approval (the "Wow!" factor). Often, a combination of text colors and background colors, which look good on screen, results in pages that cannot be read when printed. (Try printing a Web site that uses white text against a blue background—you'll probably get a series of blank pages.)
- **Hard to navigate**. Many complain about the difficulty involved in locating information. Few Web sites practice what direct marketers have always done, which is to put their most compelling arguments up front. Even fewer Web sites include an effective search engine that helps visitors locate informa-

> The increasing number of Web sites, the failure of search engines to keep up-to-date, and the increasing bombardment of traditional mass media advertising with advertisements intended to drive traffic to large, well-funded Web sites forces a new approach to Web sites. Old formulas are no longer valid. A new approach to Web content is required.

tion by keywords or key product attributes. As a result, time is wasted trying to puzzle out a Web site's navigation scheme. Often, the larger the firm—and the more elaborate (and expensive) the Web site—the harder it is to find information.

- **Lack of follow-up**. Because the Web is often approached and funded from a "design" perspective, customer service is often neglected. There's often a hefty design budget but insufficient resources for the relatively unglamorous task of following-up on customer requests. Few firms have dedicated individuals—or, where appropriate, departments—responsible for responding to e-mail. As a result, requests for information go unfulfilled, leading to frustrated Web visitors who will never return to the site.

- **No incentive to return**. Web sites fail when they do not give visitors a reason to return. Most Web sites do not attempt to capture the visitor's e-mail address, making it impossible for the firm to contact previous visitors and enjoy another opportunity to sell them. As a result, most Web sites resemble static electronic brochures in that, once posted, they are not revised. Change is necessary to maintain a dialog with visitors, providing a reason for visitors to return and, again, be exposed to the businesses marketing message.

> More important, though, most Web sites fail because they fail to satisfy their visitor's information needs.

More important, though, most Web sites fail because they fail to satisfy their visitor's information needs. Most Web sites are myopic; they look *inward*—towards the business—rather than *outward*, towards the customer.

Types of Web Sites

Let's start by taking a look at the most common types of Web sites and examine some of the issues involved in creating a Web site that will build a close and ongoing relationship with your prospects and customers. This will provide you with a framework for creating your own Web site, one based on the customer development cycle.

TYPES OF WEB SITES AND WHY MOST FAIL

There are four types of Web sites: inner-directed, information-oriented, transaction-driven, and relationship-oriented. We'll examine the first three in this chapter and describe the fourth in the next chapter.

- **Inner-directed** Web sites are created from the business's point of view. The home page typically features the firm's logo and accomplishments. Inner-directed Web sites lack a focus on specific products or services. They typically fail to encourage urgency or visitor involvement. These sites typically feature photographs of buildings, lists of accomplishments, and testimonials from satisfied customers.
- **Information-oriented** Web sites provide more information about the firm's products and services. These sites function like electronic brochures in that they communicate the same types of material as found in brochures. Information-oriented Web sites reflect more of a customer focus but fail to communicate urgency or establish a two-way information exchange with the Web site visitor.
- **Transaction-oriented** Web sites assume that every visitor is ready to buy and, accordingly, place an emphasis upon price product features and benefits and place a premium on urgency; price is used to encourage visitors to order *"right now!"*. To date, the most successful examples of transaction-oriented Web sites are the numerous Web sites created by airlines, book stores, concert ticket outlets, and computer industry hardware manufacturers and software makers. Although transaction-oriented Web sites are the fastest-growing category of Web sites, transaction sites depend heavily on price incentives and—accordingly—often fail to offer visitors a reason to return until the next time customers are in the market to buy. They, likewise, make no attempt to create long-term customer loyalty.
- **Relationship-oriented** Web sites—described in the next chapter—attempt to forge long-term bonds with Web site visitors by establishing an ongoing dialog with them, fine-tuning the relationship between buyer and seller, and rewarding previ-

The four types of Web sites:
1. Inner-directed
2. Information-oriented
3. Transaction-oriented
4. Relationship-oriented

ous customers so they'll not only buy again, but also recommend the firm to their friends. Relationship-oriented Web sites are intended to advance customers along the customer development cycle.

> Relationship-oriented Web sites are intended to advance customers along the customer development cycle.

Web Site Characteristics

Web sites can be analyzed in terms of 10 major characteristics. These can be stated as questions:

1. **Information flow**. Which direction does information flow, from Web site to visitor, visitor to Web site, or is there a two-way flow of information?
2. **Information density**. How much information is presented? Information density refers to the quality and quantity of information contained on the Web site. Information-rich Web sites contain just about all the information visitors might need to know, others less information. Does the Web site contain a lot of in-depth information or does the Web site just hit the high points?
3. **Urgency**. How much point-of-sale urgency does the Web site communicate? Urgency involves motivation, the degree to which the Web site attempts to make an immediate sale. Some Web sites are set up to take the visitor's money (i.e. credit card) whereas other Web sites just distribute information and are not concerned about making the sale.
4. **Dialog**. Does the Web site invite a two-way exchange of information with visitors, or does the Web site exist simply to broadcast information? For example, how aggressively does the Web site invite visitors to provide their e-mail address, submit questions, rate the contents of the Web site, or comment on the firm's products and services?
5. **Follow-up**. Does the Web site facilitate later follow-up? What does the Web site do to make it easy for the firm to contact the visitor at a later date, providing new information or informing visitors when new content has been added to the Web site?

6. **Search capabilities**. One of the best ways you can create a user-friendly site is to include a site search capability. Visitors can enter keywords referring to the topic they want information on, i.e., "Australia," "Jaguar," or "filet mignon" and the titles of the pages containing those words will appear.

7. **Qualification**. Does the Web site invite visitors to qualify themselves, indicating their areas of interest, expertise, or budget resources? Qualification permits visitors to quickly locate information that is most appropriate to their needs, even if they do not know the specific search criteria or links that would take them to the information.

8. **Customized content**. Does the Web site provide a different experience for each visitor on the basis of their qualification or later follow-up? Most Web sites broadcast identical information to each visitor, others customize the content to the visitor's responses to the Web site's qualification options. Other Web sites provide customized, or specialized, content upon request.

9. **Updates**. How frequently is the Web site updated? Some Web sites are updated four times a year, others are constantly updated throughout the day.

10. **Size**. The size of a Web site (i.e., the number of pages in it) does not affect how fast the Web site loads, but often affects the speed with which visitors can locate desired information. Web site size should be appropriate to the amount of relevant information. One way to keep control over Web site size is to scrupulously remove outdated information (immediately remove descriptions of upcoming events after the events have taken place).

> Analyzing the four major types of Web sites will help you begin to get a better idea of the type of Web site most appropriate for your needs now and as your business evolves.

To get a better idea of these characteristics, let's see how they are reflected in the four major types of Web sites. Analyzing the four major types of Web sites will help you begin to get a better idea of the type of Web site most appropriate for your needs now and as your business evolves.

Inner-Directed Web Sites

Inner-directed Web sites are created from the business's point of view. Inward-looking Web sites are egotistical. Their underlying assumption is that visitors should be interested in reading–and will read–anything posted on the Web site. The criteria for inclusion is that the information presents a favorable, i.e. glowing, description of the business and its owner. The reality, of course, is that visitors are selfish; they're only interested in spending time at Web sites that offer them a benefit. Visitors to your Web site are always asking themselves What's in it for me? If you don't immediately answer that question, visitors are likely to quickly leave.

You can easily identify an inner-directed Web site. It usually begins with the name of the firm or association plastered like a billboard along the top of the home page, accompanied by links and text explaining what the firm is, what it does, where it's located, and how long it's been in business. Often, a vapid mission statement ("Our goal is to create happy customers!" or "A half-century of helping farmers survive by designing and building America's best fluid bushings") is thrown in as a bonus. Although links are present, they typically fail to involve the visitor and only serve as a way of helping visitors navigate from one page to another.

Although they may be elaborately designed and produced, the content of inner-directed Web sites often falls into the "brag and boast" category. They typically begin with a large logo on the home page (that, inevitably, takes a long time to download) followed by a list of company accomplishments. Descriptions of company information typically contain numerous adjectives and adverbs. The pages typically end with links to pages elaborating on the company's accomplishments.

Here are some other characteristics that make inner-directed Web sites easy to identify:

- The opening screens usually fail to immediately describe the benefits visitors will enjoy at the Web site or when patronizing the firm.
- The word "you" is rarely encountered in the text.

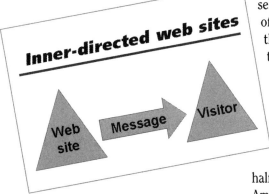

FIGURE 3-1 INNER-DIRECTED WEB SITES BROADCAST INFORMATION IN ONE DIRECTION, FROM THE BUSINESS'S POINT OF VIEW.

- The home page often contains large, slow-loading "brag and boast" graphics, like the firm's logo, motto, or a picture of the building where the firm is located.
- The home page typically lacks a featured product or service.
- Links are identified from the business or Web site's point of view rather than translated into visitor benefits.

The myopia of most typical inner-directed, or informational, Web sites is reflected in the way they handle the 10 major characteristics previously described.

Information flow

Inner-directed Web sites are like one-way streets. Inner-directed Web sites resemble print advertising in that the contents remain static and that information travels in one direction only—from business to visitor. Inner-directed Web sites reflect a one-way transfer of information. The Web site passively sits there, waiting for visitors. When visitors access the site, the site sends—or broadcasts—messages to the visitors. All visitors receive essentially the same information. With the exception of the obligatory "How to contact us" e-mail link, the Web site remains basically passive. Visitor interaction, or involvement, is limited to choosing the pages—and the order of the pages—that visitors access.

> Inner-directed Web sites are like one-way streets.

Information density

Inner-directed Web sites are usually "information light" in terms of information that will help customers and prospects make better decisions. Although there may be numerous pictures of facilities and staff—accompanied by impressive staff biographies—most of the information is of little value because it is not related in terms that customers and prospects can relate to their specific needs or problems.

Knowing, for example, that the president of the firm graduated with honors from Harvard doesn't mean very much (in fact, it might be a negative in that it could scare away people who might be intimidated because they didn't finish college).

The language used to describe inner-directed Web sites is inward-looking rather than market looking. Links entitled "Staff profiles," for example, really don't offer a benefit, as contrasted to "Meet the people with the answers to your problems."

Urgency

Inner-directed Web sites rarely project urgency. The attitude the Web sites project is "We'll be here when you're ready to buy." There are no incentives to immediate action.

Dialog

Although inner-directed Web sites usually contain contact information (telephone numbers, postal, fax, and e-mail links), they often do not include registration forms to facilitate visitor involvement. Likewise, they do not invite visitors to describe their challenges, identify their needs, or request further information.

Follow-up

Because inner-directed Web sites do not immediately involve visitors in a dialog, they usually do not capture the visitor's e-mail address. As a result, the firm not only doesn't know who is visiting its Web site, they are unable to contact the individuals in the future.

Search capabilities

Inner-directed Web sites usually do not have an internal search engine because there isn't any need for one. All of the "me-first" information can be found by clicking on the appropriate links.

Qualification

Since their approach and contents are so "me-oriented," inner-directed Web sites do not offer visitors an opportunity to prequalify their areas of interest.

- Visitors to an inner-directed bank site, for example, would not be given an opportunity to indicate their primary interests as either home banking, home buying, small business services, or corporate services.

> The language used to describe inner-directed Web sites is inward-looking rather than market looking.

- Visitors to a car dealer's site, for example, instead of being asked to indicate their desired monthly payment and type of desired category of automobile (4-door, 2-door, convertible, truck), visitors would be shown a list of all the brands the dealership represented.
- Likewise, visitors to a Realtor's site would not be given an opportunity to indicate the town where they're interested in possibly living, the number of bedrooms, or a desired price range. Instead, they would be presented with pictures of the staff members employed and a list of the awards they had received.

Customized content

Because there is no way for visitors to ask questions to qualify their interests or needs on the home page, there is no way for inner-directed Web sites to customize the visitor's Web site experience. Everybody gets to see (or avoid) the same pages.

Likewise, because there is little incentive for visitors to submit their e-mail or postal addresses, there is no possibility to provide customized content at a later date, perhaps when the Web site is updated or information appropriate to the visitor's needs appears.

Updates

Because their information is so inner-directed and generic, inner-directed Web sites are infrequently updated. In most cases, the Web sites remain the same until staff or product line changes require updating the Web site.

Size

Although their design may involve animation and movement, inner-directed Web sites are usually small by Web site standards. Sites may consist of only a dozen or so pages.

Limitations of inner-directed Web sites

Inner-directed Web sites are doomed to fail because they do not answer the question, What's in it for me? They fail to offer

> Inner-directed Web sites are doomed to fail because they do not answer the question, What's in it for me?

visitors reasons, or benefits, for remaining at the site or returning again and again. By way of contrast, Web sites that succeed are benefit oriented. They provide multiple answers to the question, What's in it for me? They make this information easy to locate by permitting visitors to qualify themselves so they don't waste time viewing information that doesn't pertain to them.

Web site visitors are in a hurry. Your Web site is competing for attention with millions of other Web sites. Unless you can immediately provide meaningful answers to the Web site visitor's unspoken "What's in it for me?" question, your Web site will fail.

When you visit a Web site for the first time, ask questions like "So What?" and "What's in it for me?" Notice how you tend to stay at Web sites that provide answers and how quickly you leave Web sites that fail to address the question.

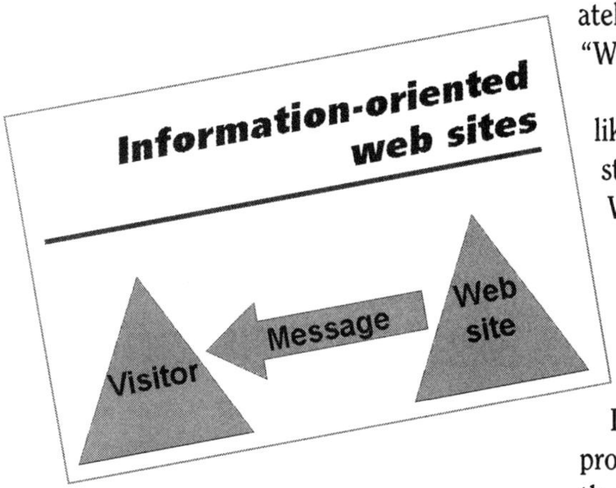

Information-Oriented Web Sites

Information-oriented Web sites are more marketing oriented. Information is chosen and presented from the customer and prospect's point of view. The starting point is usually an analysis of the visitor's information needs, and information is provided to satisfy the customer and prospect's questions.

Outer-directed Web sites, on the other hand, are created to satisfy not the business's egos but the information needs of past, present, and future customers. Outer-directed Web sites analyze the information needs of customers and prospects and provide answers to their questions. The firm or association's message is arranged and written so it will appeal to the visitor's needs.

This marketing orientation—attempting to satisfy customer's needs by preparing content that will help customers and prospects—forms the key distinction between inner-directed and information-oriented Web sites. Information-oriented Web sites succeed not because of the words, colors, or typefaces used, but because—before

FIGURE 3-2 INFORMATION-ORIENTED WEB SITES BEGIN WITH AN ANALYSIS OF THE VISITOR'S NEEDS, AND THE INFORMATION PRESENTED TRANSLATES THE FIRM'S OFFERINGS INTO EASILY-UNDERSTOOD BENEFITS.

work began—the business owner identified the information (or stimuli) customer's wanted.

Identifying information-oriented Web sites

Here are some of the ways you can easily identify an information-oriented Web site when you encounter one:

> Information-oriented Web sites are more marketing oriented.

- There may be several articles explaining the benefits of the firm's product or service category—not specific products and services—but the benefits of the product or service *category*. (These articles may be illustrated photographs showing the firm at work.)
- These articles may be illustrated by examples or case studies detailing the firm's previous experiences.
- Articles are written from the reader's point of view. The language reflects empathy; the articles are written using the customer's or prospect's language, and the word "you" frequently appears.

Here's how information-oriented Web sites handle the 10 major Web site characteristics.

Information flow

Like inner-directed Web sites, the primary information flow in information-oriented Web sites is from Web site to visitor. The same content is broadcast to all visitors. Yet, in this case, the customer or prospect's needs come first. The Web site's message was crafted *after* analyzing the Web site visitor's needs. So although information-oriented Web sites still reflect a one-way transfer of information, the customer's and prospect's needs, not the business owner's egos, came first.

Information density

Information-oriented Web sites are often information rich. They contain a lot of information intended to help visitors:

> Like inner-directed Web sites, information-oriented Web sites often fail to arouse urgency.

- Make the **right choice** by identifying their needs
- Learn the **right questions to ask** when shopping and comparing alternatives
- Find out how to **identify quality** (or the lack thereof)
- Learn how to **make the most** of their purchase
- Know **where to go for further information** or help

Urgency

Like inner-directed Web sites, information-oriented Web sites often fail to arouse urgency. The information is presented for the visitor's benefit, but there is no motivation for visitors to act right now. As a result, Web site visitors may lose interest in the purchase or they may visit another site that offers more urgency and purchase there.

Dialog

Dialog is a small part of most information-oriented Web sites. E-mail, fax, telephone, and other contact information is usually provided. Forms are sometimes used to invite visitors to provide their information, but there is rarely an incentive for immediate action. Visitors are rarely invited to request specific information.

Follow-up

Because information-oriented Web sites often fail to capture the visitor's contact information, follow-up is impossible.

Search capability

Search capability may be included when information-oriented Web sites become too large for visitors to locate information simply by clicking on links. Usually, links are enough to allow visitors to access desired information.

Qualification

Information-oriented Web sites often fail to invite visitors to qualify themselves on their information needs. The result is that most visitors encounter essentially the same information via linking, rather than requesting information that will satisfy their unique challenges or needs.

Customized content

Information-oriented Web sites rarely offer customized content. In most cases, the only customization that occurs is that visitors can choose the topics that promise to offer solutions to their problems and the sequence they visit the topics.

Updates

Information-oriented Web sites are updated only as necessary, usually when product information changes or new applications appear for existing products and services.

Size

Information-oriented Web sites can grow, especially those serving corporations with numerous product and service categories. Still, they rarely reach the size of large transaction-oriented Web sites, such as those created by online book or music stores.

Limitations of information-oriented Web sites

The major problem associated with information-oriented Web sites is their lack of urgency. By not providing compelling reasons for visitors to take immediate action, visitors are likely to leave and buy elsewhere. Information-oriented Web sites may also become too technical and turn off prospect buyers by confusing them.

Often this lack of urgency is based on a fear of upsetting current distribution channels. If the firm's products are sold by retailers and sales personnel around the country, the firm is constrained from building urgency into its message until it commits to a stronger online presence. In other cases, however, this lack of urgency is due

> The major problem associated with information-oriented Web sites is their lack of urgency.

to the educational mindset of the firm, one that feels its products and services are so clearly superior that the market will buy from them once they learn how great the product is.

As the Web evolves, information-oriented Web sites are likely to be replaced by either transaction-oriented or relationship-oriented Web sites, which recognize the growing importance of Web-based commerce.

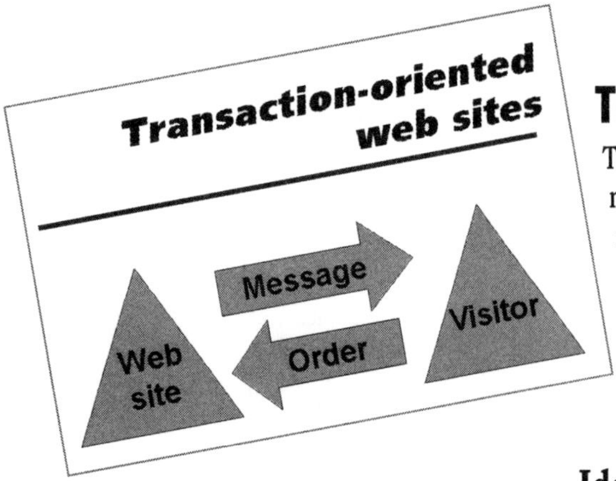

Transaction-Oriented Web Sites

Transaction-oriented Web sites represent the fastest growing and most highly publicized segment of the Web. By eliminating the middleman typically involved in distributing the product, these Web sites are revolutionizing the way many firms and industries do business. Transaction oriented Web sites ask for the sale and provide a means—usually involving credit cards—by which the sale can be immediately and securely consummated.

Identifying transaction-oriented Web sites

Transaction-oriented Web sites typically focus on one or two key products and offer extensive search capability to descriptions of other products or services. Usually, there is extensive search capability allowing visitors to quickly locate specific product information.

The content is typically very price and product oriented. Less attention is placed on positioning the company or attempting to build close, long-term relationships with the customer than making the sale right now.

You can usually easily identify transaction-oriented Web sites by the following characteristics:

- The home page typically focuses on one primary product or service offering (for example, this week's bestseller, etc.) plus contains briefer descriptions of a limited number of other "hot" products. These home page links take visitors directly to the pages promoting the products.

FIGURE 3-3 "BUY NOW!" WEB SITES INVITE A TWO-WAY, STIMULUS/RESPONSE EXCHANGE OF INFORMATION BETWEEN WEB SITE AND VISITORS.

- The home page is typically link-filled, allowing direct access to categories of products and services. In the case of online bookstores, for example, there would be links to categories such as fiction, current affairs, mysteries, self-help, automobile repair, employment, investing, home repairs, and health.
- There is usually an elaborate home page search mechanism to help visitors specify the date they want to travel, attend a concert, the group they want to hear, or the destination where they want to travel.
- Transaction-oriented Web sites usually provide full product descriptions including all necessary purchase, financing, and shipping information.
- Electronic order forms make it easy for visitors to order.

Let's take a closer look at transaction-oriented Web sites using the 10 characteristics as our guide.

Information flow
Transaction-oriented Web sites are based on a stimulus-response, four-step, two-way exchange of information.

1. The exchange begins when the visitor arrives at the Web site. The Web site invites the visitor to describe the product or service they are interested in purchasing.
2. The visitor responds by describing the product or products they're interested in.
3. The Web site informs them of current product availability and price and invites an immediate order.
4. The visitor responds by submitting an order.

Information density
Transaction-oriented Web sites are very information rich. Products and services are described in great detail. Transaction-oriented Web sites can describe hundreds, thousands, even *hundreds of thousands* of products. These products are described in great detail. There's space to provide as much marketing (benefits,

> Transaction-oriented Web sites are very information rich.

applications, usage tips) and technical information (specifications) as necessary to convince the buyer.

Transaction-oriented Web sites can become very sophisticated. Multiple photographs can be included. More important, available virtual reality technology permits visitors to view the products from multiple angles, for example, from the perspective of the driver's seat, Web site viewers can zoom in on the car's instrument panel or zoom up to the rear view mirror to check the view out the back window.

Urgency

Transaction-oriented Web sites resemble direct mail to the extent that they arouse an immediate response. Transaction-oriented Web sites are *even more* immediacy oriented, however, in that their offerings may change daily, even hourly, depending on whether the Web site is integrated with the firm's inventory. In the case of airline tickets, for example, the minute the last seat on the 3:30 plane to Paris is sold, the flight is removed from the Web site. Likewise, in the case of a model railroad hobby store selling limited-edition brass locomotives, the minute the last New York Central "Hudson" is sold, it disappears from the inventory.

Dialog

Dialog is an essential part of most transaction-oriented Web sites. The information on the Web site is static until the visitor requests it. You see only the information you request so that if you're travelling to Philadelphia, you don't encounter information about flights to Pittsburgh.

Transaction-oriented Web sites differ, however, in the attention they pay to those who don't immediately purchase. Some Web sites require you to register (fill out a form containing your e-mail and postal address), while others don't.

Transaction-oriented Web sites that are making the transition from printed and mailed direct mail to online commerce often invite visitors to request a copy of their latest catalog. The catalog request is often enough to establish a dialog with the visitor, permitting follow-up.

> Transaction-oriented Web sites resemble direct mail to the extent that they arouse an immediate response.

Follow-up

Transaction-oriented Web sites that invite visitors to register enjoy a major advantage over those that don't. Registration allows the Web site to announce special promotions and inform previous visitors when new content is added to the Web site. This permits the Web site to easily invite visitors back.

The follow-up of most transaction-oriented Web sites is shared by all visitors who have provided their postal or e-mail addresses. All visitors are likely to receive the same direct-mail catalog and all visitors are likely to receive the same e-mailed promotion.

Search capability

Because of the plethora of products offered at most transaction-oriented Web sites, they include sophisticated search capabilities. Visitors to an online hardware store, for example, can either search by category of product—such as detergents, mops, pails—or by brand name. Visitors to a Web site selling concert tickets can search by location, venue, performer, or date.

Qualification

Transaction-oriented Web sites can allow visitors to qualify their interests and needs as specifically as desired. Bookstores can invite visitors to indicate their favorite books and authors, music stores can invite visitors to indicate their favorite musicians. This information can be used as the basis of both present and future sales.

> Customized content is a key characteristic of transaction-oriented Web sites.

Customized content

Customized content is a key characteristic of transaction-oriented Web sites. This customized content can be immediately provided, or it can be sent at a later date.

On the basis of the visitor's descriptions of their favorite books or musicians described previously, for example, two types of customized content can be presented to the visitor:

- At the time of the initial visit, the Web site can make recommendations of new books or recordings by the visitor's favorite authors or performers. Perhaps the visitor isn't aware that his or her favorite author has a new book out. More important, the Web site can also suggest books by other authors who appeal to the same readers. The Web site could send a message along the lines of: "If you like X, you'll probably also like Y!"
- More important, however, this customized content can take place at a later date. For example, months after the visitor's first visit, bookstores can send e-mail announcements (with price incentives) to fans of certain authors when the author comes out with a new book. Likewise, they can inform a performer's fans when the performer is going to be in their area.

Many transaction-oriented Web sites can create customized pages for each visit. The pages that the visitor encounters are composites, created by using text and visuals originally contained at numerous points on the Web site. When a visitor to a pre-owned luxury automobile Web site requests a list of "1990 to 1992 blue Jaguars with less than 60,000 miles from dealers within a radius of 25 miles," the content they see is unique to them and differs from the content a visitor requesting a list of "1990 to 1992 blue Jaguars with less than 60,000 miles from dealers within a radius of 10 miles" would encounter.

> The best transaction-oriented Web sites are in a constant state of change because their contents are linked to the product's availability.

Updates

The best transaction-oriented Web sites are in a constant state of change because their contents are linked to the product's availability. In addition, the home pages of the site are updated as often as daily, so that each time visitors return, they will be exposed to fresh content. Retailers depending on floor traffic know that the more frequently they change their featured displays, the more often their customers will return. The same formula of "product freshness" works online.

Size

Because of the need to describe numerous products in great deal, doing a complete job of selling, in other words, transaction-oriented Web sites can quickly grow very large.

Limitations of transaction-oriented Web sites

The key limitation of transaction-oriented Web sites is that not every business sells products that lend themselves to national or international distribution. Transaction-oriented Web sites are often inappropriate for service businesses, such as lawyers, for example, whose practice is limited to individual states and involves a lot of personal, hands-on active participation. Transaction-oriented Web sites, for example, may have little to offer automobile repair shops, consultants, doctors, and funeral homes.

Extreme price competitiveness

Transaction-oriented Web sites often live or die by price. They are very trend and price sensitive. They must be very sensitive to changes in their competitor's prices.

Little opportunity to create customer loyalty

The extreme price competitiveness of most transaction-oriented Web sites forces them to cut their overhead to the bone, which means they have few resources to offer a high degree of noncomputer-based personal service. Transaction-oriented Web sites thus are rarely capable of creating long-term customer loyalty other than loyalty based on providing an expected service at a competitive price. Thus, transaction-oriented Web sites sacrifice long-term customer loyalty to short-term sales.

> The biggest problem with most Web sites, however, is that they are not fully integrated with the firm's day-to-day business activities.

Integration with Business

The biggest problem with most Web sites, however, is that they are not fully integrated with the firm's day-to-day business activities. With the exception of e-commerce Web sites, most Web sites are created and operated in isolation from a firm's ongoing marketing and operations. This is particularly true of inner-directed and informational Web sites that do little to convert visitors into prospects, prospects into customers, and customers into repeat customers.

Transaction-oriented Web sites often fail to integrate with the firm's ongoing marketing by seeing each transaction in isolation from an ongoing customer development process. Each sale is seen as a conquest and little is done to create future business. These Web sites are typically characterized by heavy promotion budgets—items are frequently given away for free in order to attract first-time customers.

The Relationship Marketing Alternative

Relationship marketing Web sites, described in Chapter 4, use the Web and e-mail to advance customers and prospects from stage to stage of a five-stage customer development cycle. Relationship marketing places the Web and e-mail firmly in the center of the firm's marketing and operations. The company's Web site and e-mail become the fulcrum around which all activities operate. This approach generates revenue as well as reduces the heavy promotion costs transaction Web sites require to stay in business.

Putting Ideas to Work

In the next chapter, we'll examine a relationship marketing alternative to these three most frequently encountered types of Web sites. In the meantime, take a few moments to evaluate your current, or planned, Web site's design and content.

1. Does your Web site load quickly?
2. Is the text on your Web site easy to read?
3. Is your Web site easy to navigate?
4. How quickly do you follow up on e-mailed requests for information?
5. Is the information on your Web site up-to-date?
6. Does your Web site encourage visitors to frequently return?
7. Does your Web site look inward or outward?
8. Is information presented from you, or your market's, point of view?
9. Does your current Web site resemble an inner-directed, information-oriented, or transaction-driven approach?
10. How often does the word "you" appear on your Web site?

> The company's Web site and e-mail become the fulcrum around which all activities operate.

For more information on this topic, visit our Web site at www.businesstown.com

Five Steps to a Successful Relationship Marketing Initiative

Overview of Section II
Premium content: How to develop information based incentives.
How to get to know your Web site visitors.
How to quality visitors and satisfy their needs.
How to transform prospective clients into returning customers.
How to convert customers into advocates.

Chapter 4

Introducing the Five-Stage Relationship Marketing Program

> A relationship, I think, is like a shark, you know? It has to
> constantly move forward or it dies.
>
> —WOODY ALLEN, *ANNIE HALL*

The relationship marketing program introduced in this chapter is designed to avoid the problems associated with inner-directed, information-oriented, and transaction-based Web sites. The goal is to help you develop a new way of viewing your Web site and, in the process, work towards a new, information-oriented and technology-based, ongoing marketing program for your business. This approach will help you better harness the powers of the Web by building on your current strengths instead of unnecessarily risking your firm's profitability and stability by attempting too much too soon.

In this chapter we'll examine the basics of the relationship marketing program and take a look at the five-stage customer development cycle. *Relationship Marketing on the Internet* is based on four key ideas:

- Customer retention versus customer acquisition
- Long-term customer value
- The five-stage customer development cycle
- Creating a synergy between information and technology

Ideas without commitment and implementation, of course, are unlikely to lead to success. Thus, this chapter ends with a discussion of the importance of commitment to a course of action.

As you implement the five-step customer development program described in this book, you'll find yourself gaining the confidence and resources you need to safely and successfully adopt the Web and transform your business over the coming years.

Customer Retention Versus Customer Acquisition

There is a startling disconnect between most Web sites and the businesses they ostensibly support. This is especially true in small and midsized businesses. Often, a firm's Web site reflects very little of what actually occurs on the sales floor or in face-to-face sales presentations.

Worse, e-mail and the Web are typically not used for effective customer follow-up. Most Web sites—especially e-commerce Web sites—are on a "treadmill to Hell," constantly attempting to attract new customers using cutthroat pricing incentives instead of focusing their efforts on satisfying and reselling the firm's current customers and prospects. As a result, profitability suffers and the firm does little or nothing to cultivate a loyal customer base.

Instead of focusing their efforts on those who have already "voted with their wallets" by buying from the firm, firms expensively attempt to recruit a constant stream of new customers to their Web site to buy products at extremely low margins. Firms that compete exclusively on price are constantly vulnerable to each new low-priced competitor that comes along. As a result, many firms spend a lot of money attracting customers to their Web sites to buy low margin products—and do little to retain the customer after purchase.

> Firms that compete exclusively on price are constantly vulnerable to each new low-priced competitor that comes along.

The fancy term for this form of economic lunacy is "churn," and it's what your stomach (and your investor's stomachs) do when you compare constantly escalating media costs with low margin sales.

A more sensible alternative for most firms is to eliminate, or reduce, churn by retaining customers. You also avoid the need to advertise and promote your Web site. By reselling current customers, you avoid the need to sell things at profit-destroying low prices. By harnessing technology to resell past customers, you are rewarded by higher margins and can convert your present customers into advocates who will do your advertising for you through word-of-mouth advertising.

Traditionally, it has been said that it costs five to seven times as much to sell (i.e. acquire) a new customer than it costs to resell a current customer. In today's highly competitive Internet world, the figure is even higher.

Firms that compete exclusively on price are constantly vulnerable to each new low-priced competitor that comes along.

The best study of the economic advantages of customer retention is to be found in a book called *The Loyalty Effect* by Frederick F. Reichheld (1996, Harvard University Press). Reichheld writes, "raising customer retention rates by five percentage points could increase the value of an average customer by 25 to 100 percent."

Customer Lifetime Value

Relationship marketing, in addition to emphasizing customer retention rather than customer acquisition, points out the need to view customers as long-term assets that must be managed, not harvested.

Currently, entirely too much emphasis is placed on sales at the expense of profits. Peppers and Cross, who wrote *The One-To-One Future* in 1993, emphasize the importance of analyzing "Customer Lifetime Value." Instead of concentrating solely on the profits from a single sale to a customer (or a firm's total sales volume in a single year), firms must analyze the total profits individual customers will generate over a period of five, ten, or fifteen years.

This long-term approach puts an entirely different spin on e-commerce and the appropriate relationship between a firm's Web site and its ongoing business. Profitability comes from reducing churn and increasing sales from existing customers. Profitability also comes from identifying your most profitable customers and having the courage to focus your efforts on them, rather than trying to please everyone (and ending up pleasing no one).

The Customer Development Cycle

One size does not fit all when it comes to the Web. Web site visitors enter with different information needs, based on their relationship to your firm. There are five stages to the customer development cycle.

Step 1: Introduction

The introduction stage is where you and your Web site visitor introduce yourselves to each other. This typically happens at the first visit, when a visitor comes as the result of a listing at a search engine or when a customer encounters your Web site address on your business card, invoice, or newsletter. The more you learn about your customers at this stage, the easier it will be to satisfy them in the future. It is imperative that you obtain your visitor's e-mail address. Your primary challenge at this stage is to develop an incentive that will motivate visitors to provide you with their e-mail address. If you fail to capture the visitor's e-mail address, you may never have another opportunity to sell that prospect.

> One size does not fit all when it comes to the Web.

Step 2: Comparison

The comparison stage is where visitors compare your product or service with those from your competitors. Meaningful content and credibility are the keys to success at the comparison stage. The more information you can provide, the higher the likelihood you'll make the sale. The comparison stage also provides you with an opportunity to learn more about the needs of your Web site visitors and, in doing so, be better able to fine-tune your offering to their needs.

Step 3: Transaction

The transaction stage is where money (or credit card information) changes hands. Unless you are giving products away for little or no profit, the transaction stage will only take place if you have played your cards right during the awareness and comparison stages. The transaction stage should be viewed as the beginning, not the end, of the relationship. The transaction stage sets the stage for the highly profitable stages that follow.

Step 4: Reinforcement

The reinforcement stage is where you *add value* to your customer's purchase by showing them how to maximize the value and pleasure their purchase can provide. The reinforcement stage presents you with an opportunity to position yourself apart from your competition by thanking your customer for their purchase and paving the way for future purchases. It's where you begin the process of creating word-of-mouth ambassadors for your firm out of satisfied customers.

Step 5: Advocacy

Advocacy is the final stage of the customer development cycle. Advocacy takes place when you provide your customers with the tools, or feeling of community, they need to become your promoters, motivating past customers to drive new visitors to your Web site and preselling your firm with word-of-mouth recommendations, the most effective form of advertising ever devised.

The Role of Information and Technology

Information is the most valuable incentive available. Fancy graphics, catchy slogans, and sophisticated Web effects, like animations, do not in themselves motivate visitors.

Visitors are selfish. They are interested only in information that helps them save money or perform a task more efficiently. Information presells visitors on your firm's competence and professionalism. Whereas advertising "claims," information "proves." It shows that you understand the needs of your customers and prospects.

In most cases, you already possess the information that your market needs to accomplish its goals. After all, you deal with your products and service every day. You're involved in your industry and understand the challenges facing your market. Individual customers and prospects only see a narrow slice representing their needs and wants. You, however, possess an overview of your market's needs. The information you take for granted is "news" to your customers and prospects. You also, typically, receive information about challenges, trends, and upcoming new products before your customers do. You have also been involved with your field long enough to have developed a perspective that permits you to interpret and explain your products and services from an in-depth, informed perspective.

Information is also free. You don't have to hire expensive graphic designers or Web site developers to prepare a white paper

> Information is the most valuable incentive available.

explaining the expected impact of recent trends in your field; you already know this information. Likewise, you don't have to hire a professional writer to prepare answers to the 20 most frequently asked questions that newcomers to your field ask; you and your staff answer these questions every day!

What's "everyday" and "common sense" to you is "news" and genuinely appreciated news to your market. All you have to do is format the information that already exists into white papers, new product introductions, and applications stories and you have a year's worth of content ready for your Web site.

Technology and content

Web-based relationship marketing is based on two types of content: open and premium. *Open content* refers to Web site pages that any Web site visitor can access. *Premium content* refers to pages containing more in-depth information. Technology is used to separate these two types of content. Premium content pages can be separated from open content pages by being password protected, unlinked, or downloaded.

- *Password protected* means that visitors must contact the Web site and submit their e-mail address. A password is then sent to their e-mail address.
- *Unlinked* pages are those that are not accessible through clicking on navigation links contained on the Web site.
- *Downloadable* pages are often fully formatted pages which, after authorization, are downloaded onto the visitor's hard disk. These can contain fancy fonts and graphics or include spreadsheets.

Open content

Open content establishes your credibility to newcomers and reinforces your credibility to previous customers. Open content is the baseline that everyone can access. But open content should never tell the whole story. Open content should be used as a teaser to motivate visitors to want to become more involved with your firm by

> What's "everyday" and "common sense" to you is "news" and genuinely appreciated news to your market.

submitting their e-mail address in order to gain access to your Web site's more sophisticated and in-depth premium content.

Premium content

Pages containing premium content do not appear on your Web site's navigation bar or text links. Premium content refers to pages with a richer, in-depth information content, content that visitors must be qualified to access. Access to premium content is limited to those who have registered their e-mail address or who have purchased from you. Current technology makes it easy to provide limited access premium content.

E-mail is the engine that provides access to premium content and propels visitors from level to level of the customer development cycle. When visitors to your Web site register by filling out a form and sending you their e-mail address, you can respond by providing the "key" that allows them access to your site's premium content. You can send them the URLs of unlinked pages, passwords to unlock password-protected pages, or access to pages containing files they can download in Microsoft Word or Adobe Acrobat format.

Content and competition

Another reason to separate content into open and premium areas is that open content is information your competitors can |access and respond to. If your competitors know that you're selling a certain product for X dollars, they can undersell you by selling it for Y dollars.

By restricting access to merchandising and promotions to those who have registered their e-mail address (and, perhaps, other information), allowing them access to premium content, you can gain a competitive edge over your competition by keeping them in the dark—or at least delaying their ability to respond to your promotions.

E-mail is the "engine" that provides access to premium content and propels visitors from level to level of the customer development cycle.

Relationship Marketing Web Sites

For most businesses, relationship-oriented Web sites represent the best investment. Relationship-oriented Web sites take a long-term view of customer and prospect development. Relationship-oriented sites are based on setting up a continuing dialog between visitor and Web site. This dialog typically involves forms and e-mail. Visitors submit forms that explain their interests and information needs along with their e-mail address. In return, the business renews the relationship at appropriate and/or periodic intervals by sending e-mail to the visitor.

Relationship-oriented Web sites combine the best of information-oriented and transaction-oriented Web sites, yet operate from a longer-range perspective. Characteristics you'll immediately notice include:

- The home page often focuses on a particular product or service, yet contains links to pages containing helpful information. Benefits other than price may be the key incentive to learn more about the featured product or service.
- Incentives to register are based on forms that request information about the visitor's opinion of the Web site, the visitor's e-mail and postal addresses, plus attempts to qualify the buyer's areas of interest.
- Relationship-oriented Web sites often contain an educational component with "How to buy" information.

Characteristics of relationship-oriented Web sites

The same criteria used to identify the previous types of Web sites can be used to identify relationship-oriented Web sites.

Information flow

Relationship-oriented Web sites involve a two-way flow of information. At their highest levels, relationship-oriented Web sites involve the same level of give-and-take that occurs in face-to-face meetings and telephone conversations. Visitors describe their unique needs and, in return, receive specialized content.

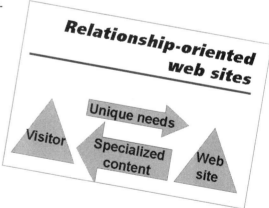

FIGURE 4-1 RELATIONSHIP-ORIENTED WEB SITES ENCOURAGE VISITORS AND CREATE A TWO-WAY DIALOG BETWEEN VISITOR AND WEB SITE.

Information density

Relationship-oriented Web sites display a high degree of information density. Relationship-oriented Web sites differ from transaction-based Web sites, however, in that the information is usually more business oriented rather than product oriented. On a transaction-oriented Web site, for example—to return to the hardware store example—the Web site would provide detailed information about each of the makes and models of mops or pails it stocked. On a relationship-oriented Web site, however, the emphasis would be on how competently the firm could deliver the mops and pails and the firm's after-sale mop and pail maintenance program and exchange policy.

Urgency

Relationship-oriented Web sites are in it for the long haul. The goal is to create long-term relationships with their prospects and customers. Thus, there is less "Buy Now!" emphasis. Time and resources are available to invest in helping prospects make the right choice, maintaining customer enthusiasm, and creating customer loyalty.

Dialog

Dialog is a key characteristic of relationship-oriented Web sites. Long-term success involves identifying Web site visitors and learning as much as possible about their needs as well as their after-sale experiences with the firm's products and services. Dialog can be as simple as offering first-time visitors a premium for filling out a registration form or as sophisticated as inviting Web site visitors to submit questions and concerns.

Follow-up

Dialog leads to follow-up. At minimum, registration should receive acknowledgement of their submission and the promised premium should be sent as soon as possible. Professionalism is the key to successful relationships; promises must be quickly fulfilled.

Relationship-oriented sites also involve ongoing follow-up. The goal is to always remain visible so that the next time the customer

> Relationship-oriented Web sites display a high degree of information density.

wants to make a purchase, the relationship-oriented firm will be the first Web site the customer thinks of. Likewise, when the customer is asked for a recommendation by a firm, the first URL that comes to mind should be the relationship-oriented Web site. The best way to do this is to send frequent e-mail messages announcing updated Web content or new products and services.

Search capability

Search capability is less important with relationship-oriented Web sites than transaction-oriented Web sites because the sites are likely to be smaller. In addition, because the relationship between business and customer/prospect will be based on personalization, the firm sponsoring the Web site can take the initiative in helping visitors locate desired information.

Qualification

Qualification is an important to part of successful relationship Web sites. Relationship-oriented Web sites are based on not only knowing who their visitors are but on knowing their customer's and prospect's specific needs. Today's computer technology makes this increasingly easy.

The key, of course, is to encourage visitors to qualify themselves on the home page at the first visit. The Web site should be constructed in a way that will enable the creation of a database that will classify visitors into whatever categories are most appropriate: geographic area, type of employment, area of concern (i.e. problem to be solved), or income. Form-based incentives must be offered to encourage visitors to share their qualifications with the Web site.

Surveys offer yet another tool you can employ when creating a relationship-driven Web site. Surveys go beyond involvement in that they permit you to fine-tune your Web site and improve it on the basis of visitor information. Surveys also allow you to determine who is visiting your Web site and qualify them on the basis of the profit opportunities they offer you.

> The key, of course, is to encourage visitors to qualify themselves on the home page at the first visit.

Customized content

Customized content can be the least expensive and most effective tool used to build long-term relationships with Web site visitors. Information can be both inexpensive and valuable: it can be inexpensive to create and valuable to both sender and recipient.

You can also involve visitors and fine-tune the information you provide by offering content at different levels of sophistication. A Web site for a ski resort, for example, could offer different content for beginning, intermediate, and advanced skiers. Likewise, a site for a tool company could have separate areas for home handymen and professional contractors. In each case, after qualification, the visitors would encounter different Web pages. But, unless they communicate this information to you, you won't be able to follow-up on the information.

Consider an example related to my own Meaningful Content Web site (*http://www.meaningfulcontent.com*). I could create a form that permits visitors to prequalify themselves on their areas of interest. I could include a form that asks questions like:

- Are you the owner of a small business?
- Do you publish a newsletter?
- Do you give frequent presentations?
- Do you hire freelance copywriters?

There would likely be little response to these questions because they're invasive and there is little incentive for visitors to respond to those open-ended questions.

Instead of asking visitors questions, I could offer those who registered their choice of valuable twenty-page articles, not available elsewhere. These could be sent either by return e-mail (as attached computer files) upon receipt of their request or by e-mailing those who registered their choice the URL, or address, of an unlinked page on my Web site. This would permit me to enjoy a much higher and much better response rate.

I could do a better job of qualifying my Web site visitors by offering visitors my choice of one of the following upon registration:

> Customized content can be the least expensive and most effective tool used to build long-term relationships with Web site visitors.

- FREE REPORT! Twenty-Five Ways to Use E-Mail to Increase Sales to Existing Customers
- FREE! The Ten Most Common Newsletter Design and Editing Errors
- FREE! Twenty Presentation Tips I Learned the Hard Way— So You Don't Have To!
- FREE! How to Get Your Freelance Copywriters to Deliver Excellence on Time—or Ahead of Time

Notice that, instead of acting "nosy," I'm setting up a win-win situation. I'm finding out the information I desire and, in return, the visitor is receiving valuable information that will help him or her do a better job. Also, notice that in each case there are no printing or postage costs involved and visitors receive immediate access to their customized information.

Updates

Relationship-oriented Web sites must be continuously updated. New, helpful content must be presented in order for visitors to return.

Whereas transaction-oriented Web sites only have to be updated in order to accommodate changing products and prices, relationship-oriented Web sites must be constantly updated with new information in order to maintain enthusiasm and enhance the Web site's credibility—and, hence, the credibility of the firm sponsoring it.

Out-of-site, out-of-mind. That's the trap that most Web sites and their sponsoring firms fall into unless they commit to constant updates.

Size

Relationship-oriented Web sites don't have to be large to succeed. Since their goal is to serve as a customer creation machine advancing customers from position to position along the customer relationship cycle, they only have to be as large as necessary to provide the necessary information. They don't have to be encyclopedias or catalogs offering information for *every* conceivable need; they can

> Relationship-oriented Web sites must be continuously updated.

be far more focused. The emphasis can be on the business and reasons to buy from the firm, rather than the products.

Limitations of relationship-oriented Web sites

The primary disadvantage of relationship-oriented Web sites relates to the time needed to set up and maintain a database of customer/prospect names and addresses and respond to e-mail. Time is needed to compile and analyze responses to survey questions. Time is required to prepare e-mail messages for registered prospects and customers.

This time commitment should not be taken lightly. As described in the following chapters, the creation of a relationship-oriented Web site is likely to require the delegation of numerous duties, including:

- Responding to e-mail
- Maintaining the customer and prospect
- Creating new Web content
- Preparing e-mail alerts
- Notifying the sales staff of new customers and prospects for personalized follow-up (when appropriate)

Challenges

This is simply an overview of a philosophy of Web site development, and there are many challenges to be overcome. Credibility and relevance are crucial to the success of a Web initiative based on the five stage customer development cycle. To succeed, most firms are likely going to have to devote more time and resources to the information resources appropriate to each level of the customer development cycle. The next five chapters explore each of the five steps of the cycle and will put you on the right track to building your own relationship-oriented Web site.

> To succeed, most firms are likely going to have to devote more time and resources to the information resources appropriate to each level of the customer development cycle.

Putting Ideas to Work

Ask yourself the following questions as you review your use of e-mail:

1. Does your Web site contain separate pages offering both open and premium content?
2. Do you use incentives to encourage visitors to submit their e-mail address?
3. Do you qualify the needs of your visitors by ascertaining their areas of interest?
4. Do you keep track of visitor e-mail addresses and organize access to addresses on the basis of their stage in the customer development cycle?
5. Do you send visitors e-mail newsletters at frequent, consistent intervals that are intended to drive visitors back to your Web site?
6. Do you send alerts and bulletins to specific market segments based on their position in the customer development cycle?
7. Do you respond quickly to e-mail requests for information?
8. Does your Web site contain information appropriate for newcomers just becoming interested in your field as well as those who are experienced, repeat buyers?

For more information on this topic, visit our Web site at www.businesstown.com

Chapter 5

Step One: Getting Acquainted at the Introduction Stage

Getting to know you, getting to know all about you!
—RODGERS AND HAMMERSTEIN, *THE KING AND I*

Carroll's Jewelers, in downtown Seattle, always has a plate of freshly baked cookies on the counter. It makes a good (and tasty!) first impression and it says they care about the people who come in to their store. Now it may be a little difficult to offer a home baked cookie to everyone who comes to your Web site, but the example illustrates the importance of making a good first impression and of offering first-time visitors something they will value.

Something else they do at Carroll's Jewelers is take the time to get acquainted with their customers—to learn their likes and dislikes. Because, realistically, there is no reason their staff should show a bracelet or any other piece of jewelry to a customer unless it matches the tastes of the customer. Once they take the time to learn about the tastes and interests of their customer and demonstrate that understanding by showing a piece of jewelry that fits those tastes perfectly, the chance of making a sale go way up. This is an important lesson. And when you do the same thing on your Web site your chances of making a sale go way up, too. And your customers will take note of that fact that you care about them.

The introduction stage is the first step in converting a visitor to an advocate. Awareness is what occurs when your prospect first visits your Web site. Often, this is the make or break point that determines the whole course of your future relationship with the visitor. Done right, the introduction stage provides an opportunity for you and your prospect to *introduce yourselves* to each other. If you both make a good impression, the stage is set for future involvement.

However, if things don't work out in the introduction stage, the prospect may quickly leave your Web site and never return. The success of your future relationship with the visitor depends on establishing your credibility and making such a positive impression on the customer that the prospect will provide you with his or her e-mail address for future follow-up.

What Should Happen When Visitors Arrive at the Introduction Stage

Four things should occur during the introduction stage:

- *Mutual introduction.* From the moment they hit your Web site, visitors should begin learning about your firm, the products and services you sell, as well as your philosophy of doing business. The benefits you offer should be immediately apparent.
- *Image.* Your Web site should project a unique image, one that is distinct from your competitors as well as appropriate for your philosophy of doing business.
- *Registration.* Visitors must register by submitting, at bare minimum, their e-mail address and, preferably, additional information.
- *Qualification.* Visitors have differing information requirements. Your Web site's structure should make it easy for visitors to qualify their information needs, which will help them quickly locate desired information and help you fine-tune your dialog with them.

> Within seconds of visiting your Web site, visitors should be able to learn a lot about you, your business, and the products or services you offer.

How to Introduce Yourself

Within seconds of visiting your Web site, visitors should be able to learn a lot about you, your business, and the products or services you offer. Your success depends on your ability to immediately engage your Web site visitor in a meaningful dialog while introducing your products and services. It's important to emphasize the importance of speed. Visitors are in a hurry and will not stick around unless they are presented with meaningful information tailored to their needs.

The biggest mistake most firms make is to create a home page for their Web site that features a big logo and their name, followed by a series of buttons with vapid titles like "About us," "In the News," "Our Products," and "Contact."

It's interesting that businesses that have mastered the art of business-to-business or business-to-consumer direct mail fall down with a resounding thud when it comes to creating their home page. Home pages that waste their visitors time and fail to offer meaningful information or engage visitors in a dialog are doomed to failure.

Is your home page effective?

Start by viewing your home page from a visitor's point of view and ask yourself, "What does the home page teach me?" If you can't provide a meaningful answer to that question, your home page needs work. Ask yourself the following questions:

1. Does the Web site load quickly?
2. Does the Web site communicate the firm's area of expertise?
3. Does the Web site describe the products or services offered?
4. Does the Web site offer news value that I will benefit by learning?
5. Does the Web site communicate how the firm differs from its competition?
6. Does the Web site invite me to participate?

The easiest way to improve most Web sites is to reduce the size of the graphics and choose more appropriate titles for the navigation links. In many cases, reducing the size of the logo—which really does not offer visitors any information or value—creates the space necessary to begin the sales process by focusing on a specific product or service that identifies the firm's area of expertise. Another advantage of this approach is that reducing the space devoted to your logo makes it possible to add news value to your Web site by frequently changing the product or service featured.

If your Web site's home page always appears the same, even if the contents are changed, visitors are unlikely to come back because the new content isn't visible.

The second simple, but major, way you can improve your Web site is to choose titles for navigation links that offer obvious benefits to visitors. Think in terms of direct response marketing. You'd never receive an envelope or catalog in the mail with words like "About us," "Our Products," and "Contact." Instead, every word on the envelope or front cover of a direct-response catalog is designed to offer a benefit and ask for an action.

Accordingly, strive to replace inward-directed links with links that offer benefits. Translate the categories of your Web site into clearly identified "benefit chunks." For example:

- "Products" could be translated into "Resources"
- "About us" could be translated into "Experience"
- "Contact us" could be translated into "Register to win" or "Free valuable report!"
- FAQ—shorthand for "Frequently Asked Questions"—can be replaced by "How to be an informed buyer"

In each case, the goal is to have every word of your Web site appeal to the visitor's point of view, rather than the business's point of view.

The home pages of many Web sites have brief "mission statements." Invariably, these, too, are written from the business's point of view rather than the visitor's point of view. "Our goal is to create happy and satisfied customers." What does that tell you about the business? Is it believable? Does it help separate the business from its competition? Does it offer a benefit?

In most cases, mission statements, taglines, or mottos simply waste space and are ignored by visitors on their first visit and irritate visitors upon subsequent visits. Why subject your visitors to the same words each time they visit? Instead of wasting space on an empty claim that cannot be proven, or a claim that is difficult to translate into a visitor benefit ("Family-owned since 1955"), concentrate on developing headlines and links that satisfy your visitor's need for information.

> In most cases, mission statements, taglines, or mottos simply waste space and are ignored by visitors on their first visit and irritate visitors upon subsequent visits.

Enhancing your Web site

Further reducing the size of your firm's logo and navigation links and eliminating empty mission statements often creates the space necessary to start selling your product or services with specific news-oriented headlines and text. You can then use this space to begin one or more text articles that can be continued on inside pages. There are several advantages to this approach:

- **More options**. By showing one or more headlines, visitors are more likely to find a topic they will want to continue reading.
- **Credibility**. By couching your marketing message in editorial, as opposed to "brag and boast," terms, visitors will treat your message as "news" rather than "claims."
- **Change**. By featuring different articles on your home page—indicated by different headlines and, when appropriate, different photographs—even if the same articles are rotated every two weeks over the course of a few months, repeat visitors will sense change and pay more attention. Visitors who weren't interested in a topic one month may be interested the next month.

The key to success is to cultivate a news and benefit-oriented approach to describing the products or services your firm offers—and begin the articles on your home page. Although this may initially be difficult, it will ultimately be extremely important to you as six months or a year from now you'll be naturally thinking of your business from your customer's and prospect's point of view instead of your own.

This attitude change will reward you with years of enhanced profitability, not only on the Web but in all aspects of marketing and promoting your business.

How to Project the Right Image

In addition to introducing yourself to visitors, you have to project an appropriate image. In contrast to words, which operate on a cognitive, or conscious, level, image operates on an emotional level. Just as you make instantaneous like/dislike decisions when you first meet someone, visitors to your Web site are likely to make like/dislike decisions based on the appearance of your Web site.

You control the image of your Web site with four design tools:

- **Color**. The colors used on your Web site project emotional images that can be described in terms of "cheap," "expensive," "friendly," or "aloof." Color choices help communicate who you want to visit your site: children or adults. The number of colors used as well as the color choices themselves instantly communicate a lot about your business. There is a world of difference between a Web site that uses bright colors like hot reds, pinks, and yellows against a black background and a Web site that uses dark blues and grays against a white background.
- **Layout**. Layout refers to the density of information on your Web site, the arrangement of text and graphics on your pages. Layout helps nonverbally communicate "amateur" versus "professional." If the various text and graphic elements on your home page appear to be randomly placed, your Web site will communicate an amateur as opposed to a professional image; this image will carry over to the way visitors think about your business. "Quiet" Web sites—those exhibiting generous margins along the top edge and left and right-hand edges project a far more professional image than Web sites filled screen-edge to screen-edge with text.
- **Typography**. Although on the Web you do not enjoy total control over the typefaces and type sizes used for "live," or HTML text, you do have the ability to project an image by setting key words—such as your Web site's title—or theme graphic, navigation buttons, and key headlines as downloadable graphics. In general, sans serif typefaces project a more contemporary image than titles and key words set in a serif typeface. Large type sizes "shout" rather than "seduce with a whisper," and project a less expensive, less polished approach.
- **Visuals**. Visuals include backgrounds, illustrations, and scanned photographs. Visuals communicate at a glance. A

> You control the image of your Web site with four design tools:
> 1. Color.
> 2. Layout.
> 3. Typography.
> 4. Visuals.

Web site that uses bold, brightly colored, cartoon-type illustrations will be perceived in an entirely different way than a Web site that uses finely detailed drawings. The size of the illustrations also communicates the firm's professionalism. Large, slow-loading graphics communicate a disrespect for the visitor's time. Thumbnails, small illustrations that can be clicked on to reveal larger images, reflect an attention to detail that communicates an image of customer care and respect. Likewise, the absence or presence of movement communicates the firm's attitude towards its customers. The gratuitous use of blinking or scrolling text communicates a "gee gosh!" amateurish image that undermines the visitor's respect for the firm.

In general, the restrained use of color, layout, typography, and visuals communicates a more professional image than the overuse of any of these tools.

Registration

It's not enough for you to introduce yourself to your visitors. Success and relationship building require your visitors to introduce themselves to you.

Creating a registration form (covered fully in chapter 14) is a matter of finding the ideal balance between quality and quantity. Registrations increase to the extent your registration form is easy to locate, short, and easy to fill out. Responses go down as you ask for increased amounts of information. But the increased amount of the information you receive enhances the value of the registrations. It's up to you to determine how much information is appropriate and how many responses you're willing to sacrifice in order to build your e-mail mailing list.

Qualification

Qualification is important because no two Web site visitors have the same information needs. By helping your Web site visitors qualify

> It's not enough for you to introduce yourself to your visitors. Success and relationship building require your visitors to introduce themselves to you.

themselves, you can make it easier for them to locate important information and you can do a faster, more efficient job of satisfying their information needs.

One of the best ways you can qualify your Web site's visitors is by asking questions on the home page. Properly handled, qualification can perform two important functions:

- *More responsive Web site.* Your visitor's responses to a series of qualifying questions can direct visitors to the pages of your Web site offering desired information. For example, let's assume you are an architect dealing with both residential and commercial construction and you ask your visitors, "Are you interested in residential or commercial construction?" These are mutually exclusive options. Choosing either the "Residential" and "Commercial" option will take the visitor to a specific page. Likewise, if you're a software publisher selling products to the legal, accounting, and banking industries, offering visitors the ability to qualify themselves by choosing one of these options saves them time by taking them directly to the information they're interested in. Even if your product is identical, your sales pitch on the linked pages can be changed to appeal to the specific interests of lawyers, accountants, or bankers.

- *Better tracking reports.* By offering visitors an opportunity to qualify themselves on your home page, and tracking the option each visitor chooses, you can add this information to the visitor's e-mail registration. Even if the visitor does not tell you that they are a lawyer or a banker, the fact that they chose the lawyer or banker option as the next page they visited can be added to your database along with their e-mail address. Later, you can fine-tune the e-mail and newsletters you send to visitors on the basis of their profession, industry, or the product/service they are interested in.

Determining your qualification criteria

There are several approaches you can take in determining your selection criteria. You can analyze your current market in terms of product or services, clients or customer categories, or purchase price. A car dealer might categorize buyers in terms of the make or model purchased, a bookstore might analyze readers in terms of fiction or nonfiction, and an oral surgeon in terms of cosmetic or "preventative" procedures. It often helps to think of your market in terms of opposites: expensive or inexpensive, local or distant, individual or corporate, etc.

Once you have established a qualification profile, preparing the text needed for your Web site will become increasingly easy as you will know which points to emphasize by remembering previous sales encounters with members of each category.

Use certificates to remember visitor preferences

Certificates are files that are downloaded from your Web site into a special folder on the hard drive of your Web site visitor's computer. Certificates can be used to identify visitors when they return to your Web site (assuming they are using the same computer and not their home computer if they first visited your Web site from their office). Certificates remember the pages a visitor has visited and also remember any information visitors have submitted.

When visitors qualify themselves by choosing "defense attorney" rather than "officer of the law," for example, not only will the visitor see information custom tailored to attorneys on their first visit, but upon subsequent visits the Web site will take them directly to updated information of interest to attorneys.

Why Visitors Leave at the Introduction Stage

Visitors to your Web site will make a decision to leave or stay within a few seconds. It is up to you to design a Web site and—in particular—a home page that encourages visitors to stick around so you both may get to know each other better. Here is a summary of why most Web sites fail to attract and keep visitors at the introduction stage:

- *No visit at all.* A failure to promote your Web site via postcards, a constant repetition of your URL in your letterhead, business cards, and other advertising, and a failure to set up

> Certificates are files that are downloaded from your Web site into a special folder on the hard drive of your Web site visitor's computer.

your Web site so that search engines locate your Web site will ensure that no one visits your site.

- *Slow loading.* Web site visitors are very impatient. You have a very short time to attract their attention. Within a matter of a few seconds, if they do not immediately see a reason to remain at your Web site, they will move on. There are too many fast-loading Web sites for visitors to want to stick around for slow-loading Web sites. Large graphics and logos are sure-fire attention killers.

- *No information.* Unless your Web site offers immediately obvious benefits, i.e., information unavailable elsewhere, visitors are unlikely to remain. Web sites live and die by information. Visitors are not interested in hearing how great you are; visitors are selfish, they are more interested in hearing how you can help them achieve their goals.

- *Difficult navigation.* Confusing navigation can devalue the best information. If your navigation is not immediately obvious, visitors will move elsewhere. "About us" or "Our products" does not offer visitors much of an incentive to click on the navigation link.

- *Lack of incentive to register.* Visitors are unlikely to provide you with their name, e-mail address, and other information unless you provide them with a reason to share this information with you. In addition, you must also promise not to share visitor information with others.

- *Difficult registration process.* Asking too many questions or rejecting registration forms with simple errors is a proven way to kill visitor interest.

> Visitors to your Web site will make a decision to leave or stay within a few seconds.

Goals

At the end of a prospect's or customer's first visit, the following should have occurred:

- Visitors respect your Web site and your firm because the Web site has communicated substantive information.

- Visitors know what business you're in and what sets you apart from your competition.
- Visitors like you because you have respected their time by creating a fast loading Web site.
- You know who your visitors are and can communicate again with them via e-mail because they have submitted their e-mail address.
- You have begun to qualify your visitor's needs and concerns.

For more information on this topic, visit our Web site at www.businesstown.com

Chapter 6

Step Two: Communicating Your Competitive Advantage

Anyone who believes that the competitive spirit in
America is dead, has never been in the supermarket when the
cashier opens another checkout line.
—ANN LANDERS, AMERICAN ADVICE COLUMNIST

*The staff at Carroll's Jewelers in downtown Seattle know their
jewelry. That expertise comes across plainly as they introduce the
features of a wristwatch or the cut of a diamond. That expertise
gives the customer respect for their knowledge and a comfort level
for making a purchase. Customers want to do business with
experts. That much is obvious. What may be less obvious to some is
that you can't just announce your expertise; you need to demonstrate it. It is at this stage that the customer begins to make a buying decision. It is at this stage that you need to stand out as the
clear best choice.*

*And when the jeweler behind the counter at Carroll's Jewelers
combines this expertise with the personal knowledge of the customer's tastes in jewelry, customers take notice and respond.
Considering this competent, personalized service delivered one on
one, you may begin to get an appreciation for the powerful results
that a well-implemented relationship marketing initiative on your
Web site can produce.*

Your goal at the comparison stage is to show how your firm or
product can better satisfy the prospect's needs than your competition's. The comparison stage is where many potential sales are lost.
Sales are lost during the comparison stage when the firm does not
re-involve the prospect (by attracting them back to the Web site) or
present an effective description of its offerings compared to the offerings of its competitors. Sales are also lost when the Web site does
not deflect the prospect's interest away from price and towards areas
where the firm enjoys a perceived competitive advantage, such as
competence, professionalism, selection, or any other criteria.

Credibility, again, is the key to success. You must be able to present facts and figures that convincingly demonstrate your competitive advantages. Success comes from a three-step process:

> Credibility, again, is the key
> to success. You must be
> able to present facts and
> figures that convincingly
> demonstrate your
> competitive advantages.

1. *Identify and analyze your competition* in order to better understand their strengths and weaknesses.
2. *Identify your firm's competitive strengths* so you can focus on areas where your firm offers a real (or perceived) advantage.
3. *Shift the battleground* to those areas where your firm enjoys the most advantages.

Information is also the key to success. All the Java scripts and pretty design in the world aren't as important as developing convincing arguments that show how your firm can do a better job of satisfying the prospect's needs than your competition.

Tools that could be used at the comparison stage include:

- Case studies of previous successes
- Background information about your firm and its people
- Testimonials from satisfied customers
- Product reviews, comparisons, or benchmarks

The problem with the above options is that they all reflect a passive or one-size-fits-all approach. They are all variations on the electronic brochure school of Web site design that provides identical content for every Web site visitor. The inevitable result of this is that many Web site visitors are presented with information that is not tailored to their specific needs.

It's like being forced to wade through airfares and schedules to Reno when you really want to go to Anchorage. Although the information to Anchorage may be present, it's difficult to locate and—once found—doesn't create an emotional bond or satisfying experience.

Importance of Qualifying Visitors

A much better approach is to *qualify* visitors and to provide them with information tailored to satisfy their particular needs. By inviting your prospects to communicate their needs and concerns, you can do a better job of addressing their specific needs.

Although it is often sufficient to gather just the visitor's name and e-mail address at the previous awareness stage, at the qualification or market segmentation stage, visitors should be invited to provide more information.

Although it is often sufficient to gather just the visitor's name and e-mail address at the previous awareness stage, at the qualification or market segmentation stage, visitors should be invited to provide more information. By encouraging and making it easy for visitors to communicate their specific needs to you, it becomes easier to provide—through either database-driven Web pages, automated e-mail or fax-back systems, or human intervention—custom information to your visitors. This information also makes it easy to tailor your firm's offerings to what your market really wants, not what you think it wants.

Qualification requires you to give more thought to the target markets you want to approach and their information needs. Before you begin creating your Web site, you have to divide it into different market segments and present—and re-present—your arguments in different ways to appeal to different audiences. It also forces you to create a Web site that has a more sophisticated navigation system.

As a starting point, let's examine some examples to see how Web site market segmentation at work. As always, it helps to start by looking at opposites, or extremes, and refining your choices.

- A restaurant Web site could segment visitors on the basis of individuals (or couples) searching for an evening out, large groups (such as corporations planning dinner meetings for large groups), and off-premises catering.

The competitive arguments that a restaurant can provide for a couple celebrating an intimate birthday are completely different than the arguments the restaurant would provide a corporation looking for a venue to celebrate landing a new account. In the former case, a quiet atmosphere, fresh flowers, and an extensive wine selection might be most appropriate. In the case of a corporation looking for a "party" atmosphere, private rooms, competitive prices on volume dining, and the ability to handle large groups of people would be more appropriate.

- A lawyer might segment visitors on the basis of opposites such as civil or criminal, individual or corporate, or matters dealing with liability, real estate, or taxation.
- Web sites for real estate agents should permit visitors to indicate whether they are interested in buying a home or selling a home. At the next level, qualification can indicate desired price range and timeframe.

Once qualification information is gathered, of course, it should be made a permanent part of the visitor's record. This can be done by creating a cookie, which stores the information for future reference when the visitor revisits the Web site. Or, the information can be placed on the Web site.

Qualification, or market segmentation, can also be used to help firms define the various markets that they serve—and, upon examination—often firms serve more markets than initially obvious. A health club, for example, serves several markets:

- Individuals and families who enroll on their own
- Doctors who recommend or prescribe membership for their patients
- Corporations seeking to reduce sick days and insurance premiums by enhancing their employees health

By targeting different messages to each market, the health club can maximize its returns. After all, individuals are unlikely to be interested in information about corporate onsite training workshops and corporations are unlikely to be interested in messages aimed at area physicians.

Likewise, a secretarial service's Web site serves two markets: corporate prospects who are in need of outsourcing secretarial work during periods of high demand, as well as prospective full-time and part-time employees. The messages sent to each market should be different and tailored to its needs. Messages to corporations should stress low costs and savings compared to full-time employees; messages to prospective employees should stress pleasant working conditions, benefits, and high pay.

Prospect Interactivity

The most effective way to argue your competitive advantage is to offer your prospects an opportunity to further qualify themselves by indicating their areas of concern in increasing detail. Asking individuals to rank their problems or concerns allows you to find out your prospect's "hot buttons" and gain information that you can use to improve your Web site in the future.

By soliciting increasingly granular, or detailed, input from Web site visitors, you will gain important information about their needs and the information you can provide to serve them better.

> The most effective way to argue your competitive advantage is to offer your prospects an opportunity to further qualify themselves by indicating their areas of concern in increasing detail.

The Role of Personalization

Personalization is one of the most effective tools you can use at the comparison stage. People respond to people. As early as possible, after capturing a visitor's name and address, assign a customer representative, by name, to respond to queries from Web visitors. When appropriate, consider introducing the e-mail you send visitors with their first name rather than a generic "Dear client" salutation.

Learning from the Case Studies

The best way to gain ideas for the comparison stage of your Web site is to review the following case studies in an effort to identify ideas you can adopt. Notice the dichotomy of in-depth information between open and premium content in most of the case studies.

Accountant

Open content at an accountant's Web site should include testimonials from previous clients and articles stressing the accountant's understanding of the current economic and taxation environment. The accountant's premium content electronic newsletter should contain articles outlining how the latest changes in the state's tax code will affect filing procedures.

Customized e-mail alerts can be sent to specific categories of businesses discussing how changes in the tax code will affect categories such as self-employed, large corporations, or two-income families.

Art gallery

During the comparison stage, open content at an art gallery's Web site should include reviews of previous gallery showings and credibility-enhancing articles about current art trends and the proper way to display and insure art. The premium content invitation sent to registered visitors should stress the works currently on display in great detail as well as the artist's background and the challenges he or she overcame in creating the works on display.

Automobile dealer

Open content should include letters from satisfied customers as well as summaries of previous reviews from automotive enthusiast magazines. Premium content should point registered visitors to pages containing the latest reviews and rumors about next year's models, plus seasonal driving tips. Model alerts should also be sent to registered visitors who have requested to be kept informed about incoming new and pre-owned models.

Bed and breakfast

Open content for the bed and breakfast Web site might include recipes for popular dining room specialties as well as reprints of comments from previous visitors. Premium content could include a monthly calendar containing a seasonal photograph and information about upcoming events in the area. Previous visitors might also appreciate an opportunity to download a seasonal screen saver stressing "signature" area activities.

Community photographer

Open content at the community photographer's Web site might include sample photographs of the area and its residents. Premium content might point registered visitors to pages describing "How to be a better client" and "How to prepare for an executive portrait."

Executive recruiter

Open content might include case studies of successful placements as well as interpretative reports on the current job market. Premium content for those seeking employment might include service pages that would help prospects prepare a better resume or adapt their resume to changing job requirements. Premium content for corporate clients could include teasers describing newly available employees and articles discussing reimbursement and benefit issues.

Financial planner

Open content might include credibility-enhancing articles interpreting recent trends and a glossary of financial planning terms, along with results of an ongoing customer satisfaction survey. Premium content might invite registered visitors to take a no-commitment survey of economic goals, which leads to an invitation to discuss a customized financial plan.

French restaurant

Open content would include reprints of magazine reviews and comments from newspaper critics plus articles describing seasonal specials. Premium content could include an invitation to download the latest recipe of the month, which is perhaps joined to a seasonal photograph.

Graphic artist

Open content would include client testimonials, case studies, plus an in-depth article discussing the problems and solutions involved in a recent project. Premium content would introduce newly available typefaces, comments about upgraded software, and links to the firms displaying the latest online projects.

> Open content would include client testimonials, case studies, plus an in-depth article discussing the problems and solutions involved in a recent project.

Health club

Open content could contain before and after member photographs, photographs of recent membership activities, plus articles by staff members on diet and exercise issues. Premium content would include an opportunity for visitors to fill out a personal health goal statement plus a newsletter announcing advance sign-up's for upcoming events.

> With open content, there are many hundreds of choices and applications.

Home theater installation specialist

Open content would include staff profiles, photographs of previous installations, plus an article on choosing, using, and installing home theater components. Premium content could include downloadable clip art for furniture and home theater components, which visitors could use in preliminary planning. Premium content would also include a newsletter discussing the latest trends in home theater and evaluations of the latest equipment.

Microbrewery

Open content for the microbrewer could include an article describing the special steps the brewery takes to ensure a high-quality product. Premium content for registered visitors would include new recipes that complement the brew of the month.

Oral surgeon

Open content would include comments from previous patients and articles describing the surgeon's background and accomplishments (educational highlights, techniques newly introduced to the area). Premium content could include features describing empowerment steps that patients can do to minimize discomfort and reduce the possibilities of surgery.

Outdoor recreational clothing store

Open content would include articles describing what to look for when choosing various categories of outdoor clothing. The store's expertise could be enhanced by showing photographs of its staff using the products they sell. Premium content would include a bimonthly or quarterly newsletter previewing the upcoming season and describing newly introduced products for the upcoming season.

Secretarial service

Open content for the secretarial service would profile previous successful job placements and outsourcing, as well as articles summarizing the advantages of outsourcing. Premium content for corporate markets could include a return on investment page showing potential employers how much their firm could save using the service. Premium content for employees could highlight skills currently in high demand plus the advantage of working for the firm.

Veterinarian

Open content would include articles on general pet health care for owners. Premium content would consist of advance warnings and seasonal alerts for various types of pets. Owners of specific breeds could read preventative health articles written specifically for them.

Wood stove store

Open content at the comparison stage would include photographs of recent custom installations, profiles of the brands carried, and information about choosing and using wood stoves and gas barbecues. Premium content could include in-depth, up-to-date recommendations helping visitors compare the various brands and models of wood stoves they sell and information about weather trends that might affect the upcoming season. During the spring, the emphasis could be placed on evaluating outdoor gas grills.

> Notice the way that premium content is always more focused and specific than open content.

Conclusion

Notice the way that premium content is always more focused and specific than open content. Open content enhances the firm's overall credibility, but premium content is tailored to increasingly specific markets—corporate versus small business, dog owners versus cat owners, etc.

The comparison stage uses numbers and specifics whenever possible. The day care center uses pictures of children at play to present a friendly image, the secretarial service uses a return on investment calculator to help employers calculate the savings that outsourcing makes possible, etc.

Putting Ideas to Work

The starting point for developing open and premium content for the comparison stage is often to ask past customers why they bought from you instead of one of your competitors. Take careful notes of their responses. What is the most frequently mentioned reason they give for buying from you? What are some of the other reasons? After talking to several customers, trends are likely to emerge. Use these trends as the basis for developing comparison content.

Then, use the following worksheet to identify some of the ways you can emphasize your firm's competitive advantage. (This worksheet is also available on the author's Web site at *www.rcparker.com/comparison*).

> The starting point for developing open and premium content for the comparison stage is often to ask past customers why they bought from you instead of one of your competitors.

Worksheet: Competitive Advantage

1. What are some of the customer benefits that set your firm apart from your competition?
2. How can you quantify some of the ways your firm differs from the competition?
3. Would it be appropriate to personalize your firm by including photographs of your staff along with brief statements describing their backgrounds and philosophies?
4. How can you help newcomers to your field identify quality in the goods or services they are considering buying?
5. What insider information regarding challenges, trends, or new products in your field could you discuss and interpret in newsletter articles or special position papers?

6. What types of electronic information can you create that you can use to reward visitors who register their e-mail addresses at your Web site?

7. Can you use customer satisfaction survey results or letters and testimonials from customers to back up your claims about superior customer service?

8. What special services, beyond the obvious, does your firm offer that you can describe to show you offer a complete solution?

9. What types of event marketing—demonstrations, seminars, workshops, etc.—can you use to illustrate your in-depth approach to business?

10. Are there ways you can visually demonstrate your firm's competence, such as before and after photographs?

For more information on this topic, visit our Web site at www.businesstown.com

Chapter 7

Step Three: Converting Prospects to Customers

I'm the world's worst salesman; therefore, I must make it easy for people to buy.

—FRANK W. WOOLWORTH

Carroll's Jewelry in downtown Seattle uses a powerful relationship marketing approach that brings the new customer smoothly to the point of purchase. Would you prefer to buy from a clerk that doesn't know your tastes and shows you styles you don't care for and who can't tell you anything about the diamond that isn't written on the tag? Or, would you buy your engagement ring from someone who has taken the time to learn what you like, who presents several choices that are just your style, and who can look at the diamond through the magnifier, make comments, and then hand you the glass and explain the nuances of cut, color, and clarity? And then, once they show you the choices and tell you about each, they ice the deal by telling you that every customer that buys an engagement ring from their jewelry store gets a ride in a beautiful, classic Rolls Royce limousine. Hardly a tough choice is it?

Turning a prospect into a customer—making the sale—is what the relationship marketing process is designed to do. And on your Web site, this is done by providing open and premium content for customers at each stage, content that builds on the strengths you are demonstrating and the personal attention you are providing and that makes the buying decision simple and the transaction pleasurable and painless.

The transaction stage involves providing specific incentives for visitors to buy right now. The transaction stage involves "harvesting the seeds" that you planted during the awareness and comparison stages. The transaction stage is where you get down to business and ask for the sale, describing a specific product or service and providing an incentive to act right now.

Often, your ability to offer the right product and incentive is based on the information you have gathered during the awareness and comparison stages when you qualified your visitors and identified areas of greatest concern for them. To the extent that you have invited your prospective clients and customers to tell you about themselves, it will be easier and easier to get them to buy.

Transactions can take place both online and offline. Increasingly, however, the success of your business will be defined by your ability to erase the line between online and offline, merging online and offline customers into a single database.

Make Your Offer Easy and Irresistible

Success comes from making the purchase as easy as possible and from following up on the numerous details that inevitably occur. Barriers to success at this point include:

- Insufficient information about product features and benefits
- Order forms that are difficult to locate and hard to fill out
- Lack of incentive for immediate action

Database Design

Whether online or offline, transactions should be carefully entered into your firm's customer database so you can easily refer to your customer's purchase history as you search for additional products and services to offer them. This requires the creation of a flexible customer database that tracks customers. This can become surprisingly difficult, as, in addition to maintaining transaction details, you have to:

- Track the point when a prospect becomes a customer so that future messages sent to the customer reflect their purchase and they do not receive "prospect" offers
- Add previous, that is pre-Web, purchases to the customer's database.
- Merge in-person sales with your Web site. Depending on the size of your business and how long you have been in business, it may take a long time to create a single up-to-date database containing customer transaction information, but, once the system is in place, it will be easy to maintain and the rewards of "data mining," or searching for trends and

> Success comes from making the purchase as easy as possible and from following up on the numerous details that inevitably occur.

making customized offers based on previous behavior, will more than offset the cost of the program.

Relating Overhead to Selling Price

One important aspect of the transaction stage involves identifying areas where you can reduce your overhead, particularly transaction costs, so you can become more price competitive. By reducing transaction costs, you can afford to lower costs for all customers or—even better—offer increasing savings as incentives to registered visitors.

Electronic ordering and fulfillment reduces labor costs, which can be used to reduce selling costs. For example, a travel agency might not currently offer products such as travel books, luggage, maps, and photographic equipment. Thanks to the low costs of Web promoting, the travel agency could add a page describing travel-related books and other products to the Web site. The travel agency would not even need to stock these items. Orders received online could be immediately sent to a partner store who would fulfill the order. The travel agent's profit on the sale might be relatively low, but little or no investment or actual work is involved!

This is just one more example of the way that, as you adapt your business to the Web, you will undoubtedly find yourself exploring new and innovative ways to expand your product and service offerings. A Realtor, for example, might expand their business to create "virtual partnerships" with house cleaning services or house painters—the goal in both cases being to make homes more presentable, and, hence, more salable, to prospective buyers.

> One important aspect of the transaction stage involves identifying areas where you can reduce your overhead, particularly transaction costs, so you can become more price competitive.

Case Studies

The various case studies that follow illustrate some of the different types of incentives that you might be able to adapt to your Web site at the transaction stage. Notice that all of the following are based on first obtaining the visitor's e-mail address so you can offer an incentive for immediate action to one, a few, or all of your registered visitors.

Accountant

Open content for professionals such as accountants usually includes a range of fees plus a description of the procedure for hiring the accountant. Premium content could be a downloadable coupon offering a free (or discounted) initial consultation. A more hard sell approach might be to send prospects to a page where they could fill out a form that would help them evaluate the performance of their current accountant.

The various case studies that follow illustrate some of the different types of incentives that you might be able to adapt to your Web site at the transaction stage.

Art gallery

Open content for an art gallery might include articles describing the firm's rental program permitting corporations to lease art for extended periods of time. Premium content could offer an affinity marketing "evening on the town" in conjunction with the art gallery, that is, free parking plus a two-for-one dinner at an area restaurant when attending the opening of a new exhibition.

Bakery

Open content for the transaction stage of a bakery's Web site could include information on special catering services and facilities for delivering fresh coffee and bagels to breakfast meetings at corporate headquarters. Open content could also include a catalog page of products associated with baked goods, such as books, home baking supplies, etc. Premium content for the transaction stage of a bakery could include alerts offering special incentives for early ordering (and payment) of baked goods for busy holiday periods. Alerts could be sent for birthday coupons for registered visitors who provided the birthdays of family members.

Beauty shop

Open content for the beauty shop's transaction stage could include a listing of available products, services, and beauty aids. Premium content could offer rewards for early reservation before important holidays as well as a limited-time coupons for slow-moving merchandise.

Everyone can use a Web site.

Bed and breakfast

Open content for a bed and breakfast would include information about various categories of pricing for different seasons. Premium content would include alerts offering pre-season/early-registration discounts and weekend getaways during slow periods.

Community photographer

The open content for a community photographer would include information describing the range of prices and services available, including both custom photography as well as products like posters, books, note cards, and coffee mugs illustrated with area photographs. Premium content would invite registered visitors to fill out and submit a project estimate sheet for an upcoming project. Transactions could also be facilitated by online scheduling and alerts to coupon pages offering discounts for early registration at photo classes or selected products.

Day care center

Open content could include sample fees plus a catalog of child development books and child care products likely to be of interest to parents. Premium content could include a coupon offering a discount on the first week of child care. Transactions could also be simplified by offering discounts for online prepayment and registration, or alerts when payments are due.

Electronics distributor

Open content would include a description of the range of discounts different categories of buyers could enjoy. Premium content would be alerts to specific categories of buyers for limited-time discounts on specific makes and models of equipment. Other alerts could be sent when models were about to be discontinued or when product shortages appeared on the horizon.

Financial planner

Open content for a financial planner's Web site could include a discussion of fees for different levels of service. Premium content at the transaction stage would include e-mail reminders about scheduled meetings, alerts containing timely investment advice, and alerts to coupon pages offering discounted (or omitted) fees for a limited time for registered visitors who have not yet committed to the program.

French restaurant

Open content at the transaction stage for the French restaurant would include sample menu costs plus a description of the range of fees for catering and take-out services. Premium content would include the ability to make online reservations, plus e-mail alerts one week before anniversaries and birthdays in the registered visitor's family. Premium content alerts could also announce special event meals, like thematic meals, fixed price meals, wine tastings, or meals hosted by guest chefs. Alerts could also offer incentive for early reservations before busy periods.

Affinity marketing could play a major role in the restaurant's transaction stage. Alerts for reduced price admission to area attractions and reduced parking fees could also be used to gain a competitive edge at the transaction stage.

> Affinity marketing could play a major role in the restaurant's transaction stage.

Gift shop

Open content for the gift shop could include an online catalog inviting online ordering for visitors after they have returned home. Premium content alerts could offer reminders before family member's birthdays or incentives for early purchase before holidays. Other premium content alerts could offer special savings on overstocked or new merchandise.

Microbrewery

Open transaction content for a microbrewery includes description of capabilities for parties and special events. Premium content alerts would offer incentives for early reservation for large groups of people as well as "get acquainted" coupons for new seasonal brews.

Graphic designer

Open transaction information could include a frank discussion of policies and payment terms. Premium content opportunities include an opportunity for registered visitors to fill out a project estimator form describing the project they want the designer to bid. This will spark a dialog with the designer because undoubtedly there will be some questions that need answering before the estimate can be returned. Additional premium content opportunities include electronic reminders of upcoming appointments.

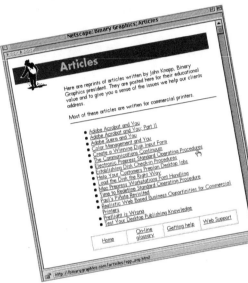

Motel operator

Open content transaction information could include pricing and information about room availability during periods of the year. Premium content could include off-season incentives for early reservation (and payment) before prime season begins. Customized premium content alerts could also be sent for get-away weekends before anniversaries.

Outdoor recreational clothing store

At the transaction stage, the outdoor recreational clothing store open content area could contain searchable catalog pages permitting visitors to order current season and preseason specials. Premium content preseason alerts could be sent to registered visitors offering special savings on new products about to be introduced for the coming season. Alerts to pages could be sent to registered visitors describing end-of-season or about-to-be-discontinued products.

Travel agency

Open transaction content could include information about travel opportunities for the coming months. Open transaction content could include affinity marketing programs for products like travel books, luggage, and camera equipment. Premium content transaction content for registered visitors could include customized alerts for travel and lodging savings to areas where visitors have previously expressed an interest in visiting or where they frequently travel. Premium content alerts could offer limited-time coupon discounts on affinity products like books and luggage.

Veterinarian

Open content for a veterinarian's Web site could include articles and information encouraging preventative health practices for pets. Premium content could include electronic reminders of scheduled appointments and alerts when routine check-ups are needed and when shots should be updated. Additional alerts could be sent when new services, like boarding and grooming, are offered. Another category of transaction alert could be to encourage pet owners to make early reservations for boarding pets well in advance during busy seasons like summer vacations or winter holidays.

> Open content for a veterinarian's Web site could include articles and information encouraging preventative health practices for pets.

Video rental store

Open content to encourage transactions could include listings of new titles and an explanation of online reservations. Premium content could describe new titles, encouraging early online reservation of new titles. If all transactions are recorded on computer, customized premium content alerts could be sent based on the customer's previous rental history. Buyers could also fill out a form indicating their preferences and automatically be informed when movies meeting their criteria appear.

Whale watch operator

Open content during the transaction stage for a whale watch operator could include the ability to make reservations and purchase tickets online. This would reduce lines at the dock and help the whale watch operator know, in advance, which cruises were likely to be most popular. Open content could also provide incentives for pre-season bookings and announcement of upcoming special cruises, such as sunset or lighthouse cruises. Premium content could include last-minute discount coupons for early morning, late afternoon, or evening cruises that are not sold out.

Putting Ideas to Work

Start by analyzing recent transactions. As you review your invoices and sales records, create three piles of invoices: one for new customers, one for repeat customers, and one for customers who were recommended by friends. Which pile is the largest? This will give you an idea of how effectively your firm is satisfying customers. Then, ask yourself questions like these:

1. What types of incentives can I use to encourage prospects to make their first purchase from me?
2. What additional product categories can I offer my customers? What other products or services are likely to be purchased along with my primary product or service? Your answer to these questions will help you develop co-marketing, or affinity, marketing programs.
3. What products or services are disposable or will expire if they are not sold? Examples of disposable products and services include tickets for whale watch cruises that become useless the moment the ship leaves the dock and winter jackets that become increasingly difficult to sell as summer approaches. Disposable products make ideal premium content coupon incentives.
4. What products or services are so profitable that I can significantly discount them and still make a healthy profit—or are worth selling at a loss in order to create a new customer?

> Start by analyzing recent transactions. As you review your invoices and sales records, create three piles of invoices: one for new customers, one for repeat customers, and one for customers who were recommended by friends.

5. Where can you identify opportunities for online transactions, like room reservations, that will reduce selling costs, allowing you to reduce prices for all customers or—even better—offer registered visitors significantly greater discounts?

6. What packaging pricing incentives can you offer, such as packages containing two, or more products or services bundled at one special promotional price?

7. What co-marketing opportunities can you develop with businesses that complement yours? For example, if your art gallery is located downtown, can you create evening out packages that include free parking, discounted meals at a local restaurant, and complimentary corsages from a flower shop?

8. What are the seasonal influences on your business and how can you create premium content rewards for registered visitors out of them? For example, what incentives can you offer based on important holidays or your registered visitors' birthdays and anniversaries?

For more information on this topic, visit our Web site at www.businesstown.com

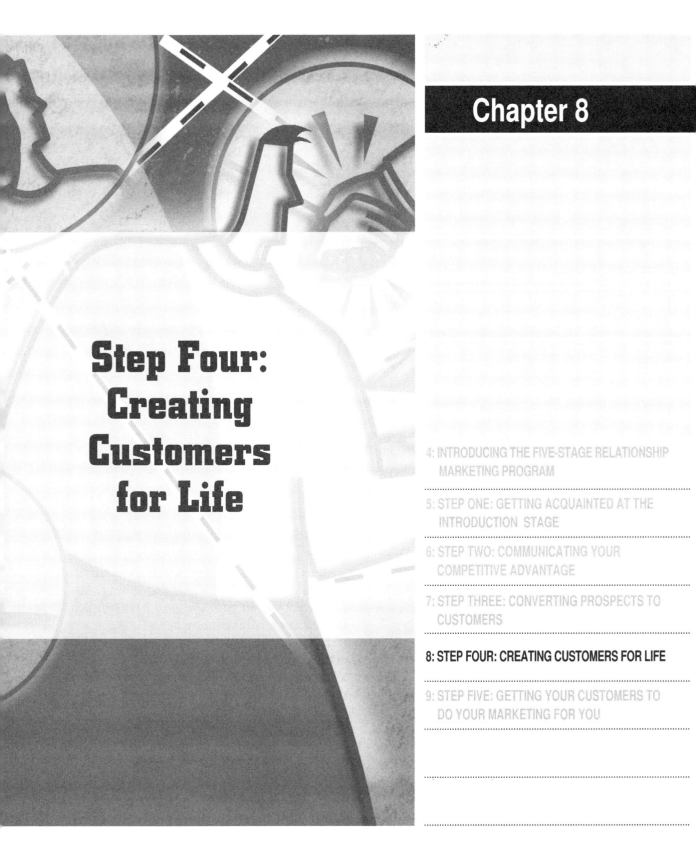

Chapter 8

Step Four: Creating Customers for Life

"Every company's greatest assets are its customers,
because without customers there is no company."
–MICHAEL LEBOEUF

*The simple envelope in the mail is scented. The card inside:
"Thank you for shopping at Carroll's Jewelers. The platinum
engagement set you chose was particularly beautiful. We certainly
hope you and your fiancée enjoyed your ride in our Rolls Royce
limousine, and to help you remember the evening, here's an 8 x 10
photograph of the two of you. You certainly look happy!*

*By the way, we just got a few of the most beautiful sterling sil-
ver picture frames in our store, so in case you're interested in displaying this photo in style, we thought we'd take this opportunity
to offer you a coupon for 10 percent off. Just come to the attached
Web address and enter your preferred customer code."*

*The word "relationship" in relationship marketing refers to
building a lasting bond with your customers, one that transcends
price competition and builds something even stronger than loyalty–advocacy. The technologies of the Web and e-mail combined
with open and premium content and creative promotions allow
you to have that personal relationship, that bond, with each of
your customers.*

"Once a customer, always a customer!" *Wouldn't it be nice if
that were always true!* But we all know it isn't. Future transactions
and referrals have to be fought for almost as hard as the initial transaction. What transpires during the reinforcement stage determines,
to a great degree, whether you will be enjoying a one-time relationship with your customer or whether the customer will become a
repeat customer and–even more important–recommend your firm to
their friends and associates.

The reinforcement stage is especially important to your firm's
profitability because, time and time again, it has been proven that
repeat customers are less expensive to advertise to and–hence–more
profitable to sell. The generally mentioned statistic is that it costs
seven times as much to sell a new customer than an existing one.
This is especially true now with e-mail, since you can advertise to

repeat customers without incurring any media, printing, addressing, or postage expenses.

The reinforcement stage is also valuable because it provides you with an opportunity to avoid buyers remorse, which often leads customers to try to return a previously purchased item. More important, the reinforcement stage provides you with opportunities to sell additional products to a customer—enhancing their original purchase. Finally, marketing to customers during the reinforcement stage makes it easy for you to cultivate word-of-mouth referrals among their friends and coworkers.

Goals

There are five basic marketing goals during the reinforcement stage. Most involve driving customers back to your Web site to take an action or learn more about the products or services you offer. The incentives are usually information and savings.

1. Build strong emotional bonds with customers by thanking them for their patronage, expressing your appreciation for their purchase.
2. Find out more about the customer's needs and possible ways you can satisfy them—including improving your firm's performance.
3. Provide incentives to purchase additional products or services that complement the customer's original purchase.
4. Plant the seed for future purchases and maintain the buyer's enthusiasm by describing new products and services as they become available.
5. Provide customers with the tools they need to become your advocates and recommend your firm to their friends and coworkers.

A few enterprising firms have always done these things. But the problems of maintaining customer records and the costs—primarily printing and postage—associated with customer retention programs

There are five basic marketing goals during the reinforcement stage.
1. Build strong emotional bonds.
2. Find out more about the customer's needs.
3. Provide incentives to purchase additional products.
4. Plant the seed for future purchases.
5. Provide customers with the tools they need.

worked against their success. With e-mail, however, reinforcement can operate virtually cost free. All that's needed is the discipline and imagination to set the program in motion and constantly search for new ways to re-approach old customers.

Start with a Thank-You

One of the most important ways you can convert a transaction into an ongoing customer relationship is to thank the customer for their purchase. The easiest and least-expensive way you can thank customers for their purchase is to send an e-mail thanking them for their purchase. E-mail is especially easy to send when the transaction, or part of the transaction, took place online. E-mail works best when personalized, that is, different messages are sent following the customer's initial purchase and follow-up purchases.

The impact of thank-you messages can be enhanced by offering a premium—something for free. Coupons worth special savings on future purchases work especially well as they give customers a reason to make an additional purchase. Premiums build future loyalty: *everyone loves to receive something for free!* Often, the thought is more important than the actual value of the product.

The choice of premium depends on the selling price—and profitability—of the original purchase. The best premiums are electronic, that is, they are instantly available and do not require postage and mailing. Ideally, the premium should reflect the firm's personality (screen savers of healthy pets at play would make an ideal premium for a veterinarian).

Customer Satisfaction Survey

A customer satisfaction survey can be one of the most effective and universally applicable marketing activities that can take place during the reinforcement phase. There are two major advantages to immediately sending an e-mail alert to customers asking them to fill out a customer satisfaction form within a few days of their purchase.

Responses to the customer satisfaction survey can provide you with statistical evidence you can use during the comparison stage to prove the claims you have made regarding your firm's superior products and service. The customer satisfaction survey can be the source of numerous, powerful customer testimonials that personalize your firm and enhance your credibility and prove your firm's ability to perform.

The customer satisfaction survey can help you monitor and solve the inevitable customer service problems that occur. Miscommunication, shipping or delivery problems, and other problems occur in even the best-run firms. Usually, they go unnoticed as customers typically complain only about the worst transgressions. A customer satisfaction survey, however, can provide customers with a way of bringing problems to light so you can solve them.

Often, what matters most in creating a satisfied customer is not whether a problem occurred, but whether the firm made any efforts to solve the problem. Over time, customer satisfaction surveys make it easy for you to identify areas in your firm needing fine-tuning.

The reinforcement stage is where you can most easily separate your firm from the numerous online and warehouse-style firms that compete primarily on price. Most Web commerce firms fail to build customer loyalty by seeing each sale as the end rather than the beginning of a relationship. Customers will not become repeat customers and advocates for your firm unless they are completely satisfied with their purchase. Problems must be dealt with competently and quickly if you are to enjoy a second chance at the customer or earn their recommendation.

> Often, what matters most in creating a satisfied customer is not whether a problem occurred, but whether the firm made any efforts to solve the problem.

Incentives

After customers have purchased from you, they are already familiar with you and you are already familiar with them. You have an idea of their preferences and the structure is in place for easy, future purchases—the customer's credit card information, shipping information, and other information is already in your computer. This reduces the costs of future purchases.

One of the most effective ways you can create future business is to offer incentives on future purchases. There are numerous opportunities for additional purchases.

Supplies offer numerous opportunities for low overhead, e-mail driven, future sales. Once you know that a customer has purchased a particular product or service, you probably can identify future compatible products that can enhance the value of the original purchase. For example, if you know a pet owner owns a particular breed of dog, it becomes relatively easy to send them information or books written specifically about that breed or health care products likely to be of interest to owners of that breed. If a customer has purchased a particular brand of inkjet or laser printer, they are a likely candidate for supplies.

In the past, you would have to print and sell a catalog or—at minimum—a postcard describing all of the inkjet and laser supplies your firm sold. Now, using e-mail and today's low-cost computer technology, you can send them an e-mail offering a limited time saving on just the inkjet or laser cartridge they need that matches the brand they purchased.

In order to reward customers for their original purchase, and to maintain the appearance of price competitiveness, price incentives should accompany your e-mail offers for supplies. Timing is also of crucial importance. It doesn't make sense to send printer buyers an offer to buy replacement inkjet or laser cartridges immediately after purchase; the offer might make more sense after a month has gone by.

A good example of an incentive-driven supply purchase would be a wood stove dealer sending customers coupons offering discounts on mid-summer stove maintenance and chimney cleaning during the summer. Another example would be the home theater installation specialist sending customers alerts about new movies as they appear on digital video discs.

Moving beyond supplies, e-mail makes it easy to sell *enhanced purchases*, complementary products that would logically accompany their original purchase. For example, if a customer has purchased a wood stove, they might be interested in products like fans, thermostats, stands for stacking wood, carriers for bringing wood in

> In order to reward customers for their original purchase, and to maintain the appearance of price competitiveness, price incentives should accompany your e-mail offers for supplies.

from outside, as well as shovels and buckets for removing accumulated ash.

The key to success is to use e-mail to bridge the gap between your knowledge of your firm's products and services and the customer's needs. By putting yourself in your customer's shoes and asking yourself "What products or services could enhance my current purchase?" you'll be able to identify dozens of opportunities for repeat purchases.

Maintaining Enthusiasm

Information is always a strategic competitive tool. By providing a constant stream of information related to the customer's needs and their purchase history, you can maintain their interest and plant the seed for future purchases. Information opportunities include:

- Setup and installation tips.
- Information on how to maximize the benefits of their purchase.
- Information about new products and services as they appear
- Information describing the challenges and trends your customers face and your interpretation and suggestions for meeting these challenges.
- Stories about how others have benefited from your product or service.

> The key to future success is to never lose visibility in the buyer's mind! Visibility is lost when the customer takes their purchase for granted and doesn't remember who sold it to them.

The key to future success is to *never lose visibility in the buyer's mind!* Visibility is lost when the customer takes their purchase for granted and doesn't remember who sold it to them.

Electronic newsletters, requiring neither printing or postage, are the ideal way to maintain your customer's enthusiasm for your business. By sending e-mail alerts informing customers of premium content electronic newsletters containing information relevant to their needs, you can maintain your customer's enthusiasm.

Customer Advocacy Program

A final goal of the reinforcement stage is to convert customers into advocates, providing customers with the tools they need to recommend your firm to their friends and associates. Although e-mail and your electronic newsletter will often be enough to maintain your firm's visibility so your firm's name will be the first to be mentioned when a friend or coworker expresses an interest in your product category, the effectiveness of your customer outreach program will be greatly enhanced to the degree you make it easy for customers to recommend your firm.

E-mail and the Web offer numerous low-cost ways you can make it easy for your customers to recommend your firm to their friends:

> You can send customers electronic postcards that they can forward to their friends.

- Your Web site can contain electronic postcards that your customers can forward to their friends. These electronic postcards can range from simple introductions to your firm to incentives offering special introductory discounts.
- If you are publishing an electronic newsletter, you can send customers electronic postcards that they can forward to their friends, allowing them to access your premium content newsletter (and, hopefully, register for future issues).
- If you are holding a special promotion, you can send customers an electronic postcard they can forward to selected friends, offering friends an opportunity to take advantage of the savings.
- Your Web site can contain rewards for recommending new clients and customers. Instead of sending a thank-you note when a customer recommends you to an associate, you can send them an e-mail alert to an unlinked page containing coupons good for additional discounts on specially priced merchandise available for a limited time.

Case Studies

The following case studies describe some of the different ways you can use your Web site during the reinforcement stage to build closer bonds with your customers. Note that most reinforcement activities begin with a thank-you message and a customer satisfaction survey.

The frequency that customer satisfaction surveys are offered depends on the frequency of purchase. It doesn't make sense to send surveys to customers who purchase frequently throughout the year. In these cases, a yearly survey would be more appropriate.

As always, two levels of reinforcement content are presented: open content available to all Web site visitors and premium content that is available only to customers who have previously purchased. The easiest way to make premium content available is to use unlinked pages, Web site pages with URLs that must be directly entered (or copied and pasted) into the visitor's Web site browser. Other options include password-protected pages, or you can utilize cookies that are updated after a customer purchases (assuming he always visits your Web site from the same computer).

Often, the same content can be presented on two levels. Open content can introduce a topic and present an overview of the subject. An in-depth look at the same topic, with specific enhancements such as downloadable software templates, can be offered as premium content to previous customers. In this case, the "overview" serves as an "advertisement" or additional incentive for visitors to purchase from the firm.

Accountant

Open content could include frequently updated articles discussing current issues and challenges facing the market—with separate content for large corporations and small business owners. Premium content could include a yearly customer satisfaction survey and advance notification and reminders about upcoming tax deadlines. E-mail reward alerts could also be sent inviting customers to a page of coupons in appreciation for paying large bills or recommending new clients.

Automobile dealer

Open content could include information about seasonal driving and maintenance tips plus information about new and about-to-be-introduced models. Premium content could be special offers or an invitation to "event marketing" promotions like opportunities to drive new models, off-premises workshops on safe driving and winter driving skills, plus alerts describing preferred customer maintenance programs. Affinity marketing might include coupons for free or reduced-price car washes.

Bakery

Open content during the reinforcement stage might include favorite seasonal recipes based on breads that the store sells. Premium content could include electronic postcards that customers could send their friends entitling the friends to a free cup of coffee and bread or cinnamon roll sample. Occasional alerts could be sent inviting customers to visit and try out newly introduced breads.

Community photographer

Open content to enhance the photographer's credibility could include articles discussing recent trends in photography as well as a upgraded samples of the photographer's work. Premium content for clients could include a downloadable screen saver of area photographs. Additional premium content could include a monthly downloadable calendar containing a sample of the photographer's work and a listing of area events.

Day care center

Open content during the reinforcement stage could include a constantly changing photo gallery showing the children enjoying the center's facilities. Premium content during the reinforcement stage could invite parents to borrow a digital camera and photograph their child during an open house or special event. Alerts could be sent reminding parents of upcoming special events.

Financial planner

Open content could include frequently updated service articles, such as "Tips for keeping good financial records." Premium content could be a monthly or bimonthly electronic newsletter containing in-depth service articles plus interpretations of recent economic and political trends affecting area businesses.

Health club

Open content could include calendars of upcoming activities or tennis and racquetball scores to emphasize the range of activities taking place at the club. Premium content could include electronic postcards offering free visits or reduced-cost, limited-time member-ships to friends as well as a reward when referrals become full-time members. An online fitness progress program could also permit members to track their progress towards health and fitness goals.

Microbrewery

Open content during the reinforcement stage includes back-ground stories (brewing secrets, how new brews are formulated) to maintain visitor's enthusiasm. Premium content could be a "Great Beers of the World" screensaver and invitations to preview new seasonal beers as they appear.

Motel

Open content could include a calendar of recent and upcoming events in the area as well as news about changes and renovations. Premium content could include a customer satisfaction survey plus a downloadable screen saver of area attractions intended to motivate recreational visitors to return. Alerts to send preseason electronic postcards to friends would make it easy for skiers and other leisure visitors to recommend the motel to their friends.

Health club

An online fitness progress program could also permit members to track their progress towards health and fitness goals.

Oral surgeon

Open content at the reinforcement stage could include an article describing ten tips for better dental health. Premium content could include a patient satisfaction survey. Premium content, keyed to the procedure the patient had undergone, could invite readers to read an article describing ways to prevent the same problem from reoccurring.

Outdoor recreational clothing store

Open content could include invitations to event marketing promotions, such as special visits by high-profile sportsmen, slide shows, lectures, or presentations by environmental groups. Premium content could include invitations to special receptions before these events take place. Alerts could be sent inviting customers to take pictures of the store's products in use on vacations in remote locales, which would help personalize the store and help customers build closer emotional bonds with it. Alerts could also invite customers to send electronic postcards to their friends inviting them to take advantage of preseason savings.

Secretarial service

Open content could include stories providing more details about the advantages of utilizing the service during periods of high demand. Service stories could help prospective employees hone their resume and skills. Premium content could include alerts for specially needed skills and reward pages for customers who recommend new business to the firm.

Travel agent

Open content at the reinforcement stage could include articles about overlooked travel destinations. Premium content could include coupon rewards for travelers who complete a survey evaluating their recent travel experience(s). Additional alerts could offer discounts on coupons from the travel agent's affinity marketing partners.

Outdoor recreational clothing store
Alerts could be sent inviting customers to take pictures of the store's products in use on vacations in remote locales, which would help personalize the store and help customers build closer emotional bonds with it.

Whale watch operator

Open content could include results from customer satisfaction surveys and best photographs from recent cruises. Premium content could include an end-of-season "Best Whale Photos" screen saver plus a statistical summary of the season's whale sightings.

Putting Ideas to Work

Use the following questions as a starting point for ascertaining the best ways to develop open and premium content for your Web site.

1. What are the key questions you can ask that will help you determine how satisfied customers are with your product or service?
2. What types of information or visuals can you provide that will help remind clients and customers of the pleasure that your firm provided?
3. What interests and passions are shared by your customers and clients? How can you electronically reinforce these interests?
4. How can you make your clients and customers feel more involved with your firm and those who patronize it?
5. What low-cost incentives or premiums can you provide to help maintain your customer's enthusiasm for your product or service?
6. What types of electronic "pass-along" incentives can you provide to customers and clients, encouraging them to recommend your Web site to their friends and associates?
7. How can you best reward current clients and customers who recommend your firm to their friends and associates?
8. How can you help customers and clients maximize the value of the product or service they purchase from you?

> **Whale watch operator**
> Premium content could include an end-of-season "Best Whale Photos" screen saver plus a statistical summary of the season's whale sightings.

For more information on this topic, visit our Web site at www.businesstown.com

Chapter 9

Step Five: Getting Your Customers to Do Your Marketing for You

Word of mouth remains our most effective advertising.
—JIM TWETEN, MAGNOLIA HI-FI & VIDEO (ONE OF AMERICA'S TOP TEN AUDIO/VIDEO RETAILERS FOR OVER FIFTEEN YEARS)

> The technologies of the Web give you powerful ways to encourage word-of-mouth referral business and make it even easier for those referrals to take place.

If you have a friend in Seattle who is shopping for an engagement ring, by now you might know where to send them. You might send them to the jeweler with the fresh baked cookies on the counter, the certified gemologists behind the counter, and that beautiful Rolls Royce limousine their customers get to ride in. Carroll's Jewelers doesn't actually do very much advertising. Fact is, they don't have to. The advocacy that grows within each of their customers and the word-of-mouth that comes from that assures them of a healthy string of new customers.

The technologies of the Web give you powerful ways to encourage word-of-mouth referral business and make it even easier for those referrals to take place. Combining promotions that are a win-win for the existing customer and his or her friend with the techniques detailed in this chapter will help your customer base grow without excessive incremental costs.

The advocacy or community stage of Web marketing is important from two perspectives. One is that this stage offers you an opportunity to create a feeling of community among past customers and Web site visitors. This feeling of community can create feelings of loyalty that transcend any temporary pricing or availability advantage your competitors might offer. By creating a feeling of community, you can encourage your visitors to become your advocates, making return visits to your Web site a regular habit, —as well as provide visitors to your Web site with the tools they need to recommend your business to an ever-increasing pool of new prospects.

More important, the advocacy stage offers the potential of changing your business model to take new advantages of the speed and information density that the Web offers. Rather than starting all over with a new business model aimed at the transaction stage, the community stage provides you with an opportunity to explore new avenues for safely evolving and transforming your business rather than "rolling the dice" and possibly losing everything by trying to embrace e-commerce too early.

Advantages of Referral Business

There are two main advantages to business generated by word-of-mouth referrals. First, similar to the previous reinforcement stage, the advantage of community marketing is that it offers you an opportunity to create something out of nothing. At the community stage, there is little obvious end-user demand. Your previous buyers are presumably satisfied. Yet, by approaching them during this period of relative calm, you can convert inactive customers, and their friends, into active buyers. Using e-mail and information, you can ignite an urge to buy where none presently exists.

Since e-mail and the Internet do not involve expensive telemarketing, printing, addressing, or postage costs, your pricing can be extremely competitive at this stage since your customer acquisition costs are so low. Instead of acquiring a customer by running an expensive magazine, newspaper, or television ad, your only cost is in posting a special page on your Web site and sending out e-mail to your previous customers directing them to send their friends to this page.

Second, word-of-mouth advertising benefits from credibility. Advertising is always viewed as, well, advertising. It is never completely trusted. This is in contrast to recommendations from a friend who has previously purchased from a firm. Because word-of-mouth recommendations are so trusted, prospects who visit your Web site or place of business are presold on your competence and professionalism. There is likely to be less price resistance or resistance to your recommendations. They're easier sales, in other words, which might, in some cases, translate into higher margins.

> Since e-mail and the Internet do not involve expensive telemarketing, printing, addressing, or postage costs, your pricing can be extremely competitive at this stage since your customer acquisition costs are so low.

Selling Tools

The starting point for converting customers into advocates is to think in terms of providing selling tools for your customers. This involves providing previous customers with both the selling tools they need to recommend your business as well as incentives that make it worth their while to recommend your business to their friends.

> Develop a system that makes it easy to track new visitors to your Web site who were recommended by a current customer and reward the customer for the recommendation.

These selling tools might be as simple as e-mail announcements sent to previous customers that you invite them to forward to their friends. The e-mail would contain a link to premium content pages on your Web site that contain money-saving coupons.

The premium page of a restaurant could contain special menu items and allow two couples to eat for the price of one. Visitors would be invited to print out the Web page and bring in the coupon. Vacation destinations, too, could provide similar incentives for couples to invite along another couple.

Another example of advocacy in action would be e-mail sent to previous customers offering discounts or other incentives when their friends register their e-mail address on a special page of your Web site or make a purchase based on the forwarded e-mail. The key is to develop a system that makes it easy to track new visitors to your Web site who were recommended by a current customer and reward the customer for the recommendation.

Gift certificates

One of the easiest ways you can set up an advocacy program is to send an e-mail to your customers, inviting them to a premium content page on your Web site where they can enter their friends and family members names and birth dates. A few days before the friend's birthday, send an e-mail to each customer offering them an opportunity to send a printable gift certificate to their friend, perhaps redeemable at a special page on your Web site.

Alternately, you can invite customers to submit their friends names, birth days, and e-mail addresses and promise to send the friend a discount coupon a few days ahead of their birthday, compliments of the friend.

Gift certificates are extremely valuable advocacy marketing tools because they force the recipient to interact with you, visiting either your bricks-and-mortar store or visiting (and buying) from your Web site. People who might otherwise never have reason to visit your business or your Web site now have a vested interest in visiting you—because they have "free money" (the gift certificate) to spend with you.

STEP FIVE: GETTING YOUR CUSTOMERS TO DO YOUR MARKETING FOR YOU

Coupon specials

One of the easiest ways to create business among friends of your current customers is to send an e-mail to your customers directing them, and their friends, to an unlinked page describing specially priced, limited-time products and services. In your e-mail, encourage your customers to forward the e-mail to their friends, explaining that they will earn future discounts (or any other rewards) when their friends buy as a result of their recommendation.

Forwardable newsletters

Another example of advocacy in action is to make it easy for customers or previous visitors receiving your e-mail newsletter to forward it to their friends. If their friends agree that the information presented is credible and helpful, and they register for the newsletter, the friend who forwarded the newsletter to them should be rewarded in some way—perhaps with a special offer or a discount on his or her next purchase.

There are several ways you can make newsletters forwardable. One way is to add a simple "Forward to a friend" area on the newsletter that makes it easy for recipients to enter a "Compliments of" notice plus their friend's e-mail address. When your customer's friend receives the newsletter, he or she should be given an easy option of either continuing to receive the newsletter (opt in) or unsubscribing to the newsletter (opt out). If the friend desires to continue receiving the newsletter, the customer who forwarded the newsletter should receive an e-mail thanking him or her for the recommendation and a reward.

Newsgroups and forums

Newsgroups, forums, and chat rooms make it easy for your customers to communicate with each other and share their experiences. Although an occasional product or service criticism may emerge, the main virtue of these communication enhancers is that they provide an incentive for your customers and prospects to return to your Web site and be exposed to your (hopefully) constantly updated home page.

The impartiality with which you moderate the exchange of messages will determine your firm's credibility. Your credibility will suffer if postings contain only favorable comments and reviews of your product or service.

You can even turn critical comments appearing on a newsgroup to your advantage. When customer service problems occur, you want to be able to solve them as quickly as possible. Unfortunately, many customers will simply avoid your business in the future—and tell their friends about their unpleasant experience—rather than communicating their dissatisfaction to you. By monitoring the forums and chat sessions that you sponsor on your Web site, you can gain an uncensored, first-hand overview of how your business is performing from the end user's point of view.

Free e-mail

Another way you can encourage previous customers to frequent your Web site is to offer free e-mail. If the technology infrastructure is already present on your Web site, it will be relatively easy and inexpensive to provide this valuable service to your customers.

Affinity Marketing

Affinity marketing offers you additional opportunities to leverage your customer's enthusiasm and create additional sales. Affinity marketing involves partnerships with other businesses that offer products or services that are complementary, not competitive, with yours.

"Come along" deals

Once you have assembled a team of affinity marketers, there's virtually no end to the products and services that you can jointly promote to past customers and friends of past customers.

For example, a ski lodge could invite noncompeting partners (restaurants, bookstores, antique stores, clothing stores, ski

> Another way you can encourage previous customers to frequent your Web site is to offer free e-mail.

rentals or repairs, etc.) in the area to participate in two-for-one offers. The goal in a single e-mail is to invite two or more couples to return to the attraction and become acquainted with other businesses in the area. Over the year, these efforts could snowball as more and more friends of friends invite additional friends to the accommodations.

Preferred customer sales

In retailing, preferred customer sales are among the most popular ways to reward customers for their past patronage. You can multiply the results of your preferred customer sales by inviting recipients of your invitations to the sales to bring along a friend. You can make the offer more legitimate by requiring advance registration for the friend. Although you can't lock out an uninvited friend, advance registration will add value to the offer by making it appear more desirable.

Acknowledging Referrals

Central to all of the above, of course, is the importance of acknowledging referrals. The urge to be recognized is a fundamental human trait. Your business will succeed if you take the time to set up a structure to reward those who recommend your business to their friends. Your goal is to make it as easy as possible for your customers to recommend your business to their friends and you want to immediately and appropriately reward them for their kindness.

The tangibility of the reward that you offer for recommended business should be appropriate to the formality of your audience as well as the dollars involved. A hat with a baseball team's logo might be appropriate if a friend recommends a buyer to your sporting goods store but is likely to disappoint someone whose recommendation leads to a million dollar purchase.

Putting Ideas to Work

Use the following worksheet as a guide to identify affinity marketing partners and put your past customers to work by becoming advocates for your business.

> Identify affinity marketing partners and put your past customers to work by becoming advocates for your business.

Worksheet: Affinity Marketing

1. What interests, needs, or passions do many of your customers have in common?
2. What topics or concerns might your customers like to share or discuss with each other?
3. What information is likely to appeal to your customer's friends?
4. What other types of businesses in your area appeal to buyers of your products or services?
5. How can you create packages or offers based on combining offers from two or more affinity partners?
6. What price, delivery, financing, or other incentives can you afford to offer friends your current customers recommend?
7. What types of incentives or rewards can you afford to provide customers who recommend friends who make a purchase?
8. How can you best track purchases resulting from word-of-mouth recommendations from friends?

For more information on this topic, visit our Web site at www.businesstown.com

Building a Relationship-Oriented Web Site

Overview of Section III

What is the importance of viewing your relationship marketing Web site as an ongoing process, not an event.

How to identify your market's needs to ensure you provide the meaningful content.

How to prepare effective e-mail.

How to optimize your Web site performance.

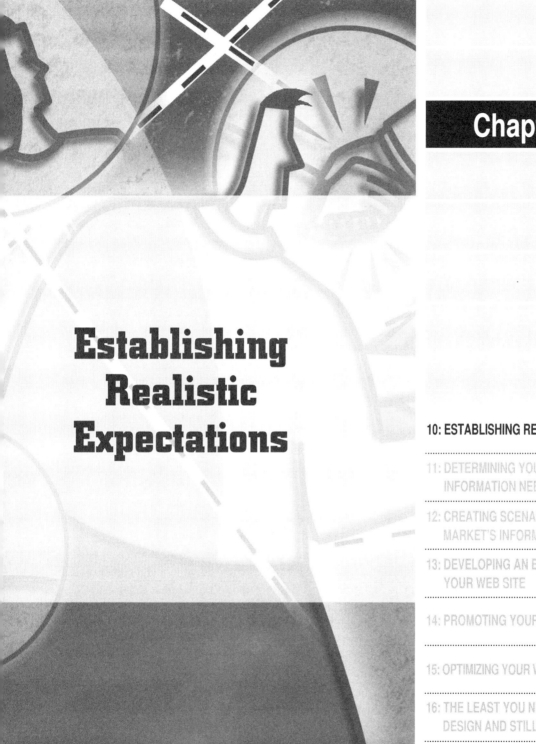

Establishing Realistic Expectations

Chapter 10

Never promise more than you can deliver!

—ANONYMOUS

If you were a talented chef about to open a restaurant, you would take stock of the resources you had available and would plan to open an establishment that was within your means and fit your goals. You would undoubtedly have a good idea about the number of tables you would have, the dishes you would prepare, and the prices you would charge before you ever got started. If you didn't have a basic sense of these things, it's likely you would not succeed.

So like the restaurateur, you must first have a solid idea of what you want to do, what you can do, and then build accordingly. In implementing your relationship marketing Web site initiative, you need to find the place where available resources align with required capabilities and functionality and work towards that goal. And as you build, you need to make sure that your results are in alignment with that goal. It's a complicated recipe but the results are worth it.

The road to disappointment is paved with overly ambitious goals. These overly ambitious goals are fueled by the media's fascination with the sales results of the Amazons, CDNOWs, E*Trades, and eBays of the world. What these glowing reports often don't tell you, however, is that their successes have been purchased with huge amounts of money, and that many ventures have not earned their creators any significant, or, in many cases, any real profit at all.

So, a word of caution. The purpose of this book is not to encourage you to dismantle your business and start a new one. It is to show you how to adopt the Web and adapt to a changed business climate and gradually transform your business on a step-by-step basis. Yes, some people achieve an overnight transformation of a traditional walk-up or bricks-and-mortar business into a Web business. But these are the isolated exceptions.

You'll probably be much better off if you follow the gradual transformation process outlined in this book that will allow you to maintain—or avoid threatening—your existing business while you use the Web to do a better job of satisfying your current customers and current marketing area as you develop a new Web-based view.

It is both unrealistic and unsafe to expect to transform your business into a Web-based relationship marketing Web business overnight. It is likely to take significant time and effort to establish the procedures and infrastructure necessary to integrate your business with the Web and create a fully relationship-oriented Web site. Unquestionably, the results of the hard work can be worth the effort in terms of expanding your business base and by increasing the value of existing customers.

What You Need to Succeed

The focus of the chapters in this section are the five sets of skills necessary to succeed in satisfying your customers at each stage of the customer development cycle. These include:

- Information
- E-mail
- Promoting
- Technology
- Design

Identifying and developing information

Information, not graphic design, catchy phrases, or gratuitous use of technology, forms the basis of your relationship marketing initiative on the Web. Success is based on your ability to provide the right information to Web site visitors, customers, and prospects as they advance through each stage of the customer development cycle.

To succeed, information must be credible, meaningful, and relevant. Your customers, prospects, and Web site visitors desire information, not advertising. Brag and boast claims are not enough. Your marketing message must be presented in a way that satisfies your market's needs rather than "we're better" claims.

Success comes from determining your market's information needs. This can be done by interviewing customers, reviewing sales encounters, or writing scenarios that detail the goals of typical visitors to your Web site.

> Information, not graphic design, catchy phrases, or gratuitous use of technology, forms the basis of your relationship marketing initiative on the Web.

The strategic use of e-mail
Your e-mail program
depends on more than just
sending e-mail. You must
make it easy for visitors to
submit their e-mail address,
you must add the e-mail
addresses of customers and
previous customers, and
you must maintain and
constantly update a
database of customer and
prospect e-mail addresses.

The strategic use of e-mail

Your relationship market Web site strategy is based on a consistent and concise e-mail program.

- *Concise.* Your e-mail must be short and to the point. Your "selling" must begin in the subject heading of your e-mail, which must promise recipients a reason to click on your message and begin reading it. The first screen of your e-mail message must contain numerous benefits that will motivate the reader to continue reading or visit the relevant page of your Web site.
- *Consistent.* An on-again, off-again e-mail program is certain to fail. If you promise to send an e-mail newsletter on the first Monday of each month, your relationship marketing Web strategy begins to unravel the first time you miss sending a scheduled issue. Consistency, retaining awareness in your customer's and prospect's mind, is the key to success.

Your e-mail program depends on more than just sending e-mail. You must make it easy for visitors to submit their e-mail address, you must add the e-mail addresses of customers and previous customers, and you must maintain and constantly update a database of customer and prospect e-mail addresses. This process should be as automated as possible.

Promoting your Web site

Although search engines will send a certain number of visitors to your Web site, one of the biggest challenges you face is promoting your Web site offline to customers and prospects who have not yet visited your Web site. You have to develop a program that will motivate visitors to your office or store to become familiar with your Web site and visit it frequently.

Your Web site address should appear on every piece of paper your firm's name, address, and phone number appears on. Your customers and prospects should become as familiar with your Web site as they are with your office or store.

Technology

Putting together even the simplest Web site involves an understanding of technology. It's a rare business that can afford to say to an outside designer or Internet service provider, "Do it!" An understanding of the underlying technology is needed so that the right choices can be made. Although you, as business owner or manager, do not need to know how to create HTML pages or set up an e-mail database, you need to know what needs to be done, who is most capable of doing it, and judge the quality of the work.

Equally important, an understanding of today's fast-moving Internet technology is necessary to take advantage of sound, video, animation, and virtual reality modeling as appropriate. As the convergence between the Internet and television gets closer, more is going to be expected.

You have to keep up with your visitors and you have to keep up with your competitors. Visitors who were once content with static text on pages are being trained by hours of watching television to expect animated text. And, if your competitor's Web site is capable of presenting a virtual tour through a simulated home environment and your site isn't, which site do you think will attract the most attention and make the most sales?

Most important, an understanding of technology is necessary for you to be able to identify new opportunities as they occur. By better understanding the structure of information exchange over the Web, you might be able to uncover ways to reduce the costs of doing business by using the Web to reduce administrative or ordering expenses or identify other ways to use the Web to reduce operating costs.

> **Technology**
> You have to keep up with your visitors and you have to keep up with your competitors.

Design

Customers and prospects form an immediate opinion of your firm from the appearance of your Web site. It's important that you, as business owner or manager, can recognize the difference between good and bad design and direct the activities of those responsible for creating your Web site.

Designers often err in the direction of decoration—of adding color, text, and background elements for their own sake. Simple is always better. The design of your Web site should be as simple as possible in order to allow your message—not the medium—to attract your Web site visitor's attention. Graphic elements that distract from your message undermine the effectiveness of your Web site.

Preparing for the Task Ahead

Do not underestimate any of these tasks or dismiss them as rudimentary. Each will be more involved than estimated and will likely take more time. Be ready for this. The overall project may take more time and resources than initially anticipated. Success demands you anticipate problems that will show up as you transform your business to a Web-based relationship marketing business. Success requires a step-by-step process.

However, as you undertake this process of embracing the Web for relationship marketing, you'll find yourself gaining a new knowledge about your entire business, which will help you improve customer satisfaction, sales, profits, productivity, and nearly every facet of your business. It is also highly likely that you will enjoy it more. In other words, it may be hard but it will be worth it.

Define your goals in real terms

An effective Web initiative requires more than hiring an outside design firm or learning another software program like Microsoft FrontPage or Net Objects Fusion. What are the goals of your Web site initiative? What do you hope to accomplish? Use the following worksheet as a starting point in examining your existing business

Worksheet: Customer Knowledge

1. Who are my customers?
2. What are they buying?
3. Who are our competitors?
4. Why do our customers buy from us and not our competitors?
5. How are we promoting?
6. How do our competitors promote?

> Success demands you anticipate problems that will show up as you transform your business to a Web-based relationship marketing business. Success requires a step-by-step process.

7. Who are our most profitable customers?
8. What are our most profitable products and services?
9. Who are our least profitable customers?
10. What are our least profitable products and services?
11. How much are we spending to maintain our existing customers?
12. How much are we spending to attract new customers?

Addressing these twelve simple questions can provide you with a new perspective on how your business currently operates as well as help you focus your thinking about your new Web initiative. It will allow you to identify strengths to be leveraged and weaknesses to be eliminated.

Identify and gain access to necessary resources

Resources involve both tangible and intangibles. Tangibles revolve around *money, people,* and *information.* How much money is available to create, promote, and maintain your Web site? Who is available to do the work? Where are you starting from?

Examine your current advertising and promotion budget and ascertain whether your Web site initiative investment will be on top of your existing spending or whether you can trim your existing media investment to fund your relationship marketing Web initiative.

> Resources involve both tangibles and intangibles. Tangibles revolve around money, people, and information.

Worksheet: Financial Resources

1. What is our total current advertising and promotion budget?
2. How much do we spend in traditional broadcast and print media (newspapers, magazines, radio, and television)?
3. How much do we spend on point-of-purchase advertising (brochures, literature, displays, trade shows)?
4. How much do we spend on customer reinforcement (thank-you letters, postcards, newsletters)?
5. How much do we spend on graphic design, copy writing, and production?
6. Where will the money for creating and posting the Web site come from—will we increase our marketing budget or where will we trim money from the above categories?

The true costs of your current marketing program involves human as well as financial resources, of course.

Worksheet: Human Resources

1. Who handles your firm's current marketing activities (or interfaces with outside suppliers)?
2. How much time do they spend each month on marketing activities (meeting with art and copy people or writing copy)?
3. Who responds to e-mail from prospective buyers?
4. How much time do they spend each month?
5. Which of your employees appears to both enjoy marketing and promotional activities as well as show a natural aptitude for it?
6. Which of their other duties can be trimmed back to create the time necessary to devote to marketing activities?

Information—customer and prospect names, addresses, and buying information—is the final resource you need to inventory. As you undertake a relationship marketing Web initiative, your firm's activities are going to increasingly revolve around customer and prospect names and addresses maintained in a *single, up-to-date, easily accessed, and easily updated database*. A successful Web initiative involves more than Rolodexes transcribed from business cards and paper invoices stored alphabetically in file cabinets.

Worksheet: Information Resources

1. Do you know who your prospects are? (Do you depend on information from distributors, retailers, your sales staff, telephone inquiries, magazine coupons, visitors to your trade show booth, or what?)
2. Do you know who your customers are? (Do you collect information from direct sales, warranty registration cards, shipping labels, customer support calls, names forwarded from distributors, retailers, or your field sales staff?)
3. Does your firm maintain a single, computerized, up-to-date customer and prospect database?

4. How far back does your customer and prospect database go?
5. How often is your customer and prospect database updated?
6. Does your customer and prospect database include e-mail addresses?
7. When was the last time you cleaned your mailing list by mailing to it?
8. Who is in charge of updating your customer and prospect database?
9. Is full customer and prospect information available to everyone in your organization?
10. Is e-mail available to all appropriate employees?
11. How often is e-mail to "information" checked?
12. Who is in charge of backing it up off premises?
13. Does your database contain all the information—full contact information, position, purchasing authority, past purchase interest, area of interest—needed for customer follow-up?
14. How often do you analyze your customer and prospect database, looking for trends and new opportunities among customers and prospects?

> Your task, as business owner or manager, is to understand the possibilities within the context of your business.

Identifying Possibilities

The Web offers a wide range of opportunities. Your task, as business owner or manager, is to understand the possibilities within the context of your business, not someone else's. This is important to avoid initiating misguided Web initiatives that may serve another business well but not yours. To help you in this task, here is a listing of opportunities. Not all of these will be valuable to your business, so think about them in personal terms and relate them to your unique situation. You can use the Web to:

- Introduce your business to new prospects (this is the traditional advertising model, the electronic brochure).
- Learn more about your prospect's needs—those you can and those you may be able to meet in the future.

- Sell directly to buyers at current prices, perhaps expanding into new geographic areas.
- Improve your ability to compete by reducing the costs of doing business, passing the savings along to your customers.
- Help customers do a better job of selecting the product or services they need.
- Increase repeat sales to existing customers and generate referral business.
- Improve customer service and, at the same time, reduce after-sale support costs.
- Analyze how well you're currently satisfying existing customers.
- Inexpensively explore new business opportunities, building on the industry-specific information you already know and integrating it with your existing customer and prospect base, slowly transforming your business into a new and different business.
- Completely abandon your current business model and jump into a whole new business model.

As the above shows, you can become as involved with the Web as you want to. It's up to you to choose a direction, allocate resources, and establish a timeline.

> You can become as involved with the Web as you want to. It's up to you to choose a direction, allocate resources, and establish a timeline.

For more information on this topic, visit our Web site at www.businesstown.com

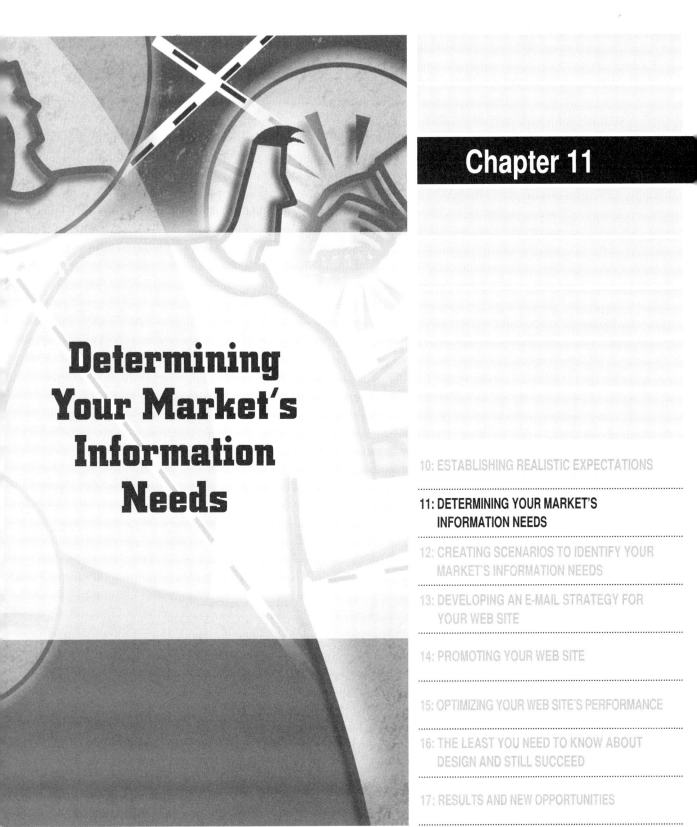

Determining Your Market's Information Needs

Chapter 11

Get inside your customer's head and find out what they want!

—JIM TWETEN

Think for a moment about the businesspeople you like and respect. You probably like them because you have similar interests, and you probably respect them because they have meaningful things to say. Perhaps their knowledge or their information helps you in some way. Think now about the process you go through when you make a new business acquaintance—the natural assessment that takes place where you are listening to them and deciding if they know what they are talking about and if the knowledge they possess will help your business in some way. This is how visitors to your Web site assess your business.

Everybody wants to be liked, to make a good impression. Think about meeting someone you want to impress. Think about the way you talk to them about relevant matters and try to talk in terms to which they can relate. Think about how you might, while listening to them, modify what you say and how you say it. Now, of course, that's easy when you are face to face with a person. It's easy to gauge their facial expression and see if your words are connecting with them. If you are to present an information-rich Web site to your customers and deliver the right message, you need to figure out what the right message is and determine how to present that message to get the desired results. Because where your Web site is concerned, it isn't about being liked; it's about generating the results you want.

Information is the lifeblood of your Web site initiative. Information is the propellant that drives Web site visitors through the five stages of Web involvement.

1. The promise of Web-based information in print, broadcast, and point-of-purchase promotional materials (ads, business cards, flyers, invoices, letterheads, newsletters, postcards, etc.) drives visitors to your Web site.

2. Information delivered at the awareness stage compels visitors to remain at your Web site and motivates them to provide their e-mail address for later follow-up.
3. Information at the comparison stage separates your firm from your competitors by enhancing your credibility.
4. Information at the transaction stage motivates visitors to act right now by providing incentives for immediate action.
5. Information at the reinforcement stage adds value to the purchase and encourages future purchases.
6. Information at the community stage creates word-of-mouth recommendations.
7. Information, and promises of information, in your monthly or bimonthly e-mail to previous site visitors drives visitors back to your Web site.
8. Information improves your Web site's performance by attracting more attention from search engines. Many search engines go through your Web site, searching for key words (proper nouns, key phrases, etc.). The more information you provide in your Web site, the more likely search engines will encounter these words and list your Web site.

There's no bluffing information, though. It has to be real or visitors will quickly see through your design or Java-based camouflage and leave your site—never to return. Attractive Web site designs and special effects may *enhance* information, but can never *replace* information.

Information represents the biggest challenge you face beginning and throughout your Web initiative. Information forms the heart and soul of Web site success. To succeed, you must continuously provide meaningful content—information that will help turn prospects into customers, customers into repeat customers, and repeat customers into ambassadors.

As you increasingly fine-tune your Web initiative, you'll become more adept at hitting the "sweet spot," where the information you present on your Web site and in e-mail follow-up hits the intersection between your market's information needs and your firm or organization's marketing needs.

> Attractive Web site designs and special effects may enhance information, but can never replace information.

An Information-Driven View of Web Site Design

The goal of a successful Web initiative is to find the perfect fit between information your market wants or needs and information that supports your firm or organization's marketing goals.

A poor Web site is one-sided. It emphasizes information solely from the business owner's point of view. A popular Web site is one that provides information the market wants but doesn't support the firm or organization's marketing goals. An *effective* Web site, however, provides information that satisfies both the firm's and the visitor's goals.

There are several approaches you might take to determining your market's information needs:

1. **Intuition**—provide the information you think they need.
2. **Historical**—base your Web site's information on previous sales experiences.
3. **Goal-driven**—provide content based on your firm or organization's marketing goals.
4. **Competitor**—survey your competitor's Web sites and see what types of information they provide.
5. **Analytical**—base information on an analysis of Web site traffic.
6. **Partnership**—create a partnership with your market and let them determine the information you provide on your Web site.

These approaches can be described as "me first" or "market first."

"Me First" Approaches

As you begin your Web site initiative, the approach you choose will probably be based on a combination of the first three alternatives.

> An *effective* Web site, however, provides information that satisfies both the firm's and the visitor's goals.

Intuitive approach

The intuitive approach is the weakest approach of all. Interestingly enough, it's also the most stressful and time-consuming of all because you're forced to *guess*, rather than rely on more solid forms of evidence.

The intuitive approach is based on putting yourself in your prospect's shoes and asking, "If I were a prospect in the market for the product or service I'm offering, what information would I need to make a choice?" The problem is that you—as a business owner or organization executive—know too much; you suffer from knowledge-induced myopia. What's important to you may not be important to your prospects and customers. More important, what's boring or common sense to you may be news to your prospects.

This is a battle that you'll be facing throughout your Web initiative—the battle to view your Web site from the market's point of view.

> **Intuitive approach**
> What's important to you may not be important to your prospects and customers. More important, what's boring or common sense to you may be news to your prospects.

Historical approach

Another approach is to review the concerns and questions that are typically brought up during previous sales presentations and identify the issues that are important to your market. The goal is to identify the questions that you and your sales force are asked over and over again and incorporate as much of this information in your Web site your Web site as possible.

Asking questions represents the best way to do this. Typical questions include:

1. What are the three most frequently asked questions your customers ask when purchasing your product or service?
2. What other questions typically come up?
3. What are your qualifications for providing the product or service?
4. How is your firm or organization different from others providing your product or service?
5. What are the procedures involved in buying and using the product or service?
6. What are the next purchases customers frequently make, or ask about?

To the degree that you view your Web site as a sales presentation, you'll be on the road to identifying your market's information needs.

Goal-driven

Another approach is to identify your firm's or organization's marketing needs as specifically as possible. What are the goals of your Web site? Increased business and referrals is not a sufficient answer. Instead, break your business down into the categories of products or services you provide and establish goals for each category:

If you're an author and consultant, for example:

1. How many copies of each book do you want to sell direct over the Web each month to new readers?
2. How many copies of each book do you want to sell each month to readers who previously purchased other books?
3. How many requests for information about speaking engagements do you want to generate each month?
4. How many requests for information about your consulting services do you want to generate each month?

After you have identified your goals, try to identify the information that your market will need in order to accomplish these goals. For example, if you want to sell 35 books, you will probably want to include a table of contents, copies of reviews from satisfied readers, and possibly a sample chapter. Once you have established your goals, it becomes a lot easier to identify the information necessary to achieve them.

Use the following worksheet as a guide to establishing realistic marketing goals.

- How many new prospects do you want to contact you each month?
- How many C-level clients do you want to upgrade to B-level clients? How many B-level clients do you want to upgrade to A-level clients?
- How many new consulting clients do you want to generate per month?
- How many books do you want to sell per month?
- How many support calls do you want to eliminate?
- How many repeat sales?

> **Goal-driven**
> After you have identified your goals, try to identify the information that your market will need in order to accomplish these goals.

Competitor

Your Web site should never be developed in isolation from your competitor. There are several reasons you should closely monitor your competitor's Web sites

Worksheet: Marketing Goals

1. At the very least, you want to makes sure that your Web site is dramatically different from your competitor's. If your primary competitors use red, you should use blue. If they use a serif typeface, you should consider a sans serif typeface. Your marketing communications should never be confused with your competitors.
2. A glance at your competitor's Web site may suggest categories of information you may have overlooked.
3. In the worst case scenario, you may be forced to react to prices or promotions on your competitor's Web site. You don't want to appear to be more expensive or less qualified than your competitors.
4. How frequently updated? Monitoring your competitor's Web sites will give you a clue as to how frequently you should update your Web site. If your competitor's Web site is updated weekly, yours should to. If you don't, you'll be sending out a "less professional" image.

> A glance at your competitor's Web site may suggest categories of information you may have overlooked.

Analytical

A more advanced approach is based on monitoring the performance of your Web site. Web site traffic reports can provide you with information like:

1. How many visitors did your home page attract?
2. Which pages enjoyed the most traffic?
3. Which pages were visited first?
4. Which pages enjoyed the least traffic?
5. How long did visitors stay at each page?
6. What was the last page of your Web site visited?

This information can be invaluable. By identifying your most popular pages—pages that are frequently visited and where visitors stay a long time—you can identify the topics of greatest interest to your market. Conversely, after a short time, by identifying Web site traffic reports, you will be able to identify the topics that are of least importance to your market as evidenced by fewer and shorter visits. Then it's simply a matter of providing more articles on topics that treat popular topics in greater detail.

There are numerous software programs available that permit you to analyze Web site traffic. If you are hosting your own Web site on your own server, you'll have to purchase these programs and interpret the results yourself—increasing your investment, learning curve, and workload. In most cases, however, your Internet service provider already has these programs and, for an additional cost each month, can prepare reports analyzing Web site traffic on your site, identifying the most popular pages and the time spent on them.

These Web site traffic reports can also indicate the order in which pages were visited at your site. After they arrived at the home page, for example, which page was usually the first one visited? Web site traffic can also indicate the sequence of page visits; which pages are typically visited first, which pages are rarely visited—or visited last.

> By analyzing Web site traffic reports, you can learn from your visitors.

By analyzing Web site traffic reports, you can learn from your visitors. Instead of guessing which topics are of most importance, you can analyze your visitor's behavior and learn from it. You can replace guesswork and hunches with information and knowledge.

Partnership

A more fruitful approach is to constantly ask your Web site visitors to evaluate your Web site's content and be guided by their reactions. Forms represent the easiest way to do this. Forms permit Web site visitors to quickly communicate their likes and dislikes to you.

If your Web site includes a visitor registration form, a simple pair of text boxes asking "What was the most useful part of this Web site?" and "What was the least useful part of this Web site?" can provide you with valuable information.

An even better approach is to include an opportunity for visitor evaluation or feedback on each page of your Web site. Option boxes represent the best approach since they make it easy for visitors to respond. Option boxes offer visitors a choice of several mutually exclusive options (visitors can't respond that the page was both "very useful" and "not very useful"). Added to the bottom of each page, along with a Submit and Reset buttons, option boxes don't take up much space, and it is easy to compile the results.

A typical option box might read "How would you rate the contents of this article?"

- Very useful
- Somewhat useful
- Not very useful
- A waste of time

You can assign values to each option, for example:

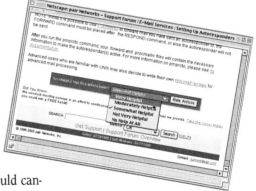

"Very useful" would be assigned the number 2
"Somewhat useful" would be assigned the number 1
"Not very useful" would be assigned negative 1
"A waste of time" would be assigned negative 2

Visitor evaluations could go directly into a database on your Web site, permitting easy evaluation. There would be a separate column for each article. Negative responses would cancel positive responses, making it easy to score each article by simply adding up the responses.

Another approach would be to add a "Comment" or "Feedback" text box to the bottom of each article. Comments and feedback for each article could be directed to a different database or e-mail address. To succeed, your comment or feedback box should have a specific headline: "What other topics should have been covered in this article?" or "Does this article suggest any questions you'd like answered?"

Depending on the goals of your Web site, you could build a dialog with your Web site visitors by adding (copying and pasting) comments to the end of each article. This would dramatically show visitors that you were interested in their responses.

Your Market's Information Needs

It is important to separate long-term from short-term information needs. Short-term information needs are transient; they reflect your firm's changing product and service offerings. These information needs may be seasonal. For example, the Web site of a landscaping supply store will offer seeds in the spring, lawn mowers in the summer, and leaf grinders in the fall. Short-term information needs may be event driven, occasioned by events in the news such as candles before a hurricane or stock trades following changes in the interest rate.

Your market's long-term information needs are likely to remain constant, however. These are based on your market's and your firm's underlying motives. Long-term information needs involve issues that remain constant from year to year, for example:

- What are the generic advantages to your firm's products or services?
- How can your market identify quality so they make the right choice?
- What are the fears or misunderstandings that prevent more of your market from purchasing your firm's products or services?
- How does your firm differ from the competition?
- What types of clients or customers buy from you?
- What are the questions you're asked over and over again?
- What information will help buyers maximize their investment in your product or service?
- What other products or services should they be buying?

To the extent you answer these questions, you'll be able to develop the information needed for your Web site.

> Short-term information needs may be event driven, occasioned by events in the news such as candles before a hurricane or stock trades following changes in the interest rate.

Where Does Information Come From?

The key to a successful Web initiative is to establish an ongoing flow of information. It's not enough to post a Web site and expect it to continue of its own accord. Successful Web sites are not static. Someone has to be in charge; someone has to be given the responsibility and the resources necessary to develop your Web site's information flow as well as the information flow needed for your ongoing e-mail program.

Separate information from design

Strive to separate information from production and design. The ability to design a good-looking page—in terms of color, layout, and typography—and the ability to create HTML pages or use a Web site authoring software program has little to do with the ability to identify the information needs of your firm and translate your firm's features into compelling benefits Web site visitors can instantly grasp.

There are likely to be any number of qualified designers in your area, and there are likely to be a large number of individuals who are comfortable producing Web pages with today's popular software programs. There are likely to be far fewer people who understand your business—your firm's products and services—and are able to understand your market's information needs. You may need to cultivate these key players or cultivate the required skills yourself.

One of the biggest problems of the Web is that it is a graphically and technologically demanding field that depends, for its ultimate success, on a finely tuned marketing ability. Graphic designers and HTML programmers may come and go, but the person who determines the content to be placed on your Web site should be a long-term player, one who fully understands your firm and your customers and is willing to direct the design and programming activities of others.

Information stages

Success depends on developing a *systematic approach* to information development. Your Web site and your e-mails must offer dif-

> The key to a successful Web initiative is to establish an ongoing flow of information.

ferent information at each stage of customer development. The questions you have to answer are:

1. What information is most appropriate for the introduction stage?
2. What information do visitors need at the comparison stage?
3. What information is needed to convert visitors into buyers at the transaction stage?
4. What information is most appropriate for the reinforcement stage?
5. What information is necessary to build loyalty at the community stage?
6. What information should be included in your monthly or bimonthly e-mail newsletters?

> To succeed, your Web site must be constantly changing. Visitors will not return to a Web site that does not offer new information or information restated the same old way.

The success of your Web initiative depends on answering these questions with increasing detail as time goes by. To succeed, your Web site must be constantly changing. Visitors will not return to a Web site that does not offer new information or information restated the same old way. Your Web site's content must be in a constant flux and new information must be added to satisfy visitors as they progress through the customer development cycle.

Case Studies

As you review the following case studies, notice how the businesses profiled use the World Wide Web, not in an attempt to cultivate customers from international markets, but to cultivate local businesses. Yes, the World Wide Web may ultimately permit you to expand the geographic base of your business, but in many cases this should not be your primary concern. Start by satisfying your local clients and customers and then expand your horizons (if necessary).

Oral surgeon

Consider the case of an oral surgeon. Obviously, a great deal of his patients are referrals from area dentists. This means that at some point his Web site should qualify visitors between patients and peers; one section of his Web site should offer content for patients and prospective patents, another level should feature content for peers.

- At the **introduction** stage, the oral surgeon's Web site should be aimed at introducing the surgeon and building patient confidence by reducing fear of the unknown and by emphasizing the surgeon's experience and compassion. "I understand" should be the underlying message.
- At the **comparison** stage, the oral surgeon should describe the procedure in slightly greater detail, building the patient's confidence by bonding with the patient, realistically describing the amount of potential discomfort, and, most important, showing how the patient can control the discomfort. The prospective patient's confidence in this particular surgeon can be enhanced by case studies or testimonials from previous satisfied patients.
- As the **transaction** stage approaches, financing, payment, and scheduling options can be described. Patient fear can be further reduced by describing relaxation techniques for the night before the procedure as well as what to do—and what not to do—the day of the procedure. An e-mail reminder should be sent the day before the procedure.
- During the **reinforcement** stage, a "how are you doing?" e-mail should be sent immediately following the procedure. This e-mail can describe what to do in case of discomfort. A few days later, an e-mail survey can be sent asking the patient to rate his or her experience with the surgeon. This, more than any other step, will communicate concern and compassion.
- During the **community** stage, e-mail can be sent to patients directing them to the Web site where they will find information about preventing similar problems in the future. An online forum on the surgeon's Web site can provide an opportunity for patients to ask the surgeon questions and—most important—communicate with new patients just arriving at the introduction stage. Soon, previous patients will be cre-

> The World Wide Web may ultimately permit you to expand the geographic base of your business, but in many cases this should not be your primary concern.

ating a virtual "fan club," which will attract more and more patients, doing the surgeon's marketing for him!

In addition, while all this is going on, a separate section of the Web site—perhaps a password-protected area—can be used to maintain the surgeon's credibility among referring dentists by summarizing recent accomplishments, new techniques developed, as well as reporting recent advances in his area.

As you review the worksheet, jot down ideas that you may adapt from the case study and apply to your own Web site. And, as you review the various worksheets, be aware that none of the information options are written in stone; some of the information may "float" between adjacent stages. View the five stages of the customer development stages as a loose, rather than rigid, framework for developing a feel for the varying information needs of each stage.

Restaurant

Restaurants offer other opportunities to take advantage of the World Wide Web and, in doing so, may suggest ideas you can adopt to your business.

- At the **introduction** stage, the restaurant's Web site can emphasize the basics necessary to attract new business. At this stage, visitors are interested in the type of food sold (French, Italian, Chinese), ease of accessibility, and—most important—typical price range. Introduction information does not have to be too detailed; visitors will immediately disqualify the restaurant if they want Italian food and the restaurant specializes in French cooking.
- Visitor information needs at the **comparison** stage are more important. Here, visitors have probably narrowed their choices down to one or two options and are looking for information or reasons to choose one restaurant over the other. Visitor information needs are more intense here and can be

satisfied by reprints of restaurant reviews, a profile of the staff, or an interview with the chef. The restaurant's credibility can be enhanced by a sample recipe.

- At the **transaction** stage, the restaurant must do everything possible to close the deal by featuring a special menu (or entree) of the day or special promotions, such as an early-bird or two-for-one coupon specials that can be printed out from the Web site. Transactions can be expedited by online reservations, with perhaps a complimentary desert or appetizer used to push undecideds over the edge and motivate them to visit the restaurant.

- At the **reinforcement** stage, if the reservation was made via e-mail or if the restaurant collects business cards from patrons using a free meal as an incentive, the restaurant should send the previous day's patrons an e-mail along with a survey asking them to rank their experience. (Again, an incentive should be used to motivate patrons to respond.) At the reinforcement stage, the restaurant can place articles about preparing seasonal menus, or patrons can be sent a recipe of the month via e-mail. Customer loyalty can be further enhanced by adding notice of special events, like wine-tasting, theme meals, or special events.

- At the **community** stage, the restaurant might offer "bring a friend" nights promoted on special "members only" unlinked Web pages and announced via e-mail. Other promotional activities at the community stage could include tie-ins with local movie theaters or parking garages, as well as links to similar restaurants in other cities of the country.

> E-mail propels the customer development cycle. E-mail should not tell the whole story but tease visitors into returning to the Web site to print out a coupon or learn more about a seasonal menu or special event.

E-mail is essential to the success of motivating restaurant patrons to return to the Web site at each level. E-mail propels the customer development cycle. E-mail should not tell the whole story but tease visitors into returning to the Web site to print out a coupon or learn more about a seasonal menu or special event.

Consultant

The varying information needs for each stage of the customer development cycle can also be gained from analyzing a consultant's Web site.

> The customer development cycle can be garnered from analyzing a consultant's Web site.

- At the **introduction** stage, the goal is to communicate the consultant's field of expertise and background. Information needs are as critical at this point as they are in the next stage, because at the introduction stage, visitors are analyzing their options and choosing the consultants whom they will later examine in greater detail. At the introduction stage, it's enough for visitor to make simple pass/fail judgments.

- Information needs at the **comparison** stage are much more demanding. Here, visitors are interested in choosing between roughly comparable options. At this stage, the consultant's goal is to build credibility by stressing competence and experience. This can best be done by presenting information that demonstrates a knowledge of his or her field. Case studies can demonstrate past competence and resources like a glossary or books written enhance the consultant's credibility and provide a competitive edge over their competition.

- At the **transaction** stage, the consultant should motivate visitors to commit by making a purchase—even if it a simple purchase like a book or special report. Full contact information should be provided along with a detailed explanation of procedures and costs. In order to begin creating a bond of familiarity with prospective clients, the consultant might offer incentives for purchasing books and tapes, or offer a specially priced brief telephone or online consultation that will permit prospects to determine if they like working with the consultant.

- At the **reinforcement** stage, the consultant can maintain visibility among past clients by adding new case studies to his Web site as well as writing articles that reflect an understanding of the client's challenges as well as demonstrate the consultant's mastery of the latest techniques. News value can also be added to the Web site by summarizing articles of interest to their market and, when possible, adding links to articles in periodicals.
- At the **community** stage, the consultant can post a question and answer forum, which will create new business by bringing in new prospects as well as provide an opportunity to oversee the challenges facing his or her clients.

Email should be sent to previous Web site visitors each time new information is posted on their Web site, driving previous visitors back to their Web site. The new information should be as easy to locate on the Web site as possible.

> Email should be sent to previous Web site visitors each time new information is posted on their Web site, driving previous visitors back to their Web site.

For more information on this topic, visit our Web site at www.businesstown.com

Chapter 12

Creating Scenarios to Identify Your Market's Information Needs

Today the tyrant rules not by club or fist, but, disguised as a market researcher, he shepherds his flocks in the ways of utility and comfort.

—MARSHALL MCLUHAN, *THE MECHANICAL BRIDE*

Hello and welcome to our Web site! Look how we made our logo spin around and around. Isn't it cool! Click here to buy our fine product because we are having a sale.

Perhaps you've heard the saying, "If you're a hammer, every problem is a nail." Fact is, this approach to business simply doesn't work in the modern business environment. What works instead is understanding the problems your customers face and solving them—on their terms. Given the fact that you can't easily meet with the visitors to your Web site, it is necessary to devise another approach in order to get a deep understanding of their needs and desires. Also, since your Web site is dealing with large numbers of individuals, it can sometimes be difficult to think clearly and deeply about the needs of your customers in the aggregate.

But this challenge doesn't excuse you from carrying out this important exercise. Fortunately, there is a proven approach that will allow you to gain a sufficient understanding of your customers needs so you can present your solution on their terms, which will compel them to take action and buy from you.

Before you even begin to think about site design and content, write several stories identifying typical visitors to your Web site and the information needs that brought them there. The time spent writing these scenarios will help you avoid myopia. Instead of creating your Web site from your point of view, the scenarios will help you focus your site's content and navigation on your visitor's needs, making it easier for you to create a truly useful Web site.

Many Web sites fail not from just the obvious reasons, such as home pages with huge, slow loading graphics, long lines of hard to read text, or cluttered backgrounds. Most Web sites fail because they are written from the site creator's perspective rather than from the Web site user's perspective. These "brag and boast" sites emphasize the Web site creator's accomplishments but don't address their visitor's information needs.

Using Scenarios to Avoid Myopia

To create an effective Web site, you must struggle to overcome the challenge of myopia. To overcome your myopia, you must experience your Web site—and the message you want to present—from your visitor's perspective. You must put yourself in your visitor's shoes and think like your visitors in order to design a Web site that presents your message in a way that best reflects needs.

Visitors are selfish. They are not really interested in your business except insofar as your business can help them achieve a goal. Visitors are at your site because they have a problem that they hope you can solve. Scenarios help you identify your visitors' goals by developing a better idea of their problems and how they relate to your solutions. Scenarios help you overcome your myopia by making it easier for you to get a better idea of your Web site visitors' information needs so you can better provide the information they need (which happens to involve buying your product or service!).

> Put yourself in your visitor's shoes and think like your visitors in order to design a Web site that presents your message in a way that best reflects needs.

Creating Scenarios

Scenarios are detailed, fictional stories you write describing typical visitors to your Web site, the challenges they face, and the information they need to be persuaded to buy your firm's product or service. Ideally, you should create a series of four or five scenarios, each describing a typical buyer for each category of product or service you offer.

The more details you include in your scenarios, the easier it will be to create your Web site and the more effectively it will satisfy your visitor's needs. Details bring your story alive, helping you get a better understanding of your visitor's information needs. Details help you humanize, or personalize, your visitors. Instead of thinking of your visitors as a "faceless mass," scenarios help you think of your visitors as individuals with specific information needs.

Limit your scenarios to one page. This makes them easy to scan at a glance, easy to share with coworkers and those working on your Web site, easy to photocopy, and easy to arrange in the right order.

Enforcing a one-page limit also forces you to write as tightly as possible, avoiding the temptation to fluff up your scenarios with unnecessary verbiage. One-page scenarios encourage you to focus on quality rather than quantity.

Start by creating a minimum of ten scenarios. *Create a different scenario for each type of customer or prospect that is likely to visit your Web site.* Or, create a different scenario for each of the products or services that you want to promote. Be sure you create different scenarios for Web site visitors at each of the five levels of the customer development cycle. This will help you identify the open and premium content appropriate for each level of the cycle.

Be as focused as possible when creating your scenarios. Focus on individual visitors to your Web site. Avoid scenarios that describe the characteristics and challenges of two or more types of customers.

Scenarios are a bargain, especially compared to the cost of purchasing Web site graphic design from independent design firms or hiring a freelance graphic designer. Scenarios perform best when they are created in-house rather than purchased by outsiders who may not be as familiar with your customers as you are.

If you are uncomfortable writing, of course, you can always hire a freelance writer to take notes and organize your thoughts as you discuss the various customers you and your employees have dealt with in the past.

Scenarios should be written by those most familiar with the business's customers and prospects. As a business owner or manager, you are uniquely qualified to write scenarios because you have probably been dealing with customers longer than anyone else in your firm. Your ability to write scenarios is determined by the extent that you have had, and continue to have, extensive customer contact. *After all, no one knows your business better than you do!*

Several employees also should be invited to write scenarios. Scenarios are too important to be limited to one person. Different employees are likely to be able to bring different perspectives to the scenario-writing process. Your sales staff, for example, is ideally quali-

> Be sure you create different scenarios for Web site visitors at each of the five levels of the customer development cycle.

fied, as are customer support personnel who deal with your customers on the phone.

Often, the best approach is to create a small "Scenario Team" consisting of four or five key individuals. Schedule a "scenario writing afternoon" in your conference room. Instruct the rest of your staff that you and your team are not to be interrupted and provide laptop computers for everyone.

Start the meeting off with a description of the goal of the scenario-writing session and begin by "brainstorming," identifying typical customers or customer categories. Then have individuals prepare their scenarios. Don't assign an unreasonable workload. As an attainable goal, consider your session a success if each employee writes two scenarios during the afternoon.

> Your ability to write scenarios is determined by the extent that you have had, and continue to have, extensive customer contact. After all, no one knows your business better than you do!

Six steps to success

There are six steps to creating successful scenarios. Follow these steps and you'll find it easy to create scenarios.

1. **Describe the Web site visitor**. Start by identifying each scenario with a specific fictional name and a position at a fictional association or corporation; *"Betsy Parker is the program chairman for the Parker Software Collaborative located in Dover, New Hampshire."* You'll find your scenarios easier to write when they focus on a specific person who comes alive as you go through the process of writing your scenario.
    Identify the individual's occupation, age, income, and education level as well as personal interests and work habits.
2. **Identify the challenge.** Next, describe the challenge or problem that the individual is facing, the goal they want to satisfy; *"Betsy Parker's goal is that she needs to locate a keynote speaker for the forthcoming User Group Meeting in June at the Portsmouth, New Hampshire, Hyatt Regency Hotel on June 14, 2000."*
    The challenge identifies the reason the visitor is at your Web site. Identifying the challenge guides you in identifying the

categories and types of information your Web site needs to
provide to satisfy the visitor. After all, how can you provide a
solution if you don't know the question?

3. **Provide as many details as appropriate**. The more specific
   details about the individual's challenge you provide, the more
   you identify the information your Web site must provide in
   order to satisfy the visitor's challenge. Don't be afraid to be
   as specific as possible (taking into account the one-page
   length for each scenario).

   *"Approximately four hundred users will be arriving from
   throughout the United States. The keynote speaker must not
   only understand the software, but be an entertaining, high-
   energy individual who can begin the conference with an
   enthusiastic, fast-paced, forty-five minute presentation outlining the progress the firm has made in improving customer service during the past year."*

4. **Identify the characteristics of a successful solution**. Identify
   the types of information the Web site visitor needs in order
   to choose you to solve their problem. In the case of the program chairman seeking a speaker, the ideal solution might
   include the following information: *"The keynote speaker
   must be a recognized authority, well known to the target
   audience, or possess credentials reflecting their area of
   expertise (i.e., published books, articles, etc.). The speaker
   must also be able to document his or her experience comfortably speaking in front of large groups. Evaluations from
   previous speaking engagements must contain terms like
   dependable, entertaining, and responsible."*

   The more effort you put into identifying the characteristics
   of a successful solution, the easier it will be to complete your
   Web site and the more you'll identify the information your
   Web site should contain.

5. **Provide a complete solution**. Complete the "sales" job by
   providing additional detailed information. Answer the question, *"Is he or she really good and are they available?"*
   Viewing the program manager's challenge from his or her
   point of view (*"I can't take a chance on an unknown quan-*

> Your firm's Web site visitor scenarios should be updated at least once or twice a year, preferably quarterly.

tity; the keynote address is crucial to the success of the conference") drives home the importance of quantifying the speaker's qualifications.

To satisfy the visitor's fear factor, the Web site could include a list of previous keynote speech topics or workshop presentations plus a list of previous clients. A list of references or copies of attendee evaluations would enhance the speaker's credibility. To address the question. *"What does the speaker actually sound and look like?"* your Web site could include pictures of the speaker in action or—even better—an opportunity to download and view a short audio/video clip showing the speaker at a previous presentations.

A list of current and future speaking engagements would provide further evidence that the speaker is an active, successful candidate. An updated list of upcoming speaking engagements would also help the program chairman find out if the speaker is available on the date of the event.

6. **Close the deal**. The Web site should conclude by answering the question, *"How can I contact the speaker in order to discuss the project in greater detail and find out how much it will cost?"*

   The speaker's Web site should make it as easy as possible for the visitor to contact the speaker and establish a dialog. Each page of the Web site should contain the speaker's e-mail, fax and telephone numbers, or an information request form to simplify communications so the visitor doesn't have to return to the home or "contact us" page to contact the speaker.

Updating scenarios

Your firm's Web site visitor scenarios should be updated at least once or twice a year, preferably quarterly. Each scenario review provides you with an opportunity to identify new market challenges and, in doing so, identify new products and services your firm should offer.

Scheduling frequent scenario updates also keeps you and your scenario team on its toes and constantly on the lookout for new market opportunities. Soon you may find yourself, or your key employees, voluntarily writing customer scenarios outside of company time, while the details of a particularly significant customer or prospect interaction are still fresh.

> Written scenarios influence both your Web site's content and the way it's organized.

Case Study

Written scenarios influence both your Web site's content and the way it's organized. Let's take a detailed look at another scenario, this time identifying a typical visitor to a Web site created for a mail order hobby shop that specializes in model railroad products and accessories.

As you read this section, you may be surprised by the amount of Web site content ideas that the deceptively simple scenario suggests. Consider the following simple five-paragraph scenario:

> *Christopher Parker is a financial investment analyst. He lives in Tilton, New Hampshire. Christopher is currently 55 years old and has been a model railroader ever since he received his first train set while in grammar school.*
>
> *His current particular interest involves O-scale brass locomotives. Since he works such long hours, and his eyesight isn't what it used to be, he prefers to purchase his models already painted rather than painting them himself like he used to. Christopher particularly likes models imported by Overland Models.*
>
> *Christopher models the Santa Fe railroad during the mid-1980s. He has a variety of engines and rolling stock (i.e., freight and passenger cars) typical of the era. He is always looking for new models to complete his collection. Since Overland models are produced in extremely limited quantities, it is often difficult to obtain models no longer available. Since he began to model the Santa Fe only a few years ago, he missed out on several mod-*

els that were previously available. He is particularly interested in obtaining a Santa Fe caboose and observation car for the end of his 12-car passenger train

One of Christopher's frustrations is that part of his collection is inactive in that it includes models of steam engines for other railroads that are more appropriate for an earlier time period.

Christopher subscribes to four model railroad magazines. Twice a year he flies to national model railroad conventions. One of his reasons for attending is to see if other individuals or dealers are selling the models he needs to complete his collection. When he finds what he's looking for, he may spend several thousand dollars on the models he desires to complete his collection.

Translating scenario into Web site

From this scenario, you can see that Christopher's needs would be best satisfied by a Web site with extensive search capabilities. This would make it possible for Christopher to frequently visit the Web site and quickly search for specific Santa Fe diesel engines or passenger cars imported by Overland Models. Since Christopher's visits to the model railroad store's Web site is very information driven, that is, he knows what he's searching for, the design of the Web site in terms of appearance and formatting is clearly secondary to quick access to the firm's current inventory.

Since Christopher owns models he no longer values as much as he once did, the Web site should include a Classifieds section or information about how the hobby shop handles consignment sales, trades, or outright purchases of models that are no longer wanted.

Finally, being in Tilton, New Hampshire, Christopher probably has few local friends who share his interest. A question and answer form or an opportunity for online chat might attract Christopher back to the Web site and allow him to share tips and techniques with other Santa Fe modelers located around the country.

The fact that Christopher travels long distances to locate models indicates that he should clearly be placed on the hobby shop's "priority" prospect list.

Generalizations based on scenarios

Not only do scenarios help you tailor your Web site for specific categories of visitors, the scenarios often provide clues that will help you in more general ways.

For example, the above scenario suggests that most model railroad collectors model specific railroads or specific eras. Hobby shops interested in attracting repeat visits to their Web sites might consider surveying their visitors to find out which railroads or eras the visitors are most interested in, and then, on the basis of the results of these surveys, run occasional articles or photographs on the most popular railroads. This would clearly increase the likelihood of repeat visitors to the Web site.

Likewise, the fact that Christopher models a particular railroad in a particular scale indicates that it might be worthwhile to create a prospect database organized by scale and railroad using e-mail to alert modelers when models meeting their needs are announced or arrive in the store. (Many models are in such high demand that the entire production run is sold out before the models arrive in the United States.)

The fact that Christopher subscribes to four model railroad magazines suggests that there may be a significant overlap in readership between the publications. One implication is that there should be an advertisement for the Web site in at least one of the magazines. Another implication is that there may be a way to survey your Web site visitors and find out which publication is most read, and then run a single, larger advertisement in that publication.

Notice, once again, how the scenario helps make the abstract become concrete, focusing your Web site on your visitors' needs. By focusing on satisfying a typical Web site visitor's needs, you avoid going off on tangents, such as spending a lot of time and money including large, slow-to-download photographs of prototype railroads or including pictures of your warehouse or your employees. Scenarios force you to focus your priorities on your visitor's needs.

Scenarios force you to focus your priorities on your visitor's needs.

Conclusion

Too often, Web sites are created from a design, or aesthetic, point of view with content being secondary to image and impact. Scenarios offer an alternative that helps you place the emphasis on the needs of your Web site visitors—your current customers and your prospective buyers. By making it easy for you to view your Web site from their perspective, scenarios can help you create a Web site that better serves your visitor's needs, and, hence, better serves your needs.

As the previous example shows, scenarios force you to view your firm's information from a different perspective than the typical "brag and boast" Web site. Scenarios make it easier to provide answers to the real world questions your visitors are asking. After analyzing the preceding scenario, you will probably find yourself thinking differently about the types of information you place on your Web site and the way you organize it.

By creating scenarios focused on the major product or service categories you are promoting on your Web site, your Web site will inevitably present information in a different way than if you write it from an impersonal, chronological point of view. By identifying the information needs of your typical Web site visitor, you will present the information in a more empathetic way, one more appropriately in touch with your visitor's needs.

Scenarios not only influence the information you present on your Web site, but the way the information is presented. By identifying your visitor's information needs, and the sequence in which they seek to satisfy them, you'll find it easier to create a navigation system that helps visitors quickly locate the information they desire.

> By making it easy for you to view your Web site from their perspective, scenarios can help you create a Web site that better serves your visitor's needs, and, hence, better serves your needs.

Putting Ideas to Work

Ask yourself the following questions as you review your use of scenarios:

Scenarios not only influence the information you present on your Web site, but the way the information is presented.

1. Are scenarios a formal part of your Web site creation process?
2. Is the information on your Web based on scenarios describing fictionalized individuals representing ten or more categories of customers and prospects?
3. Did you invite the assistance of your sales staff and others with customer experience in writing your scenarios?
4. Have you limited each Web site visitor scenario to one page in length?
5. Do your scenarios describe the specific challenges or problems your customers and prospects face?
6. Do your scenarios include revealing details that will help you identify the information that should be included on your Web site?
7. Does your Web site provide all of the information visitors need to choose your firm in order to solve their particular challenge or problem?
8. Do you review your scenarios and prepare new ones on a scheduled basis?

For more information on this topic, visit our Web site at www.businesstown.com

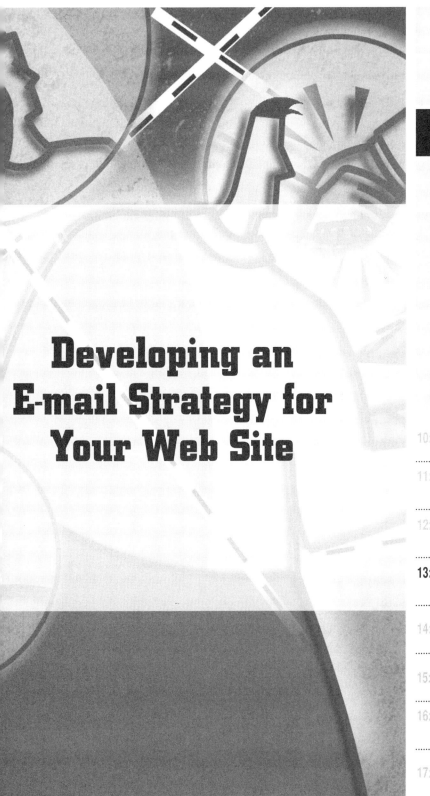

Developing an E-mail Strategy for Your Web Site

You've got mail!
—AMERICA ONLINE

The Web can be an impersonal place. Visitors to a Web site are rarely given a sense that the Web site exists for them and them alone. On the other hand, there is hardly anything more personal than direct and relevant communication. Consider this sample e-mail drawn from the scenario in the last chapter:

"Dear Christopher,

We wanted to let you know that we have just received an Overland Models O-scale Santa Fe Caboose. Since we know you are collecting from this series, we thought you would be interested in seeing the Web page showing the beautiful finish and quality of this rare find. Just click the link below. And in case you would like to make a purchase before the end of the week, just enter your preferred customer code on the order page for a 10% discount."

E-mail makes it happen, not anonymous spam, but focussed, targeted, personalized, relevant e-mail. The impact and response rates for this type of communication eclipse most forms of marketing you could employ. And a properly designed relationship marketing Web site, which gets to know the needs of the visitor, using a well designed database and e-mail system makes this process nearly automatic and with no real incremental costs other than the time to make it happen.

Since e-mail is the engine that propels your customers from step to step along the five-stage customer development cycle, it's important that you develop an attainable, consistent, and effective e-mail strategy.

- Your e-mail strategy has to be *attainable* in that, once you commit to it, you can be reasonably certain that you have the resources to maintain an e-mail mailing list, can develop your messages at appropriate intervals, and have the talent necessary to write compelling e-mail.
- Your e-mail strategy has to be *consistent* in that success comes from predictability. An on-again/off-again e-mail strategy will alienate your customers and prospects. If you

promise to send a once-a-month e-mail newsletter or bimonthly e-mail alerts, the success of your relationship marketing strategy is undermined the first time you miss your self-imposed deadline.

- Most important, your e-mail has to be *effective*. Unread e-mail is a waste of Web resources, your time, and the recipient's time. Your e-mail has to be more than "brag and boast" advertising. It has to be interesting in style and relevant in content. More important, it has to be meaningful enough to motivate visitors to visit the relevant premium content areas of your Web site.

It's important to remember that your customers and prospects are receiving more and more e-mail every day. Unless your e-mail message stands out by virtue of its brevity or extremely relevant content, it's unlikely to be read. Your e-mail will either sit in your customer's in-box, waiting until a later (that often never arrives) to be read or the recipients will delete your message. Worse, they may request that you remove them from your e-mail distribution list.

Using E-mail to Drive Visitors to Your Web Site

E-mail should be sent to previous Web site visitors or new prospects each time new information is posted on the Web site. The new information should be as easy to locate on the Web site as possible. Some of the ways this is done include:

- E-mail **alerts** inform customers when new content has been added to your Web site. You can include the URL of an unlinked page in your alert so that recipients can click on a link and go directly to the desired page.
- You can send e-mail **teasers**, which are a bit longer than alerts. E-mail teasers typically list the headlines for new information placed on your Web site along with a paragraph or two amplifying the headline and further describing the

> Unless your e-mail message stands out by virtue of its brevity or extremely relevant content, it's unlikely to be read.

FIGURE 13-1 AT A GLANCE YOU CAN READ AN ENTIRE
E-MAIL MESSAGE FROM AUDIO FOREST AND DECIDE
WHETHER YOU WANT TO VISIT THE RELEVANT PAGE.

information that has been added. Teasers will also include
the URLs of the specific pages of the Web site the new information is placed on, permitting visitors to go directly to the
new content.

- Your bimonthly or monthly e-mails can function like a
  newsletter, telling the whole story—or enough of the story—
  so that visitors do not have to go back to the Web site to
  learn more. Although the text will be unformatted, visitors
  will be reminded of your constant efforts to provide meaningful information. More important, visitors may choose to
  forward your newsletter to friends and business associates
  who might benefit from the newly added content on your
  Web site.

Long e-mails *are* read if they offer the recipient compelling and
relevant information. The 1to1.com e-mail newsletters sent by
Peppers and Roger fall into this category. Each e-mail contains several full-length articles. Although tightly written, each e-mail contains enough information to communicate a key point.

- Another approach is the **summary** approach. This involves
  sending information that updates your customer's or
  prospect's knowledge of your Web site. One of the best examples of this is the weekly alert that E. P. Levine sends out
  informing camera lovers of additions to their inventory of
  used equipment. Summary e-mail can be read at a glance and
  avoids the necessity for visitors to launch their Web browser
  and visit the Web site itself.
- Your e-mail can also contain **attached files**, such as formatted word processed documents, PowerPoint presentations, or
  sophisticated publications created using page layout programs like Adobe PageMaker and saved using Adobe
  Acrobat.

Adobe Acrobat permits you to distribute fully formatted publications that appear on screen exactly as they looked when they
were created and can also be printed on the recipient's printer.

Acrobat publications contain all of the formatting attributes found on a the original print version of the publication, including typefaces not available on the individual's computer. Adobe Acrobat documents preserve all of the design nuances, such as subtle letter and line spacing, found on the original document. The Adobe Acrobat Reader has already been widely installed on computers and can be downloaded for free from the Adobe Web site. (Always provide a link to the appropriate page of the Adobe Web site for the convenience of those who may not have already downloaded Adobe Acrobat.)

There are three primary disadvantages of distributing attached documents.

1. Acrobat files take time to download and occupy valuable computer hard disk or network space.
2. Many corporations, in order to prevent the transmission of computer viruses, do not allow attached files through their firewalls or e-mail security systems.
3. Attached files do not drive e-mail recipients back to your Web site, which, after all, is the whole purpose of sending the e-mail.

Choosing the right option

Any one of the above options might be enough to guarantee success. More important than the perfection with which these options are executed is the consistency in which you implement your e-mail campaign.

A one-page e-mail "teaser" that goes out like clockwork on the first and fifteenth of each month is far better than an occasional four-page e-mail newsletter that disappears from view for months at a time. Your goal is to constantly keep your prospects and customers aware of your presence and, whenever possible, to drive visitors—and their friends and coworkers—back to your Web site for more information.

The very fact that you consistently send an e-mail teaser or e-mail newsletter to your customers and prospects reminds them of your professionalism and your commitment to providing the informa-

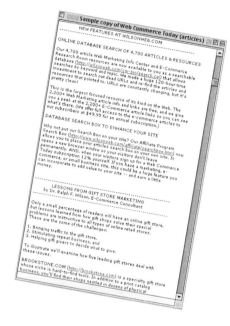

FIGURE 13-2 EACH E-MAIL NEWSLETTER FROM 1TO1.COM CONTAINS SEVERAL TWO- TO FIVE-PARAGRAPH ARTICLES THAT REINFORCE THE FIRM'S CREDIBILITY BY PROVIDING RELEVANT INFORMATION.

tion they need to do their job better or enjoy their pleasures with more satisfaction. Consistency equals success.

It's hard to overestimate the importance of using information and e-mail to propel the customer development cycle. Information used to be frightfully expensive to communicate to prospects and customers. Producing, printing, and mailing postcards and newsletters can be expensive and it can take weeks—often months—for even the simplest project to get designed, produced, printed, addressed, and mailed.

All in all, the best e-mail approach combines brevity and meaningful content with one or more hyperlinks that take visitors to a specific premium content page that interests them.

Elements of a Successful E-mail Message

You can learn a lot about creating effective e-mail by studying the characteristics of successful direct mail. Many of the characteristics that contribute to the success of a direct-mail program contribute to the creation of successful e-mail. There are eight elements that must be considered.

Subject line

The subject line of your e-mail is similar to the headline of an advertisement or direct response letter. The subject line of an effective e-mail message is short, telegraphic, and—whenever possible—memorable. Most important, it should tease the recipient by promising an easily understood benefit. The subject line should summarize the message that follows as well as indicate its relevance to the recipient.

Remember that the subject line will be the first thing that visitors read when they encounter your e-mail in their incoming mail box. If the subject line is left blank or does not indicate an important message follows, the e-mail is unlikely to be opened or it may be immediately deleted.

> It's hard to overestimate the importance of using information and e-mail to propel the customer development cycle.

Knowing the importance of motivating recipients of conventional mail to open the envelopes containing their offers, direct-mail marketers often spend as much time on the short phrase or one sentence headline placed on the outside of the mailing envelope as they do preparing the remainder of their message! You, too, should devote a great deal of time developing subject lines that will attract the reader's interest without, of course, overselling the contents of the message.

Avoid vague generalities. Which would you rather read: an e-mail with a subject line like "Monthly Newsletter," or one that says "Limited-time Valentine's Day weekend getaway"?

Avoid "shouting" in your subject lines. Avoid setting your message exclusively in uppercase type. Messages set entirely in capital letters are harder to read than messages set in a combination of upper and lowercase type.

Personalization

Whenever possible, begin your e-mail with a personalized salutation. Most competent e-mail programs can insert the recipient's first name following the salutation.

Avoid inadvertently insulting your e-mail recipient with a generic salutation, i.e., "Dear Customer," "Dear Satisfied Buyer," or "Dear Colleague." Even though the recipient of your e-mail is perfectly well aware that your e-mail is probably computer generated, the personalized salutation starts your message off on a friendlier tone than when you use a general salutation. Don't provide a salutation at all if you can't personalize it.

Address

Use your e-mail program's BCC, or Blind Carbon Copy, feature to hide the names and e-mail addresses of the other recipients of your message. It's a frightful invasion of privacy to broadcast names and e-mail addresses to strangers. Only one name should appear in the address panel.

FIGURE 13-3 THE SUBJECT LINE OF YOUR E-MAIL IS THE FIRST THING THAT RECIPIENTS WILL NOTICE WHEN THEY ACCESS THEIR IN BOX.

Beginning your message

Your message should begin with an elaboration on the subject line. The best e-mails begin by providing a short summary of the information that is contained in the e-mail.

Remember that, depending on their e-mail software program, recipients of your e-mail will only see a small portion of the message panel, in some cases, only a few lines. It's imperative that those first few lines grab the reader's attention and motivate them to scroll downward through your message. Otherwise, you've lost the sales opportunity for good. Just like you're unlikely to continue reading a newspaper article that begins with a boring first sentence, the recipients of your e-mail are just as likely to jump ship and go on to the next e-mail, or delete your message, if the first lines of your message do not attract their interest.

It's not necessary to use full sentences at the top of your e-mail messages. If your message covers more than one topic, list the topics at the top of the message area of your e-mail. This way, if a recipient is not interested in the first topic, they might be interested in the second topic.

Avoid messages that begin with housekeeping information or an advertisement from a third party, like a firm handling your e-mail. It's far more important to begin selling your customer or prospect by describing the benefits they'll enjoy when they read your e-mail message and visit a premium content page of your Web site than it is to remind recipients why they received your message or—worse—subject e-mail recipients to reading the same advertisement at the top of each message.

Formatting your message

Always build as much white space into your e-mail messages as possible. Unlike the instructions found in every word processing and desktop publishing design book ever written, press the Enter or Return key on your computer keyboard twice after each paragraph. Your readers will appreciate the band of white space this will introduce between paragraphs.

FIGURE 13-4 BEGIN THE MESSAGE AREA WITH ONE OR MORE SHORT PHRASES THAT EXPAND UPON THE PRIMARY BENEFIT OUTLINED IN THE SUBJECT LINE AND—WHEN APPROPRIATE—INTRODUCE ADDITIONAL TOPICS.

Keep your paragraphs as short and to the point as possible. Ruthlessly edit your message. Replace long words with short words and eliminate all unnecessary words. Remember—your goal of e-mail in a relationship marketing program is not to tell the whole story but to drive customers and prospects back to your Web site for the full story. Include just enough information about the contents and benefits of your premium content pages to intrigue your visitors into visiting, and leave it at that.

Keep your e-mail messages as short as possible. This will encourage visitors to read them rather than putting them off until later.

Other formatting options

Feel free to employ style options like bold and italics to help organize the contents of your e-mail message. Use boldfaced type to introduce new topics and use italics to emphasize individual words or short phrases within your message. Do not, however, set your entire message in bold or italics, as this will make it harder, instead of easier, to read.

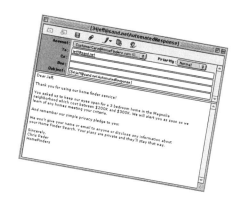

Likewise, use color and different type sizes with discretion. Words set in color are often so distractingly bright that they discourage, rather than encourage readership.

Many e-mail programs, like Microsoft Outlook, allow you to include graphic elements such as your firm's logo, photographs, or seasonal illustrations in your e-mail. These programs also allow you to choose a colored or textured background for your message. You may want to consult with your customers and prospects and find out how they feel about formatted versus unformatted e-mail. Remember that graphics take longer to download than text, and that all e-mail programs may not be able to download the graphics.

E-mail signature

Do not be afraid to personally sign your e-mail. Depending on the size of your business and the formality of your customer and prospect relationships, you may want to personally end your e-mail message with your name and position.

Depending on the sophistication of your relationship marketing program and your database and e-mail software capabilities, you might want to consider having the e-mail signed by the customer sales representative who has direct responsibility for the product (or product line) or the product department manager. *Never be afraid to be personal in an increasingly impersonal world!*

Don't be too concerned about employee promotions and changes. If the original individual leaves your firm, consider sending out a "let's get acquainted" e-mail introducing the new personal contact, perhaps linked to a premium content page that contains a photograph and biography—as well as a carefully camouflaged selling message.

Your e-mail signature should contain all of the information necessary to contact your firm. Although your firm may hand out tens of thousands of business cards, brochures, and newsletters each year, it's a great convenience to have your firm's address, phone, and fax numbers available at the bottom of the message area of your e-mail. This way, if a visitor wants to pick up the phone and call you, he or she doesn't have to search through a desk draw or wallet, or visit your Web site, in order to find your contact information.

Housekeeping and privacy statement

At the end of your e-mail you might include a brief message indicating why the recipient received the e-mail. "You're receiving this e-mail alert because you have registered for our monthly newsletter or provided your e-mail address when you purchased from us."

Although you hope the recipient will never use the information, you should also describe how the recipient may be removed from your e-mail list.

Your firm's privacy statement should also be prominently featured at the end of your e-mail. Throughout your relationship marketing Web initiative, you should reassure customers and prospects that their e-mail address, purchase information, and any other information they may provide will not be shared with any other firm or organization. And you should scrupulously live up to this promise.

> Although your firm may hand out tens of thousands of business cards, brochures, and newsletters each year, it's a great convenience to have your firm's address, phone, and fax numbers available at the bottom of the message area of your e-mail.

Sending Unsolicited E-mail

The use of e-mail as the engine of a relationship marketing program is based on the idea that your e-mails are limited to those who who have previously dealt with you, either by visiting your Web site, visiting your place of business, or by purchasing from you. Resist the urge to send unsolicited e-mails to purchased lists or to prospects whose names you see on discussion forums or other publicly distributed lists.

Unsolicited e-mail is extremely intrusive. It is an invasion of privacy. The dislike of unsolicited direct mail, derogatively called "spam," is a result of the unsavory products and reputations of companies that send unsolicited direct mail.

The only time you might possibly get away with sending unsolicited direct mail is when you make it clear that the mail is being sent as the result of a request or a recommendation from one of the recipient's friends or business associates. There is a world of difference between receiving referral e-mail as opposed to unsolicited e-mail.

If you do send e-mail to an individual you have not previously dealt with, be sure to mention the source of the recommendation at the top of the message area of your e-mail; "You are receiving this e-mail because—Name of Friend—suggested you might be interested in reading about it."

> Resist the urge to send unsolicited e-mails to purchased lists or to prospects whose names you see on discussion forums or other publicly distributed lists.

Handling Incoming and Outgoing E-mail

Creating an effective e-mail program involves developing answers to the following questions:

- Who will write the e-mail messages necessary to drive registered visitors back to your Web site for more information each time new premium content is posted?
- Who will develop or write the automated responses that can respond to the majority of registered visitors to your Web site?

- When a request for literature arrives at your Web site, how long will it take for the request to be fulfilled and the information sent? Who will write a covering letter to accompany the literature?
- What happens when questions requiring a personalized or carefully researched response appear in your firm's incoming e-mail? Who will either respond to the request or route it to the appropriate individual?

What's needed is an individual who can "triage" e-mail and forms. This individual has to know just about everything that's going on in your firm so as to be able to answer questions or—if the answers aren't immediately available—know where to find the answers.

As your Web site grows in importance as a marketing tool, the volume of e-mail is likely to dramatically increase. If you're running a small business and you leave for a day or two you may come back to find hundreds of e-mails from customers and prospects waiting for you.

> As your Web site grows in importance as a marketing tool, the volume of e-mail is likely to dramatically increase.

Consolidating Customer and Prospect Information

Data management is perhaps the biggest challenge while implementing your Web initiative. Data management implies creating access to the following information:

- *Maintaining an active e-mail database.* Not only must there be a database of visitor e-mail addresses, this database should be coded so that different e-mail messages can be sent to visitors at different stages of the customer development cycle. This database is likely to be very volatile in that there will probably be a constantly growing stream of new names coupled with numerous requests for deletion from the list.
- *Coordinating e-mail with transactions.* It's not enough to know the e-mail addresses of visitors at each stage of the cus-

tomer development cycle. This list must be constantly updated as new information becomes available. The e-mail database must be flexible enough to grow as more and more information about each visitor becomes available. Visitor contacts that begin with a simple e-mail address must be updated when the visitor makes a purchase, responds to an invitation to visit a premium content page, or when the visitor recommends the business to a friend.

- *Integrating old and new customers.* Perhaps the biggest data challenge is integrating previous customers with those created by your new Web initiative. Your business files may already contain information about tens, hundreds, or even millions of customers. Chances are, this information does not include customer e-mail addresses. One of your biggest challenges is to bring old customers "up to speed" by creating an incentive (see the next chapter) for them to visit your Web site and register their e-mail address so—in the future—you can use e-mail to promote from a single database.

> The e-mail database must be flexible enough to grow as more and more information about each visitor becomes available.

Assembling an e-mail database

One of the first questions to consider is where the e-mail database will be maintained. Will it be maintained on your firm's computers or on the computers of your Internet service provider? Who will have access to this database? How easy will it be to update, backup, review, and maintain by deleting those who wish to unsubscribe to your e-mail newsletter or messages?

The advantages of maintaining your e-mail database on your Internet service provider's computers are the relative low cost and ease of operation. The negatives involve the costs of maintaining the database as well as the firm's stability. What happens if they go out of business or are merged with another firm? How much access will you have to the database? Will you be able to backup the database on your own computers in case their database is compromised? How secure do you feel the data will be?

Another major problem with a remotely administered database concerns the flexibility of the database. Will you be able to "code" visitors as they progress along each level of the customer development cycle? Will you be able to easily enter transaction information on a database maintained off premises?

The advantage of maintaining your e-mail database in-house is that you have total control over it; you can easily create a customer and prospect database that contains the information you need and can generate the reports you need as desired. Your valuable customer and prospect information is as secure as you want it to be—and can afford to make it. Firewalls—protecting the information from competitors, outside hackers, or snoops—can be as secure as you want and can afford it to be.

The problem, of course, is that information management requires budget resources for hardware, software, and the trained personnel necessary to make it all work. In deciding whether to handle this in-house, consider the following:

- Do you presently have the resources for administering an in-house information system?
- When do you think you will have the resources for an effective information system?

Another choice you will face is deciding whether it will be easier to add an e-mail field to your existing customer and prospect database or create an e-mail database and add transaction information to it. The ultimate result of both alternatives is the same; you will be able to send e-mail to individuals who have contacted your firm, visited your Web site, or purchased from you—but the direction of information input will be different.

As your business makes the transformation to a single database, there will likely be a lot of issues involving changed addresses and duplicate information. How do you coordinate previous purchase information with Web site visits? Who will develop a procedure to eliminate duplicate entries so that a John Smith who visits your Web site and submits their e-mail address is the same as the John Smith who purchased from you six years ago? What will be your criteria for identifying duplicates—name, address, phone number, invoice number?

The advantage of maintaining your e-mail database in-house is that you have total control over it; you can easily create a customer and prospect database that contains the information you need and can generate the reports you need as desired.

Another issue involves e-mail that is returned as undeliverable. Each day, tens of thousands of individuals change their e-mail address. When an e-mail is returned as undeliverable, what will be the procedure to contact the individual—perhaps by telephone or the United States Postal Service—and update their e-mail address?

Coordinating e-mail with transactions

After establishing a flexible database that contains online transaction information plus e-mail addresses, you have to ensure that information from offline and online transactions are consolidated into a single database.

- If your business sells from a walk-in location (a bricks-and-mortar business), you want to make sure that you consistently capture your customer's or prospect's e-mail address. If a purchase occurs, what will be the procedure for entering transaction information that will be part of the customer's database, permitting them to receive e-mail based on their location in the customer development cycle?
- Likewise, how will you ensure that information from online transactions will be integrated with previous sales?
- What happens when the same individual buys both online and from your bricks-and-mortar location?

Setting up a relationship marketing program using e-mail to drive customers along the five-step customer development cycle is information intensive and involves database technology issues that require specialized treatment. You are unlikely to have all of the answers from the start. What's important, however, is that you recognize that these issues need to be addressed.

> When an e-mail is returned as undeliverable, what will be the procedure to contact the individual—perhaps by telephone or the United States Postal Service—and update their e-mail address?

Putting Ideas to Work

Ask yourself the following questions as you review your use of e-mail:

> You are unlikely to have all of the answers from the start. What's important, however, is that you recognize that these issues need to be addressed.

1. Have you established a structure for maintaining the e-mail addresses submitted by visitors to your Web site?
2. Have you chosen an e-mail style in terms of length and content?
3. Does each e-mail begin with a meaningful, benefit-oriented subject line?
4. Can you personalize the message area of your e-mail with the recipient's first and/or last name?
5. Do the first words visible in the message area of your e-mail tease recipients into reading further?
6. Does the "housekeeping" area of your e-mail remind recipients why they are receiving the e-mail and make it easy for them to discontinue receiving your e-mail?

For more information on this topic, visit our Web site at www.businesstown.com

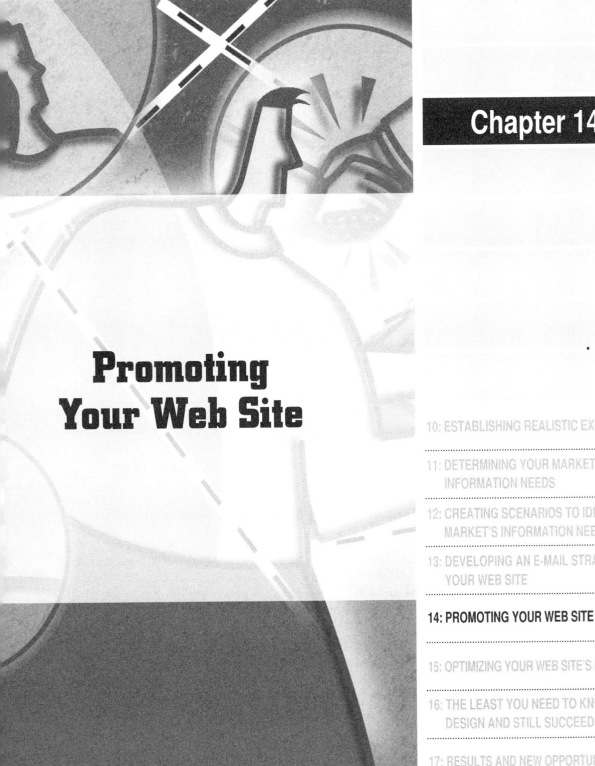

Chapter 14

Promoting
Your Web Site

> Doing business without advertising is like winking at a girl
> in the dark. You know what you are doing, but nobody else does.
> —STEWART HENDERSON BRITT

Imagine you just got a new computer with a modem and were going to connect to the World Wide Web for the very first time. What is the first Web page you would want to see? Maybe some of the basic things like the weather forecast in Seattle or perhaps the latest developments in sailboat racing? What if you wanted to find information on renal angioplasty?

Think of the process you would go through: First you would have to find Web sites at a directory or search engine on that particular topic. Next you would have to sift through all the information on the Web directory to get what you were interested in finding. The fact of the matter is that with a couple of clicks you will find thousands of pages on the topic. Now think about the people who are looking for what you sell. They will go through the same process.

If you are going to win the game, you need to get onto the playing field. As far as your Web site is concerned, that means making your Web site easy to find. You particularly want the right people, those in the market for what you sell, to be able to find you easily.

How to Attract Visitors to Your Web Site

Attracting visitors to your Web site is a precondition for the success of your Web initiative. Although promoting your Web site should take place at all stages of your Web initiative, it is particularly important at the start. There are a few keys to attracting and promoting visitors to your Web site:

1. Choose the right URL, or Web site, address.
2. Make your Web site visible on the various search engines.
3. Place banner advertisements that link to your Web site on other Web sites.
4. Promote your Web site to your existing customers and prospects.

URLs

Your Web site address should be short, logical, and memorable so that someone could remember it without writing it down. Many new Internet companies will actually choose their name based on the availability of a domain name. You may not have this flexibility. It is also best to choose a domain within the "dotcom" top level domain. This is the premium real estate on the Web and will continue to be so even if or when additional top level domains become released.

> Your Web site address should be short, logical, and memorable so that someone could remember it without writing it down.

Search Engines

Businesses have gone to a great deal of trouble making sure their Web sites show up on the various Web search engines. There are two types of search engines:

- Many Web site search engines require you to submit your Web site address and a brief description of the content on your Web site. Sometimes these search engines automatically list your site, other times employees evaluate your site to make sure that what you promise is what you deliver.
- Other search engines work quietly in the background, constantly searching the Web for keywords located in the text at the top of each of the individual pages of your Web site or elsewhere in your Web site, categorizing your Web site on the basis of the keywords.

Checking your current listing

If you already have a Web site, you can see how effectively your Web site is listed by visiting a popular search site such as *www.yahoo.com* (an individual search site) or a site such as *www.ask.com* that simultaneously submits your query to several search engines. Enter your name or the name of your business in the "find" box. The number of times your Web site's correct Web address appears will give you an idea of how well you're doing.

If your Web site address doesn't show up frequently enough (or at all), you might consider devoting some time to visiting each of the search Web sites, locating their search criteria, and submitting (or resubmitting) your Web site address.

Increasing your visibility

There are some inexpensive ways you can ensure that search engines that actively search the Web will locate your Web site. One is to be sure that you clearly identify the contents of each page of your Web site in the title area at the top of each page.

Another approach is to add HTML meta text to the top of each page below the title area. Meta text consists of keywords that describe the contents of each page. Meta text does not show up on the screen of your Web site visitor, but it is visible to the search engines who silently visit Web pages and inventory the meta text located at the top of each page.

If your Web site contains important text, like headlines and pull quotes formatted as graphic files that are downloaded along with each page of your Web site, you can use alt text to make sure that the formatted text is searchable. Although the graphic files themselves are not indexed by search engines, alt text (which appears on the screen of your visitor's computer as the graphic text is downloaded) is searchable and indexable.

Pros and cons of search engines

The advantage of being listed by a search engine is that a lot of potential visitors to your Web site depend on them. However, if you are totally absent from the search engines, you will undoubtedly miss out on some sales opportunities.

Other problems involved with search engines are that not every Web visitor is aware of them or uses them, and the explosive growth of the Web has meant that the search engines are unable to keep up with new sites. Some research indicates that less than 16 percent of all Web sites are listed on search engines. Search sites are overwhelmed by the number of Web sites out there.

It makes more sense to concentrate your attention on developing open and premium content for visitors at each stage of the customer development cycle, and backing up your efforts with a consistent and targeted e-mail program aimed at those most likely to buy from you.

The primary emphasis of this book is on using the Web as a tool to develop closer relationships with existing customers and prospects and those you encounter during your day-to-day business activities. For this reason, it makes more sense to concentrate your attention on developing open and premium content for visitors at each stage of the customer development cycle, and backing up your efforts with a consistent and targeted e-mail program aimed at those most likely to buy from you, rather than investing a lot of time on marginal prospects.

Banner Advertising

Many Web sites contain banner advertisements. Banners are ads that, when clicked, bring the visitor from the current site to your Web site. Banner ads are either traded or sold. The purpose of trading banner ads is that, hopefully, when your ad is seen by visitors at a site attracting the same market as yours, the visitor will click on the banner and visit your Web site. You can also purchase banner ads on Web sites that, presumably, attract visitors who would enjoy visiting your site.

The pros and cons of banner ads

The advantage of banner advertisements is that your name and brief advertising message is viewed by tens, perhaps hundreds of thousands, of visitors to other Web sites each day, thereby increasing your firm's visibility. Also, since payment for many banner advertisements is based on the number of visitors who click on the banner and visit your site, you pay only for the actual site visitors, even though your advertising message may have be seen by far more people. And, of course, there is no charge for banner ads that are exchanged or traded with other sites.

The problem of banner ads is that—at best—they are intrusions. They interrupt the primary reason the visitor is at a Web site, which is to learn something.

When trading banner ads on your site for banner ads on another site, of course, each time a visitor clicks on a banner on your site and leaves your site, there is a chance they might never return.

Another problem is that it is very difficult to obtain actual statistics on the number of purchases that result from banner advertising. Although many individuals may click on your banner advertisement and visit your Web site, it is very difficult to relate these visits to actual sales. You might end up spending a lot of money on banner advertising and find that only a few actual sales can be traced back to the originating advertisements. Your banner advertising might be attracting curiosity seekers rather than serious buyers.

> Your banner advertising might be attracting curiosity seekers rather than serious buyers.

Look to your competition

When evaluating banner advertising, pay attention to your competition. See how many businesses similar to yours in size and product mix use banner advertisements and where they are placed. This will give you a rough indication of whether others similar to you have successfully employed banner advertisements.

Promoting Your Web Site to Existing Customers and Prospects

A far better alternative to get visitors to your site is to promote your Web site to your core market—your current customers and prospects. There are three ways to do this:

- You can promote your Web site's address wherever possible, such as on all of your existing print communications.
- You can obtain your customers' and prospects' e-mail addresses whenever possible.
- You can create a direct-mail or telemarketing promotion designed to drive visitors to your site.

Let's examine each of these alternatives.

Promote your Web site address everywhere

Free advertising is always the least expensive and most cost effective. Thus, once you establish a Web presence your Web site address should appear in all of your marketing materials, including (but not limited to):

- Advertisements
- Billboards
- Brochures
- Business cards
- Envelope stuffers (inserts sent along with invoices or checks)
- Invoices
- Mailing and shipping labels
- Letterheads
- Newsletters
- Posters
- Product packaging
- Rubber stamps

Indeed, as you prepare a budget for promoting your Web site, you might allocate funds for reprinting and updating your print communications to add your Web site address. You should also include your Web site address in your broadcast advertising and the credits of any articles you write or e-mail that you send.

> Once you establish a Web presence your Web site address should appear in all of your marketing materials.

Obtaining customers' and prospects' e-mail addresses

One of the biggest challenges you face in creating a relationship marketing Web initiative is driving current customers and prospects whom you deal with on a face-to-face basis to your Web site and encouraging them to register their e-mail address. *Few businesses take the time to ask for e-mail addresses as part of their day-to-day operations.* This is a tremendously expensive mistake because asking a customer or prospect for their e-mail address doesn't cost anything. Businesses of all types should routinely request the e-mail addresses of customer and prospects.

> Make it easy for visitors to do your advertising for you by encouraging them to direct others to your Web site and register.

But you have to develop reasons for visitors to register at your Web site and provide their e-mail and other information. In this day and age, people are very concerned about privacy. As use of e-mail increases, visitors are likely to think twice before submitting their e-mail address, increasing the amount of e-mail they will receive in the future. You must overcome these obstacles to registration. You can do this by offering an incentive and making registration as easy and obvious as possible. Registration takes more than a "contact us" e-mail link.

Upon receipt of a registration, consider sending a confirmation via return e-mail–necessary, of course, if you are sending passwords or attached files. This confirmation, as with all future e-mail, should contain information about how visitors can pass along your Web site address and registration incentive. Make it easy for visitors to do your advertising for you by encouraging them to direct others to your Web site and register.

Providing an incentive

What type of registration incentive should you provide? As a rule of thumb, avoid the temptation to use physical or tangible items as a registration incentive. Physical or tangible incentives cost money to obtain and they cost money to ship or mail. Because your Web site may attract visitors from around the world, you may end up spending money to send incentives to people located far outside of your marketing area.

Your incentive could be a gift certificate towards their next purchase. After the customer visits your Web site and registers their e-mail address, after verifying that the visitor *did*, indeed, make a purchase, you could e-mail the address of a page containing a thank-you gift certificate that the customer could print out and use or share with a friend.

As an alternative, information (your premium content) represents the least expensive incentive you can provide. Information is the best incentive you can offer visitors to register their e-mail address because:

- *Information is free.* The only cost is preparing the information. The information probably already exists—it just has to be "repackaged." You already know the challenges, frustrations, and problems your market faces and you know how your product or service addresses these challenges. By repackaging your selling message as information—giving it an editorial spin and backing it up with facts, figures, and case studies so your message looks like "news"—your incentive is ready to be sent.

- *Information enhances your credibility.* People like to buy from experts. Consumers are, by nature, insecure and afraid of making a mistake. (This fear increases as the price of the object increases.) The more information they can get, especially information from an editorial or third-person perspective, the more comfortable they will be in making a decision, and the more they'll trust the firm offering the information.

> Information is the best incentive you can offer visitors to register their e-mail address because:
> - Information is free.
> - Information enhances your credibility.

Creating information premiums

Information premiums gain value to the extent they offer meaningful benefits that help your market better address its challenges and problems. The point of developing an information premium is to package information that you may take for granted as "news" and give it extra value by making it scarce. Perception equals reality. Freely available information is less appreciated than information that has scarcity value. If everyone can read an article, it won't be perceived as valuable as inside information that visitors have to do something to earn access to.

As always, to the extent that your information premium looks good (is graphically attractive), its value will be enhanced. The contents of an ugly typewritten sheet are not perceived as valuable as the contents of an attractive page, which is typeset using good-looking typefaces, has generous margins and white space, and contains photographs and subheads that guide the reader through the page.

Worksheet: Determining your information incentive

1. What non-selling, strictly helpful, information can you share with Web site visitors who take the time to register?
2. What are the challenges facing your market?
3. What other problems does your market face?
4. How can you help your market better face these challenges and problems?
5. What are the major changes or trends occurring in your industry or consumer product group?
6. How does your approach to the above problems or changes differ from that of your competitors?
7. Can you develop problem/solution case studies illustrating the superiority of your approach?
8. How can your customers identify quality in the product or service category you sell?
9. What are the pitfalls prospects should watch out for when investing in your product or service category?
10. What changes do you foresee in the coming years and how can you help visitors accommodate or adjust to these changes?
11. What topics are frequently discussed in your product or service category's trade publications?
12. What are the limitations of yesterday's approaches to current challenges?

Distributing an information incentive

There are several ways you can avoid postage and printing costs and electronically distribute information. The most common alternatives include:

- *Passwords to unlock protected pages.* Your information incentive can be placed on password-protected pages of your Web site. Upon registering their password, your e-mail program can automatically (if desired) send an e-mail to the registrant containing the password necessary to unlock the pages containing the information premium. The advantage of

---

You can avoid postage and printing costs and electronically distribute information. The most common alternatives include:

- Passwords to unlock protected pages.
- URLs to unlinked pages.
- Attached files.

this approach is that there is no fulfillment (i.e. printing or mailing) costs and that the information is immediately available. The disadvantages are that visitors may not print it out, you have little control over its appearance, and there is little "permanence" or "pass-along" value to the information.

- *URLs to unlinked pages*. You can also place your information incentive on unlinked pages on your Web site. Again, upon receipt of a visitor's e-mail address, you or your e-mail program can send back the full Web site address of the page, or pages, containing premium content. Visitors must then return to your Web site and either append the page location to your domain name or enter the full Web site address. This approach suffers from the same pros and cons: the option is free, you have total control over formatting, but the pages lack pass-along permanence.

- *Attached files*. Your return e-mail acknowledging your visitor's registration can include attachments. There are two options for these attachments. One option is to send the document as a Microsoft Word document. Visitors can open attached Word documents using just about any Macintosh or Windows word processing program. The advantage is that you have a bit more control over the formatting of the document because you can embed TrueType fonts in the document and you can control margins and column widths. The other option is to send the documents in the Adobe Acrobat format. File sizes may also be smaller than Word documents, but many people dislike the need to download the free Acrobat reader.

Use privacy as an incentive

In addition to offering a registration incentive, promise Web site visitors that you will not share their names, e-mail addresses, or any other information with other firms . . . and live up to your promise! Place a short, noticeable privacy statement right next to your registration form promising visitors that you will respect their privacy and not sell, share, or rent their names to other firms. When you send an e-mail confirming receipt of their registration, repeat

> In addition to offering a registration incentive, promise Web site visitors that you will not share their names, e-mail addresses, or any other information with other firms . . . and live up to your promise!

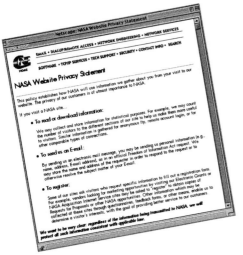

your privacy statement. Guard your Web site visitor's privacy as carefully as you guard your own!

Employees should be trained to respond with a statement that offers a benefit ("We'll be able to keep you up-to-date with information about maximizing the pleasure of your purchase as well as, from time to time, invite you to special preferred customer events and promotions") when asked why this information is being requested. Your staff should also be trained to reinforces your firm's privacy statement when customers ask why your firm wants their e-mail address. Your staff should be trained to emphasize that you will treat their e-mail address as sacredly as you treat their telephone number and mailing address and that their address will not be shared or sold to any other organization.

Making it easy for visitors to register

Instead of placing the registration form on a special page of your Web site, consider adding a registration form to your home page or the bottom of your featured article. Consider including more than one registration form to encourage visitors to impulsively register after they have finished reading an article or case study.

When designing your registration form, resist the temptation to ask too many questions. Once you have established an initial contact with your visitor, you can always go back and ask for additional information. Here are some registration form options:

- At minimum, simply ask visitors to provide their e-mail address. This will reward you with the highest return. The advantages are that it's easy for visitors to submit this information and there is little implied "commitment." The disadvantage is that you will be unable to address future e-mail to them on a first-name basis and, should you call them, you will not be able to address them by name.
- The next step is to ask visitors to provide their name, mailing address, and—where appropriate—position. This personalizes the relationship as you can include their name in the salutation field of your e-mail. In addition, by finding out their mailing address, you can send them print communications

such as brochures, newsletters, and other information. By finding out their position and business name, you also can determine the likelihood of their purchasing from you. The disadvantage is that visitors may hesitate to provide this additional information as it involves more of a commitment.

- You can request as much information as you feel is appropriate, depending on the complexity and cost of the product or service you're selling and the value of the registration incentive you're providing. You can ask visitors to identify the product or service they're interested in, the need they want to satisfy, or the challenge or problem that frustrates them. You can ask them how close they are to making a purchase. You can ask them to identify the size of their business and how soon they're likely to buy. You can also ask them which parts of your Web site they found most or least interesting.

When creating a registration form, avoid user-unfriendly or "totalitarian" forms that reject a submission if one or more fields are not filled in. Forms that reset to zero, forcing visitors to start filling them out all over again if a zip code, phone number, or position field are not filled in are certain to cause visitor rebellion in the form of unsubmitted forms. If your form contains numerous fields, you might consider highlighting required fields by placing an asterisk next to them.

Using direct mail to drive visitors to your site

Postcards offer an easy and cost-effective way to encourage your existing customers to visit your Web site and become e-mail accessible, which permits you to send them a continuing (and no-cost) stream of information-filled e-mail. In contrast to newsletters, postcards take very little time to produce, cost little to print, and cost less to mail than newsletters or more elaborate mailings. Postcards don't need envelopes, like brochures or newsletters do. They can be quickly prepared and easily printed, addressed, and mailed.

Your "Visit our Web site and register!" mailing does not have to be an elaborate production. Two-sided postcards are ideal. This is

> If your form contains numerous fields, you might consider highlighting required fields by placing an asterisk next to them.

one of those cases where smaller is better. Avoid the temptation to overdesign or spend too much on design, printing, and postage. Since there is likely to be a high amount of "waste" circulation in a mailing sent to a list that hasn't been consistently utilized, you want to spend the absolute minimum necessary to drive visitors to your Web site to register their e-mail address.

Most important, it's difficult to ignore a message on a postcard. Your message can be communicated at a glance. The front of your postcard should contain a concise description of the incentive you're offering to customers and prospects who visit your Web site and register their e-mail address. The incentive you offer can consist of premium content options like discount coupons or gift certificates.

Postcards sent to rented mailing lists offer a cost-effective way to develop new prospects for your business, prospects that you can later keep informed with e-mail. You should never send unsolicited e-mail to prospects with whom you have not previously communicated. Postcards permit you to politely approach new prospects and allow them the option of submitting their e-mail address for later follow-up.

For some reason, people do not mind receiving unsolicited direct mail through the United States Postal Service as much as they mind receiving unsolicited e-mail. After identifying your most logical prospects, contact a list broker who can sell you address labels based on industry classifications, employment position, income, geographic area, education, product ownership, or just about any other criteria. Send prospects one or a series of postcards inviting the prospects to visit your Web site—where, hopefully, they will be motivated to register their e-mail address.

Add "Address Correction Requested" to the address panel of your postcards. This provides you with an opportunity to clean and update your mailing list. The post office will inform you of undeliverable postcards as well as update mailing addresses when customers have moved.

Locating partners

If your firm has been in business a long time, the costs of printing, addressing, and mailing a print publication to your entire past customer base might appear to be prohibitive. However, there are ways to get around this problem.

As always, look for affinity partners—preferably firms with more money than you to spend—who would be willing to split the cost of the mailing with you in exchange for featuring one of their products or services on your mailing. Your mailing partner's message can appear on the back of the postcard, next to the address label.

- If you are a retailer, for example, you could devote part of your mailing to promoting one of the vendor's new products.
- If you're a running a ski lodge, you could share the cost of a mailing with an airline, car rental agency, or restaurant in your area.
- If you are an executive recruiter, you might share the cost of the mailing with a publication that focuses on the corporations and job seekers you deal with.
- If you are an automobile dealer, you might find an ally in a motor oil company or a firm that sells after-market parts for the brand or brands you sell. Or you might find a bank or lending institution willing to share the cost of your mailing.

Once you get into the mindset of searching for strategic partners with whom you can share promoting costs, you will probably find it relatively easy to locate a partner willing to share the cost of your "visit our Web site and register!" mailing.

> Add "Address Correction Requested" to the address panel of your postcards. This provides you with an opportunity to clean and update your mailing list. The post office will inform you of undeliverable postcards as well as update mailing addresses when customers have moved.

Getting Past Customers Involved

An even bigger challenge involves getting past customers and prospects to visit your Web site and register their e-mail addresses. This challenge will likely cost money, but, in most cases, it will be money better spent than money spent on banner advertising on other Web sites or print or broadcast advertisements in traditional media.

Taking inventory of your data resources

If your business is like most businesses, you probably have a large mailing list that is contained in one or more computer databases. (Hopefully, these databases are up-to-date and frequently backed up.) These databases are probably less than perfectly organized in terms of accuracy and relevance. The value of the names and addresses of your past customers depends on how old the addresses are, how frequently you have made a mailing to the list, and whether duplicate names and undeliverable addresses were deleted from your database.

Since 20 percent of the country's population moves each year, if you have not frequently communicated with your past customers, it's a safe bet in most cases that many of the names and addresses in your customer and prospect database are out of date. If you have not frequently mailed your mailing list and asked to be informed of address changes or undeliverable mail, you have to prepare yourself for the trauma of making a mailing and receiving a considerable amount of returns.

> Making a mailing, any type of mailing, to your previous customer list is almost guaranteed to generate immediate sales, even if your promotion does not mention a specific product or service but focuses exclusively on your Web site and e-mail registration.

Bonus sales

Making a mailing, any type of mailing, to your previous customer list is almost guaranteed to generate immediate sales, even if your promotion does not mention a specific product or service but focuses exclusively on your Web site and e-mail registration. The very fact that you send anything to your customers is bound to remind them that your firm is in business and ready to serve them. Although they may or may not visit your Web site and register their e-mail address, they might be in the market for a new car, a night out on the town, or a proposal for a home remodeling. Thus, even though you might view your mailing as a "cost," it will almost inevitably generate revenue.

Updating your mailing list

Although your goal is to replace print mailing with e-mail communications, you should update your mailing list by making address changes and removing undeliverable addresses from your customer records. It's probably not a good idea to delete the names, addresses, and purchase histories of customers whose mail forwarding has expired, but you should indicate that the customer's address is no longer active and mail should not be sent to them in the future until a new address is obtained.

"Rolling" mailings

If resources are tight and your past customer list is very large, consider sending out a "rolling" mailing. Instead of mailing every past customer at once, divide your mailing over several months.

There are several advantages to this, not the least of which is that a promotion that is *too successful* might overburden your Web site, slowing down its performance or, worse, causing it to crash.

There are several ways you could mail just portions of your mailing list:

- You could divide your mailing list alphabetically and mail to customers with last names beginning with A through C in month one, customers with last names beginning with D through F in month two, etc.
- You could work your way backwards, mailing your most recent customers first, that is, mail to last year's customers during month one, mail to customers who purchased two years ago in month two, and mail to customers who have purchased three or more years ago in month three.
- You could also categorize your customers by the product or service they purchased or the dollar amount of their purchases. You could mail your most frequent and top-dollar customers first, then follow-up with mailings to customers who purchase less frequently or spend less money.

The key, of course, is to develop a strategy that is efficient and consistent.

> It's probably not a good idea to delete the names, addresses, and purchase histories of customers whose mail forwarding has expired, but you should indicate that the customer's address is no longer active and mail should not be sent to them in the future until a new address is obtained.

Testing your incentives

Before mailing to your entire mailing list, you might consider testing your incentives. You might select a relatively small number of names—perhaps five hundred—and prepare and mail an A-B test mailing. An A-B test mailing involves sending *every other name* a postcard or newsletter with a different registration incentive:

Your A mailing would promote Incentive One, perhaps a limited-time, two-for-one offer available following e-mail registration and a visit to a certain page of your Web site. Your B mailing would promote Incentive Two, perhaps a limited-time discount or an extended warranty, accessed from a different page of your Web site.

By tracking the results of the number of people who visit Page A and Page B and comparing the results, you will be able to see which incentive has the most power to motivate your market. When it comes time to mail your entire mailing list, you'll know which incentive to feature.

Conclusion

The key to success is to concentrate your promotional efforts where they will pay the highest dividends by motivating both past and current customers and prospects to your Web site where they will be motivated to register their e-mail address.

You will enjoy a far higher likelihood of profitable future sales from past customers and prospects who have previously dealt with your firm than you will from "casual" visitors who click on your banner advertisement on another Web site. Such an approach, for most businesses, will almost certainly be more profitable than making low-margin "customer acquisition" sales from customers who have not previously purchased from you.

> "Rolling" mailings instead of mailing every past customer at once, divide your mailing over several months.

Putting Ideas to Work

Think about the following questions as you review your Web site's promotional program.

> The key to success is to concentrate your promotional efforts where they will pay the highest dividends by motivating both past and current customers and prospects to your Web site.

1. Does your Web site's address appear in most search engines when you enter your firm's name?
2. Do many of your competitors trade or purchase banner advertisements?
3. Do you and your staff routinely gather the names and e-mail addresses of current customers and prospects?
4. Can you and your staff comfortably answer the question "Why do you want my e-mail address?"
5. Does your firm's Web site address prominently appear on all of your print communications, including business cards, letterheads, brochures, and newsletters?
6. What kind of premium content incentive can you offer to motivate past customers and prospects to visit your Web site and register their e-mail address?
7. What kinds of business can you work with in developing affinity, or comarketing, incentives designed to encourage customers to visit your Web site and register their e-mail address?
8. Which of your vendors or other firms in your areas might be a partner in a mailing made to your past customers and prospects?
9. Does it make sense to do a "rolling" mailing to selected portions of your mailing list instead of mailing everyone at once?
10. Are you going to test your incentive by offering different incentives to a small portion of your mailing list before committing your resources to the entire list?

For more information on this topic, visit our Web site at www.businesstown.com

Optimizing Your Web Site's Performance

Whatever is worth doing at all is worth doing well.
—PHILIP DORMER STANHOPE

Imagine reading a restaurant review about a great new French restaurant in your town. Their menu sounds superb and you can't wait to go. You call them, reserve a table a few days in advance, and tell your spouse to plan for a special evening out on the town. She buys a new dress and you even book theater tickets for afterwards. Now imagine that the long anticipated evening comes, you go to the restaurant, sit down, look over the menu, open a bottle of wine, then the waiter tells you that their stove is too busy cooking meals for other customers so you will have to leave. The same thing happens all the time on the Web.

Perhaps you've heard the horror stories about Web sites whose servers can't handle the volume of traffic they experience. People are turned away to never return. You can call your Web site successful if it is easy to find and if it provides meaningful information to customers at each of the five stages, but given that we are dealing with a Web-based relationship marketing initiative that is almost totally dependent on technology, you can expect success only if your Web site works from technical standpoint.

Your Web site consists of a combination of hardware and software that must be chosen to serve your unique needs and support your relationship marketing efforts. These tools must first of all be suitable to the task at hand in terms of volume of traffic they will support and your informational and transactional needs. These tools need to be flexible enough to accommodate the inevitable changes that will take place as your business grows. They need to be powerful enough to support surges of activity and traffic (like when you have a special offer or a live event), and they need to be powerful and expandable enough to support overnight growth without needing replacement.

Not only should each of these points be addressed, but the resulting information infrastructure should be integrated with your relationship marketing initiative. This does not happen by accident. It happens though careful planning, equipment selection, design, implementation, and operation.

Adequate Internet Connection

Traffic to your Web site comes to your Web server through your Internet connection. Your connection needs to be fast enough to support the highest anticipated traffic and reliable enough to make sure your site visitors can reach your site 24 hours a day, seven days a week. If your connection is down or simply too crowded, and visitors cannot reach your Web site they may never return.

If you will host your own Web server, you will need a high-speed Internet connection to the physical location of your server hardware. The typical minimum Internet connection for self-hosted Web sites is a T1 connection, which can support up to 1.544Mb/s (megabytes per second). This is sufficient for fairly large Web sites but can become a bottleneck at periods of peak usage such as live chats, product announcements, or special offers. Advanced media like streaming audio can place enormous demands on your Internet connection.

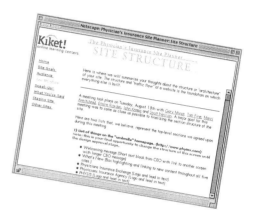

Internet service providers (ISPs) have their own high-speed Internet connections to their upstream provider. If an ISP is hosting your Web site, your site will share their upstream connection with all other Web sites they host. If one hosted site is experiencing a lot of traffic, your site can suffer. You should talk with your ISP about their upstream connection and get them to assure you they have sufficient upstream capacity today and in the future. Also ask them if they have "multiple, redundant connections" with multiple upstream connectivity providers. That way, if one of their upstream providers goes down, or if one of their physical connection lines goes down, people can still reach your Web site. The reliability that comes from multiple, redundant connections is one of the primary benefits of having an ISP host your site.

Capable Web Server Hardware and Software

If you will be hosting your own Web site, make sure you have the hardware to easily support your highest anticipated traffic and 6 to 12 months of anticipated growth. Web servers benefit from large amounts of RAM memory (512 Mb or more) and fault tolerant fea-

> Your Web server should also have an uninterruptible power supply in case the power goes out for a short while.

tures like multiple power supplies, redundant disk drives, and networking cards. Your Web server should also have an uninterruptible power supply in case the power goes out for a short while. Basically, anything that can fail needs to have a backup, preferably "hot-swappable," which means it can be replaced without turning the computer off or rebooting.

An increasingly common approach to increasing the availability of Web sites is through a hardware redundancy technique called "clustering." A cluster is two or more identical computers configured to share the traffic the site receives. Each is equipped with a special "failover" capability so that if one machine fails for any reason, the Web site is instantly served from the remaining machine, or machines, in the cluster. When the failed machine is repaired, it rejoins the cluster. Also remember that the physical facility where your Web server is installed must be secure and have good environmental characteristics and adequate and reliable power. And your Web server should be backed up regularly with tapes or other backup medium kept at another physical location.

If your Web site will need to process a large number of transactions, the processor speed and the number of processors should be increased over the basics. In this case, the I/O throughput of the hard disks on your server should also be increased.

The operating system and Web server software will be determined by your overall information needs and should be chosen to be compatible with your database, Web site reporting, and e-mail integration needs. If an ISP will be hosting your Web site, your Web site will probably share a computer with several dozen other Web sites. Rarely will you have the opportunity to impact the configuration of their hardware.

Compatible Database Software and Application Server

Most likely, you will want to create a database-driven Web site, which means that most of your open and premium content is stored in a database. When a visitor comes to your Web site and views a page, the content is called up from the database and gets formatted and sent to the visitor as HTML. This significantly simplifies ongoing site maintenance and the integration of your Web site visitor tracking and e-mail databases.

The selection of a database and an application server (the software that integrates the Web site and your database) should be made to insure compatibility with your other information integration needs. Most popular software tools in this category today are quite interoperable, but you need to investigate carefully and specifically address the compatibility with your e-mail system and other pre-existing information infrastructure components.

Remember that depending on the anticipated volume of your Web site, you may need separate computer hardware on which to install your database. Typically, all but the smallest Web sites have one or more computers functioning as Web servers as well as one or more computers functioning as database and application servers. Larger Web sites can have dozens or hundreds of servers. Make sure that the tools you select can accommodate the growth, or "scalability," you require. It would be a terrible thing if you had to abandon your system in a few months and start over. With careful planning, growth can be seamless. As your needs magnify, you can add additional computers, more storage, additional high-speed Internet connections, and the software that makes it all work.

If your site will be hosted by an ISP, you will have little choice over the database and application server programs they use. You should select your ISP based on the compatibility of their database with your overall information needs. You should also discuss your anticipated growth and let them describe to you their plan for keeping up with your needs.

> Most popular software tools in this category today are quite interoperable, but you need to investigate carefully and specifically address the compatibility with your e-mail system and other pre-existing information infrastructure components.

Flexible and Suitable Reporting Software

Statistical Web site reporting software packages are an essential tool for optimizing your Web site. These packages offer you critical insight about what is working and what isn't—which campaigns are getting results and which aren't, which pages are keeping user's attention and which are gathering dust. Reporting software analyzes the raw server log files kept by your Web server and makes attractively and sensibly formatted reports available containing meaningful information. This software allows you to view your Web site's performance in real time, as it occurs, or it can be used to compile and analyze reports daily, weekly, or monthly. The most important information for you will be:

Who came to your Web site

You identify visitors to your site by name, usually by relating them (with cookies) to personal information provided in an earlier visit and already stored in your database. Another way to keep track of visitors is by tracking their IP address. Corporate Internet users typically have fixed addresses that identify a particular workstation. This is also true for many cable modems and DSL connections that are becoming increasingly popular with home users. Almost all users connecting with a dial-up modem do not have fixed IP addresses. Knowing which computers connect to your site (and knowing the person at the keyboard) can be used to gauge the effectiveness of various marketing campaigns.

Where did they come from

You can tell where visitors came from by which HTML e-mail message, banner ad, or Web directory they came from. This is called the "referrer" and is information the browser maintains. Using codes embedded in your Web pages, you can request this information from the browser and store that information in your database. That information can be useful in determining which site promotion activities are working.

What pages did they view in what order

This tells you their point of entry to your Web site (their landing page may rarely be your home page) as well as their "click trail" so you can tell exactly what pages they saw. This information is accumulated by using the same "referrer" mentioned above. Companies

> You can tell where visitors came from by which HTML e-mail message, banner ad, or Web directory they came from.

like Amazon.com spend a great deal of time analyzing click trails to learn user behaviors and to increase the effectiveness of their site.

How long did they view those pages

This is very useful for continuing to improve your Web site. Your Web server logs which pages were sent to who and when, and by integrating this log information into your reporting package you can easily learn which pages people find interesting or irrelevant.

What did they buy

This, of course, is good information to know, but there is real power in tying all of this information together. Knowing the path someone took from their point of entry to your site, how much time they spent on which pages, and what they ultimately purchased gives you tremendous insight into their thoughts and wants. Leading online companies are expending great effort in analyzing this information and extracting meaning from it.

In addition to these things, a good reporting package can also let you know the date and time of day the page was visited and the last page visited before the visitor left your Web site.

A good reporting package will let you customize the reports and add graphs and summaries as required. The resulting reports are typically presented as private Web pages so anyone with access to the right URL can view them with only a Web browser. Reports can often be exported to spreadsheet format for further analysis.

The raw server logs from which people sometimes extract information like the number of "hits" are practically meaningless. For example, a single Web page with a logo, 5 graphical buttons, and 10 product illustrations will be counted as 17 hits! There is no measure of quality, no way to relate how often the same visitor has accessed the page. There is also no way to track where in the customer development cycle that visitor is. However, a reporting package would count only one "page view" for your premium content where users need to register, which is much more meaningful.

Internet service providers may own and operate reporting software that you can use or they may simply offer you the raw logs.

> Your Web server logs which pages were sent to who and when, and by integrating this log information into your reporting package you can easily learn which pages people find interesting or irrelevant.

Again, your needs in this regard should be part of your selection criteria in choosing an ISP. If you will be operating your own servers you simply need to make sure you purchase a reporting package that has the reports and flexibility you need.

About Cookies

Cookies are small files sent from your Web server and stored on your visitors' hard drive. They are one of the best ways to monitor the performance of your Web site and are in broad use throughout the Web. In fact, some Web sites are so dependent on them that the site will not work for users whose browsers can't or won't accept cookies. You can determine when a cookie gets sent and what it contains by embedding codes in your Web pages and integrating those pages with your database. By embedding similar codes in other pages on your site, you can read cookies from the hard drive of your site visitors and vary the content on the pages you see.

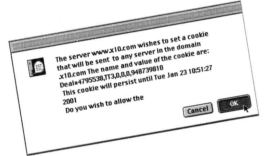

Users find this convenient since by storing passwords in cookies they don't need to be re-entered, and they can gain immediate access to the premium content they are qualified to receive. Cookies can also be used to make sure visitors do not see the same banner ad or sale offer twice. Some online retailers are using this capability to add powerful immediacy to their sale offers as they are literally able to make "one-time" offers to compel the user to the point of purchase. Over time, and as you develop a more knowing relationship with your customers, cookies can tailor the content and offers you present to the individual, eliminating offers they wouldn't be interested in and emphasizing the ones in which they would.

There are several disadvantages associated with cookies. One is that visitors can disable them, that is, they can configure their browsers to not allow cookies to be added to their hard drive. This often occurs in corporate settings where, because of security concerns, files may not be downloaded. Another disadvantage of cookies is that they are computer dependent. If a visitor visits your site from two different computers—a home computer and an office computer— the information is not shared between the two computers.

Appropriate Technical Design of the Web Pages and Navigation

In addition to having the right hardware and software, the technical design of your Web site is important, too. You need to understand your site's visitors: What Web browser do they use? What is the resolution of their computer monitor? How fast is their Internet connection? Knowing this information, you can design a site that is suitable. The browser is important so you don't use features not found in their software. The monitor resolution is important so you don't design pages too large for them to view. The speed of their Internet connection is important so you don't use graphics that take too long to download or other forms of advanced media that require a high-speed connection.

Integrating Your Information

One of your greatest challenges and most important steps is to tie information about a visitor's activities on your Web site with his or her personal information and your evolving relationship with that person. Doing this requires compatible and tightly integrated technology between your Web site, your e-mail, and your marketing efforts. Selecting the right hardware and software is the first step; planning, designing, and building compatible systems is the second step. Assuring that members of your staff have the time, skills, and resources to use and maximize all this information is the third.

This requires an overall commitment to the process. It cannot be stressed enough that it is only when all of these elements are integrated that powerful, positive results are had.

Putting Your Tools to Work

Once you have put all the right pieces in place you are ready to get down to business.

Integrating Your Information

Selecting the right hardware and software is the first step; planning, designing, and building compatible systems is the second step. Assuring that members of your staff have the time, skills, and resources to use and maximize all this information is the third.

Track where visitors come from

By analyzing the source of Web site visitors, you might also determine whether it is worth spending more or less time fine-tuning your Web site from the point of view of Web site search engines. This has numerous implications.

If the majority of your Web site visitors come to you from just one or two search engines, you can spend more time exploring ways to raise your Web site's visibility among the other Web site search engines.

If few Web site visitors arrive via a search engine, you might conclude that you don't *need* the search engines as much as you thought and can spend more time using print or telemarketing communications to induce previous customers to visit your Web site.

If you are running banner advertisements for your Web site or exchanging reciprocal links with other Web sites, you can evaluate which sites are doing the best and worst job of referring visitors to your Web site.

> If the majority of your Web site visitors come to you from just one or two search engines, you can spend more time exploring ways to raise your Web site's visibility among the other Web site search engines.

Track open content popularity

By analyzing which pages of open content your visitors visit and how long they spend at each page, you can identify your most popular pages and, hence, your site's most popular topics. By building on your successes, adding new topics similar to your site's most popular open content, and removing pages that are rarely visited, you can build constant improvement into your Web site.

By analyzing the order in which open content pages are visited, looking for trends common to many of your Web site visitors, you can begin to think like your visitors. You can avoid the myopia of seeing your Web site from your own instead of your visitor's perspective. You might also want to change the hierarchy of your site's navigation based on the order in which most of your visitors explore your Web site.

Tracking premium content popularity

Perhaps the most valuable service that page tracking software can perform is to track visitors to your premium content pages. By tracking the number of times an unlinked or password-protected page is accessed, you can test the validity of the premium content incentive you are offering. You can try out various offers, the same way that direct marketers test their offers before committing to a major mailing.

The testing procedure is simple. Send 1,000 e-mails to customers at a certain level of the customer development cycle. If offer A results in 500 visits to an unlinked page and offer B results in only 175 visits, you can safely conclude that offer A is far more effective than offer B and that offer B should be discarded. This information will help you avoid wasting your time offering incentives that do not generate the desired degree of response. By constantly testing your offers on small segments of your e-mail list, you can fine-tune your offers so that only the best survive.

Tracking sales results

Sales, of course, represent the best test of all of your Web site's performance. Your goal is to relate visits to your premium content pages to the resulting sales. It's imperative that you keep careful records of sales that result from e-mail and premium content incentives presented during the transaction stage of the customer development cycle. Likewise, you should also track redemption of premium content offers made during the reinforcement and advocacy stages.

The easiest way to do this is to prepare premium content coupons or certificates that visitors can print out, and then keep careful track of the coupons that are actually redeemed.

One of the keys to fine-tuning your Web site is to compare the number of people who visit a premium content stage containing an incentive to buy with actual sales that are made. Something is obviously wrong if lots of visitors access your premium content pages but few take the time to print out the coupon or take advantage of the price offer. A high correlation between visits to premium content pages and sales indicates that your offer is on target. A low correlation between visits and actual sales indicates that your offer should be re-examined and a stronger incentive developed.

> By constantly testing your offers on small segments of your e-mail list, you can fine-tune your offers so that only the best survive.

Putting Ideas to Work

Here are some questions to ask as you strive to replace opinion with facts in improving your Web site:

A high correlation between visits to premium content pages and sales indicates that your offer is on target. A low correlation between visits and actual sales indicates that your offer should be re-examined and a stronger incentive developed.

1. Is your Internet service provider or in-house Web server capable of providing you with detailed reports of Web site activity, including analyzing the number of unique visitors to each pen and premium content page?
2. Can you identify your most popular information topics on the basis of the number of visits to each page or the time spent visiting each page?
3. Do you regularly test your e-mail and premium content incentives on small quantities of customers and Web site visitors at each level of the customer development cycle in order to identify which offers pull the best or weakest response?
4. Do you constantly monitor the source of new Web site visitors? Are visitors coming directly to your Web site or are they coming from search engines, links from other Web pages, or as a result of banner advertising?
5. Do you regularly compare the number of e-mails sent inviting visitors to visit the premium content pages to the number of visitors who actually access the premium content pages?
6. Do you regularly compare visits to premium content and incentive offers to the resulting sales?

For more information on this topic, visit our Web site at www.businesstown.com

Chapter 16

The Least You
Need to Know
about Design and
Still Succeed

Being good in business is the most fascinating kind of art!
—ANDY WARHOL

Imagine you went to a new restaurant to find the tables too small, the chairs uncomfortable, the lighting harsh, the plates chipped, and the silverware dirty. Would you care if the food was the best you ever tasted? You probably would be so turned off by the atmosphere that you wouldn't even wait for your meal to arrive. And would you recommend the restaurant to your friends? What would you tell them about it?

On the Web, good information loses impact if it's poorly presented. If it's hard to find or hard to read people won't care if it's well written. If the graphics are too big, making the site too slow to load, they won't even wait. They will leave and go elsewhere. But this presents an opportunity as well. Given that many Web sites today are poorly designed, you have a great chance to stand out by applying tried and true principles of design.

Since it permits color, sound, and movement, including virtual 3-D effects, there are virtually no limitations to the graphic effects you can include in your Web site. Indeed, the problem with Web sites is not what you can do, but what you should do. As technology continues to improve, computer monitors will more and more resemble television sets and the Web experience will increasingly resemble the viewing experience.

Do not be mislead by the many sophisticated effects you observe on many of the Web sites you visit and the continuing avalanche of Web design software. Web design can be simple or it can be complex. Ultimately, your Web site will contain elements of both. Until you acquire a war chest containing several million dollars to invest in developing your Web site, blind yourself to the possibilities and focus on the practicalities. Many of the Web sites you have visited may have cost tens of millions of dollars to create. The vast majority of popular, "recommended" Web sites reflect design fees in the hundreds of thousands of dollars. Unless you have the resources to compete in this arena, you're much better off competing with logic and simplicity.

Logic implies appropriateness; your Web site should be based on your market, your message, and your competition.

Effective Web site design involves both art and science. The art part involves creating a "look" that effectively reflects your business and presents information in a pleasing format. The science involves making information available as transparently and quickly as possible. The best Web sites are those that don't even appear to be "designed" because your focus is on the message not the messenger.

Rather than concentrate on the many factors that can complicate your Web site, let's examine six nontechnical things to bear in mind as you design—and continually redesign—your Web site. Follow these simple rules, and you'll end up with a better Web site than the vast majority of Web sites out there—regardless of the millions of dollars that may have been thrown at them while they were being created.

> Effective Web site design involves both art and science.

Create a Brand

A brand consists of two parts: an immediately identifiable "look" that sets your Web site apart from others, and a style or tone of writing that adds further personality to your message. Brands, or looks, are the result of four basic tools: color, layout, typography, and visuals.

Color on the Web can be used for the site's background, text, borders, graphic accents (such as horizontal lines separating topics), illustrations, and—most important—the links that take visitors from one page to another.

Layout involves the placement of page titles, headlines, subheads, body copy, captions, links, and white space. Many layout decisions involve the placement of navigation link; should links appear along the top of each page, along the left-hand edge of each page, or along the bottom of each page? Another important layout consideration involves column width or line length for extended text.

Typography decisions include the typeface, type size, and color used for titles, headlines, subheads, and body copy. There are two kinds of Web type: HTML type loads immediately on your Web site visitor's browser but can look different on each visitor's computer monitor depending on the text preferences they have chosen, and words set in a distinctive typeface and type size that download as graphics. The ideal Web site contains mostly fast-loading HTML type with just enough use of a "signature" typeface to project a unique image.

Visuals can be of two types, atmospheric or literal. Atmospheric visuals create a mood—skyscrapers forming an urban skyline create a different mood than a field of yellow daisies leading the eye to a well-kept barn. Literal visuals provide specific information through illustrations, photographs, charts and other business graphics. Visuals slow down Web sites because they must be downloaded as individual files.

> Keys to branding success:
> * Maintain your firm's existing identity
> * Create as much visual distance from your competitors as possible
> * Consistency

Keys to branding success

There are three keys to using design to create an effective brand. The first is to strive to *maintain your firm's existing identity* on the Web. If your letterhead, envelopes, and newsletter are printed on cream paper using black plus a dark brown ink, for example, maintain the same look on your Web site. Likewise, if your "signature" typefaces in print are Century Schoolbook and Futura, use the same typefaces for titles, headlines, and other locations where appropriate on your Web site. If your Web site looks radically different from your print identity, visitors to your Web site may not associate your Web site with your firm. If you send follow-up materials printed in different colors and typefaces to prospects who request it from your Web site, they may not associate the information with your firm.

The second consideration is to *create as much visual distance from your competitors as possible*. Notice how much different McDonald's signage is from Burger King's or Wendy's. It's no accident that Ford's logo is different from Mercedes-Benz's. Each is striving to create a unique and easily identifiable look. You should, too. Check out the IBM Web site and compare it to Compaq's, Dell's, and Hewlett-Packard's. Note how each uses color, layout, typography, and visuals in completely different ways.

Consistency is the third important branding element. Not only must your Web site be consistent with your print communications, but the various pages of your Web site should be consistent with each other. If you place navigation links along the top of your home page, make sure you place the links along the top of every page.

Using restraint

Colors, backgrounds, and typefaces should be consistent from page to page. Restraint is the hardest characteristic to build into your Web site. Restraint, however, pays better dividends than any other design characteristic. Let's examine some of the benefits of restraint.

Typographic restraint

Use a few signature typefaces for the titles and key design elements of your Web site, such as pull-quotes summarizing adjacent text and initial caps introducing new articles. These signature typefaces should be set as downloadable graphics and used to maintain visual consistency between your Web site and your firm's existing print marketing and promotion materials. One typeface used with restraint is often enough to brand your Web site, even if it is only used for titles, subheads, and initial caps.

If you use graphic text for titles or subheads or pull-quotes, be sure to insert Alt tags. Alt tags download before the text and can be used to identify the words before the graphic is downloaded. Alt tags are also important because they can guide visitors who are visiting your Web site with graphics turned off. Alt tags are also indexed by search engines that compile site lists based on keywords and topics.

The use of a limited number of typefaces unifies your Web site. By setting page titles, headlines, or initial caps in a single, unique typeface, each page of your Web site will visually relate to the others. If every page uses different typography, however, your Web site will present a chaotic image.

Color restraint

The best Web sites use a minimum number of colors. Restrict your color choices to the 216 Web-safe colors that can be used on the broadcast base of computers running the Apple Macintosh or Microsoft Windows operating systems. If you go beyond the 216 Web-safe colors, and your visitor's computer does not have extended color capabilities, the colors will be dithered, or approximated, and, as a result, present an unpleasant image. The colors will likely look even worse if the page is printed on the majority of printers.

It is amazing the effects that can be achieved by using just three colors for a Web site. Consider using three key colors consistently in the following way:

- One color for broad areas, or panels, such as backgrounds and borders around photographs
- A second color for titles, pull-quotes, subheads, and initial capitals set as downloadable graphics
- A third color used for occasional highlights, such as horizontal or vertical lines, end-of-story markers, or "up" or "next page" links.

> One of the virtues of using color with restraint is that when you do include color photographs, the photographs will emerge with greater impact.

One of the virtues of using color with restraint is that when you do include color photographs, the photographs will emerge with greater impact. A four-color photograph in a two- or three-color Web site will have far more impact than the same photograph surrounded by competing colors.

Layout restraint

Web site unity and easy navigation is based on using a consistent page layout throughout your Web site. Frustration is certain to result when visitors have to search for navigation links in a different location on the page as they change from page to page.

More important, by using a consistent layout throughout a Web site, change becomes more visible and dramatic when it is introduced. If visuals are placed to the left of text on most pages, placing the visual within a text column on one page clearly indicates that it is more important.

Visual restraint

The restraint with which you place visuals—photographs, illustrations, and business graphics—also communicates your firm's professionalism. As always, the key to success is to adopt a single style and apply it consistently. If you place a thin rule around some photographs, place the same rule around all photographs. If you place photographs against a yellow background, or silhouette the photographs (that is, drop out the backgrounds) in one location, do it consistently.

Design for Speed

The purpose of your Web site is to communicate information. But visitors to your Web site are in a hurry. They don't want to wait. Statistics indicate that visitors to your Web site give you approximately 8 to 24 seconds to capture their attention. If, at the end of that time, you're logo is still downloading, they are likely to move on to another, faster Web site.

Whether you are creating a Web site or hiring a professional graphics design studio to create your Web site, consider that your equipment is probably significantly faster than the computers and Internet connection that most visitors to your Web site will be using.

Smaller is better

The best way you can create a fast-loading, responsive Web site is to use as much HTML text as possible and keep graphics, such as logos and visuals, as small as possible.

It's tempting to place a large logo of your firm on your Web site's front page. Inevitably, the logo takes a long time to download. Yet what information does a large logo really provide? That's right—nothing. Large logos take a lot of time to download and do not provide benefits to any visitors or reasons for remaining at the Web site.

Web sites with large logos on their home page project an amateurish image. Web sites with small logos and lots of fast-loading,

> The key to success is to adopt a single style and apply it consistently.

benefit-oriented headlines or text links provide a significantly richer experience for your visitors.

Each time you make your logo smaller, you're able to include more headlines and text links onto your home page, which offer more opportunities of capturing your visitor's interest and motivating them to stay.

A thumbnail is a small version of a photograph (illustration or chart) that visitors click on if they are interested in an enlarged view of the photograph or visual.

Text links

Another way to speed up a Web site is to replace buttons—graphic navigation links—with text links. Like large logos, buttons reflect a newcomer's approach to Web site design. Buttons slow down Web site performance because, being graphics, they take time to download. Text links, however, are immediately available to guide Web site visitors to areas of interest.

Web sites often use two levels of links. Your Web site's primary navigation level organizes your pages into major categories, such as "Products," "Support," and "Experience." Secondary navigation links only appear when one of the primary links has been chosen. Click "Products" at a computer retailer's site, for example, and secondary links show up for "Computers," "Printers," "Scanners," and "Software." Click "Support," for example, and the previous secondary links disappear, replaced by links for "Home," "Small Business," "Corporate," and "Government."

Using thumbnails

Another way you can design for speed is to replace large photographs with thumbnails.

Large photographs, especially photographs that satisfy ego concerns rather than offering meaningful information to Web site visitors, are another way you can drive visitors away from your Web site. There are few frustrations greater than waiting for a large photograph to download, only to find that it does not offer any meaningful information. Remember—visitors to your Web site are in search of information, not atmosphere or entertainment.

Thumbnails represent the best way to include large visuals in your Web site. A thumbnail is a small version of a photograph (illustration or chart) that visitors click on if they are interested in an enlarged view of the photograph or visual. Thumbnails empower your visitors; they permit visitors to determine, for themselves, whether they want to wait for the visuals to download.

Provide options

One of the most important ways you allow visitors faster access to information is to include a text search engine that permits visitors to search for keywords or product names and go directly to them. Additional options include the ability for visitors to view a text-only version of your Web site. Text-only Web sites provide the fastest information transfer of all. You can also provide a "frames" or "no frames" option. Frames are static page elements, frequently containing navigation links, that remain in place while visitors scroll through the rest of the page. Frames can slow down Web performance, hindering information transfer.

Design for Easy Reading

The design of your Web site should be as transparent as possible. Information should be easy to read. Here are some tips that contribute to easy reading.

> One of the most important ways you allow visitors faster access to information is to include a text search engine that permits visitors to search for keywords or product names and go directly to them.

Short text

Avoid lines of text that extend from one margin of the page to another. Long lines of type are visually tiring. They require visitors to make numerous left to right eye movements as they scan each line of text. Worse, wide columns (or long lines of text) make it easy for visitors to lose their place when they reach the end of a line, causing them to either reread the same line or inadvertently jump down two lines. Confusion and frustration results in either case.

Reducing line length offers another advantage; it builds in a buffer of white space to the left or right of each line of text. This focuses the visitor's attention on the text and also provides space for you to insert visuals or pull-quotes that summarize the text in the adjacent column.

Strive for short paragraphs. Long paragraphs are surefire readership killers. Short paragraphs are easier to scan and read than long paragraphs. Long paragraphs look like they will be hard to read . . . and they are.

Insert space between paragraphs by pressing the Enter key twice as you create your page. This extra space will do wonders to open up your Web page and encourage readers to remain longer.

Editing is an important part of design; editing cannot be separated from design. Web pages based on short words, short sentences, and short paragraphs are inevitably better read than "bloated" pages containing unnecessary words, long words, long sentences, and long paragraphs.

> Web pages based on short words, short sentences, and short paragraphs are inevitably better read.

Freedom from distracting backgrounds

Use colored or textured backgrounds with restraint. These usually detract from, rather than enhance, readability. Easy reading is based on easy and instant character recognition; visitors must be able to easily recognize the individual letters that make up each word. Colored and textured backgrounds often compete with the characters, making the words harder to make out. This forces readers to "puzzle out" each word, slowing them down to the point where they give up and move to another, easier to read, Web site.

Black text against a white background creates the highest contrast and, hence, the easiest to read text. As backgrounds become brighter or darker, that is, bright yellow backgrounds or dark blues and greens, text contrast is reduced. Textured backgrounds often further reduce contrast, making the words harder to make out.

Frequent subheads and bookmarks

Use subheads, short phrases that introduce and summarize the text that follows, to break long articles into short, manageable chunks. Set the subheads slightly larger than the adjacent text. You can further emphasize them by inserting extra space above and below. You can call further attention to subheads by setting them in bold and, possibly, assigning a different typeface to them. For example, if you are using a default serif typeface like Times New Roman for your body copy, consider using a sans serif typeface, like Arial, for subheads.

In general, insert subheads every time a new topic is introduced. Many visitors will scroll through your Web page, searching for subheads that attract their attention, and stop only when they encounter one that interests them. Few visitors will read every word you write. One of the best ways to encourage visitors to read your articles is to bookmark your subheads, that is, list the subheads, or topics, contained in an article at the top of the article and create links to the subheads within the article. That way, visitors can go directly to the subhead that interests them.

> Insert subheads every time a new topic is introduced visitors will scroll through your Web page, searching for subheads that attract their attention.

Design for Flexibility

Your Web site should be designed for easy updating. News and information form the essence of successful Web sites. If your Web site, particularly the home page, cannot be easily updated, it is certain to fail. Visitors do not want to see the same graphics or information on the home page of the Web site each time they visit. Each visit should feature at least one new or rewritten topic.

Show rather than link

New information should be immediately visible. Visitors should not have to click on a "what's new" link to find out the latest information; the latest information should be easily located and prominently visible as soon as the site loads. Likewise, visitors should not have to click on a "Personnel" or "Products" link to locate information about the latest job openings or new products.

This becomes particularly important when visitors get in the habit of returning to your Web site; they shouldn't have to see the same graphics in order to access the latest news.

Additional reasons to avoid large graphics

The need to frequently update your Web site is one of the reasons to avoid large graphics on your home page. The bigger the logo and/or picture of the firm's facilities, the less available space there is to include text links that will take visitors to the newest information.

Text links are emphasized because text links are easier to create and load faster. You, or your staff, are less likely to update your Web site if you have to use an illustration or image-editing program to create a new headline each time one is needed. It is much easier to simply type in a new headline and description of the new information and create a link to the appropriate page, then complete the page containing the new information.

Static versus database driven

Your first Web site will probably be a static Web site, that is, pages are presented rather than generated for visitors. Static Web sites are page-centric; new pages are created or modified as information is updated. All visitors can access the same content and new links must be created as you add content.

Dynamic, or database driven Web sites are different. Information is stored in a database and pages are generated as information is requested. An example of database-driven Web sites are those that permit you to find out the five day weather forecasts in various cities throughout the country or Web sites that permit you to compare two automobiles or the cost of living in two or more cities. It would, obviously, be impractical to create new static pages each day listing the latest weather in the thousands of cities that the weather sites contain. It would be equally impractical to compile static pages comparing every combination of make and model of cars. Given the hundreds of thousands of possible city combinations and automotive make and model combinations, these Web sites could not be created as static Web sites.

The process becomes practical, however, when the daily weather forecasts are entered into a spreadsheet or database. This information is formatted into Web pages when visitors specify that they want the five day forecast for Missoula, Montana or want to

> The bigger the logo and/or picture of the firm's facilities, the less available space there is to include text links that will take visitors to the newest information.

compare the cost of living in Dover, New Hampshire with the cost of living in Hingham, Massachusetts.

Database-driven Web sites permit tremendous flexibility. For example, an electronics distributor's Web site can display only the lines that different visitors are authorized to purchase. More important, once a dealer's discount level has been determined, the prices that Dealer A views for hundreds of products can be different than the prices that Dealer B views, based on different discount structures.

Design for Easy Printing

Many visitors will want to print pages from your Web site if it contains truly helpful information. Many Web sites are difficult to print because foreground/background color combinations that look great on screen often print poorly. In many cases, pages will not look good when printed because colors that look good on screen often look entirely different when printed. This is due to the differences between projected light (the image on your computer monitor) and reflected light (how colors are perceived when printed on paper).

In addition, many times browsers have to be reconfigured to print backgrounds. Unless your visitor has chosen the "print backgrounds" option on his or her browser, when your page is printed, only the text appears. If your Web site contains white text against a blue background, nothing will print! Worse, printer supply costs greatly increase when you force visitors to print background colors in order to read the text. If your site contains yellow text against a light green background, all that will print is light yellow text on white paper—hardly an easy-to-read combination.

Frames, mentioned above, further complicate printing. Visitors have to go through an extra step and determine whether they want to print the page as it is shown on the screen of their computer or just the portion of the screen they want to refer to later or share with coworkers.

A final problem associated with printing concerns pages with animated text. If an important part of your message is animated, it may not be on screen at the moment of printing, which means that

> Many visitors will want to print pages from your Web site if it contains truly helpful information.

the printed page will not fully communicate the information you want visitors to retain.

Design for Appropriateness

Web site design should be appropriate for your market, your message, and your competition.

Appropriate for your market

Your market's expectations for the business that your firm is engaged in will determine the visual imagery, the colors, and the typefaces used on your Web site. The best way to get started thinking about appropriate visual imagery is to think in terms of opposites—the worst possible choices you could make. By starting with the outlandish and inappropriate, it becomes easier to focus with increasing accuracy on what is appropriate.

If you're Web site is promoting a service for farmers, for example, it makes no sense to include pictures of urban skylines or skyscrapers. Although this is a "no brainer," by eliminating the obviously inappropriate, you can easily focus on selecting images that are appropriate to your message. By including images that your market will recognize and feel comfortable with, you can begin the process of bonding with them.

Color choices should be made on the basis of your intended target market. Black backgrounds with splashes of bright primary colors (bright oranges, yellows, reds, and greens) are colors that a youthful market will appreciate and identify with. "Quieter," sites, with white backgrounds and darker, subdued colors, like grays and dark blues, communicate your interest in an older, more mature audience.

The complexity of your site's navigation will also be influenced by your market. Youthful markets are more appreciative of "game" or "entertainment" Web site designs than older markets that are more likely to be interested in frill-free, direct access to desired information. Web sites with significantly different, almost random size relationships between text and graphic elements appeal to youthful rather than mature markets.

> The best way to get started thinking about appropriate visual imagery is to think in terms of opposites—the worst possible choices you could make.

Appropriate for your message

Color plays an important role in the subliminal message that your Web site communicates. Visitors will perceive you as formal or informal, cheap or expensive, friendly or aloof, depending on your Web site colors.

Colors form an instantly recognizable design characteristic. Within seconds of encountering your Web site, visitors will react to the colors you have used. For example:

- Black type against bright yellow projects a cheap or discount image.
- Outdoor colors, such as greens, yellows, and blues, are appropriate for firms emphasizing environmental or outdoor concerns.

Appropriate for your competition

Web site design should never be done in a vacuum. Always consider your competition's Web site and strive to present as different an image as possible. Your Web site's colors, layout, typography, and visuals should be distinctly different from your competition's. Be sure to check out your competitor's Web site before beginning to design your Web site so you can design as many differences between them rather than inadvertently copying their look and feel, thereby confusing your market.

Design for Involvement

Designing for involvement entails making it as easy as possible for visitors to your Web site to communicate their interests, preferences, and information needs to you.

E-mail represents an unstructured approach to visitor involvement. Inviting visitors to e-mail their questions to you puts the burden on your visitors to describe their problems in a narrative, person-to-person way. The disadvantage of e-mail is that few visitors want to take the time to "write a letter" describing their interests,

> Web site design should never be done in a vacuum. Always consider your competition's Web site and strive to present as different an image as possible.

preferences, or the problems they want to solve. It is also difficult to identify trends from visitor-submitted e-mails.

Forms represent a better alternative. Forms include check boxes, radio buttons, drop-down menus, and text boxes.

- Radio buttons are mutually exclusive. Clicking one button prevents visitors from choosing another
- Check boxes allow visitors to select more than one alternative. Visitors can select as many alternatives as desired.
- Drop down menus allow visitors to scroll through a list which can be as long as necessary to accommodate all options.
- Text boxes allow visitors to enter text that does not fit one of the above categories.

Forms make it easy for visitors to submit information and also organize the information, making it easy for the Web site operator to analyze responses and identify trends.

Working with Outside Design Firms

The act of creating the basic look of your site—making appropriate color, layout, typeface, and navigation decisions that attracts visitors and separates your Web site from your competition—involves in-depth knowledge of graphic design skills that may go beyond the scope of the typical business owner. However, if you not comfortable completely handing off the job to a design firm, specify that you're hiring them to create a Web site template and to complete the first version of it, and that from then on you want to update the Web site yourself.

Templates are formatted Web sites containing boilerplate copy for you to complete by replacing *placeholder text* like "headline goes here" and "body copy goes here" with the words describing your actual offer.

Your goal is to avoid creating a "hostage" Web site that is reliant upon the design firm or a specific employee. Hostage Web sites fail because they can only be updated by constantly spending more money hiring the outside design firm each time you want to update your Web site. This inevitably involves frustrating delays (design firms typically give Web site revisions less priority than new business development) and—if the work is done by a single employee of your firm—that individual begins to feel so indispensable that they ignore their other duties and feel justified in constantly asking for raises.

Web sites that cannot be easily updated are doomed to failure. Each time visitors revisit your Web site, there should be something noticeably different about the home page as well as the premium content pages they visit.

Web sites that cannot be easily updated are doomed to failure.

For more information on this topic, visit our Web site at www.businesstown.com

Results and New Opportunities: A Month-by-Month Outline for Transforming Your Business

> Experience is not what happens to you; it is what you do with what happens to you.
>
> —ALDOUS HUXLEY

The first 90 days are crucial to the success of your relationship marketing Web site initiative. If you chart the correct course and establish forward momentum during the first 90 days, your Web initiative will be off to a strong start, one that will continue to grow with each passing month.

It's important that you embark upon your Web initiative with realistic expectations. If you expect to accomplish too much too soon, you're unlikely to succeed and discouragement will set in. By establishing realistic expectations, you're more likely to achieve realistic goals.

Web Site Review Team

The starting point is to establish a Web Site Review Team to analyze your present Web site or design a new Web site from scratch. One person rarely can achieve success because he or she is inevitably too close to the Web site; this myopia prevents this person from objectively measuring the progress.

Ideally, your Web Site Review Team should consist of five to eight members representing your business, a few key customers with whom you have dealt with for a long time, as well as outside professionals (like graphic designers or individuals with extensive Web experience). The latter may or may not be those who are actively involved in working with you on your Web site; you might find it more valuable to have a "board of directors" who understand the Web but are not financially involved in your Web site to comment on and make suggestions for your Web site based on a strictly objective basis.

Start by making a list of individuals who might serve on your Web Site Review Team. Think in terms of categories:

- *Employees*–list two or three employees who have shown an interest in marketing activities, even if they are not directly involved in marketing.
- *Customers*–list two or three long-term customers whose opinion you trust, who have offered constructive criticism in the past.
- *Local consultants*–seek out individuals from your area who have demonstrated Web competence (perhaps marketing or Web instructors at a local college) and have nothing to gain by selling their services to you. Let them know you want them strictly as advisors rather than producers. Offer them a modest stipend for their efforts.

Web Site Review Team
- Employees
- Customers
- Local consultants

Although you, as business owner, are ultimately responsible for the success of your Web site, it is useful to assemble a team representing a broad range of interests to help guide you and keep your Web initiative on track.

Month One

Schedule a weekly meeting of your Web Site Review Team. During the first meeting, outline your goals for an information-based relationship marketing Web site that offers incentives and premium content for visitors at different stages of involvement. Make sure they understand the five stages of involvement and the diverse needs of customers at each stage. Share specific examples of each stage within the context of your business.

Create a questionnaire that asks review team members to analyze and evaluate your site. Questions could include:

1. How would you rate the information my Web site offers visitors?
2. How quickly does my Web site load?
3. Is my Web site's design appropriate for the image I want to project?
4. Is my Web site's image consistent with the image my firm projects in its print communications?

5. Do I make it easy for visitors to register their e-mail address?
6. Is my Web site's design flexible enough to accommodate frequent change?

Distribute your questionnaire to members at the first meeting. Ask them to anonymously submit their answers next week.

During the next meeting, discuss the comments and review again the basic tenets of the five stage customer development cycle. At the end of the second meeting, evaluate the performance of each member of your Web Site Review Team and decide how often you want the group to meet.

On the basis of input from your Web Site Review Team, prioritize the problems facing your Web site and focus on solving just one of the problems. After your second meeting, ask each member to identify the most important problem facing your Web site and suggest alternative solutions. By the end of the first month, your Web Site Review Team should have identified the most pressing problem facing your Web site as well as prioritized the other problems affecting it.

Month Two

Although problems of design and content may be identified, in many cases, your first priority will probably be to address the failure to capture your visitors' e-mail addresses. Accordingly, devote the second month to just these simple goals:

- Identifying a meaningful information incentive that will encourage visitors to your Web site to register their e-mail address.
- Working with your internal staff or Internet service provider to establish a self-administering database that will keep track of visitors who submit their e-mail address and permit you to send our periodical e-mail messages (or newsletters) to those who have registered.

> Identifying a meaningful information incentive that will encourage visitors to your Web site to register their e-mail address.

- While some individuals are working on setting up an e-mail database and identifying a registration incentive, others on your Web Site Review Team should identify the type of information that should be mailed to Web site visitors on a regular basis. They should be identifying the content as well as the format of your first e-mail newsletter and deciding whether the e-mail newsletter itself will be sent out or just a short e-mail announcement pointing visitors to a premium content newsletter page (or pages) on your Web site.

By the end of the second month, a flexible electronic database should be in place, capable of receiving visitor registrations. Visitors should receive a notification when they have registered, thanking them for their registration, as well as information describing your firm's privacy statement and instructions on how they can be removed from the database. Your e-mail registration system should also incorporate a way of automatically eliminating duplicates. The database design should be flexible enough to accommodate future changes as your needs become more sophisticated.

Month Three

With the structure in place, you can devote the third month to developing the first of your information incentives. You and your Web team should create your first information incentive and determine the format you will use to distribute premium content. For example, will you be providing your premium content registration incentive in the form of unlinked pages, password-protected pages, or as downloadable files?

The final step for the third month is to redesign your Web site to emphasize your registration incentive. Your e-mail registration incentive should be prominently located, not hidden on a "contact us" page. You should also find a sensible way to repeat the registration incentive on more than one page of your Web site.

By the end of the third month, your Web site should be receiving a continuing stream of e-mail registrations. It is important that

> Your e-mail registration incentive should be prominently located, not hidden on a "contact us" page.

the entire registration procedure be self-administering; when an e-mail registration appears, an acknowledgement should automatically be sent out and the visitor's e-mail address and (optionally) name should automatically be added to your e-mail database. In order for your project to succeed, you need to make sure each chore is as easy as possible to do.

Someone should be in charge of monitoring this process: receiving e-mail inquiries and routing them to the people who will respond to them, capturing and storing new e-mail addresses, and keeping track of how many visitors register each day. They should be reporting a growing number of registrations at each meeting of your Web Site Review Team.

More important, by the end of 90 days, you should have already sent your first e-mail broadcast to all registered Web site visitors. This e-mail can contain the information itself in the body of the e-mail, or—preferably—the e-mail should be short and consist of teasers inviting visitors back to your Web site to visit unlinked or password-protected pages containing the articles and information you feel will be of interest to your market. The work you have accomplished during the first 90 days provides a starting point for the next phase which is focusing on the information needs of visitors at the five different levels of the customer development cycle.

Month Four

With the e-mail component of your Web site in place, you can begin to focus on identifying the information needs of visitors at the five levels of the customer development cycle. At the end of six months, your original one-size-fits-all Web site should have separate pages for open and premium content for visitors at each level of the customer development cycle.

The process of modifying your Web site to accommodate premium content and the customer development cycle also offers you an opportunity to review your Web site's design, making sure that it is easy to navigate, easy to read, easy to print, and projects an appropriate image.

> Modifying your Web site to accommodate premium content and the customer development cycle also offers you an opportunity to review your Web site's design.

During the fourth month of your relationship marketing Web initiative, your Web Site Review Team's emphasis should be on identifying the characteristics, information needs, and potential incentives of Web site visitors at each of the five levels of the customer development cycle.

At the first meeting of the fourth month, each member of your Web Site Review Team should come to the meeting with a list of topics and questions that Web site visitors are likely to want addressed at each level of the customer development cycle. Suggested topics and concerns should be as detailed as possible, along with suggested information-based incentives. Concrete answers should be developed for questions corresponding to each of the five stages. During this fourth month, the Web Site Review Team should develop answers to the following questions:

- What types of information are visitors seeking at the introduction stage?
- What open and premium content should we offer during the introduction stage?
- What incentive should we provide at the introduction stage to motivate visitors to provide information about their product or service needs (as well as to motivate them to submit their e-mail address)?
- Who has the time and ability to create, format, post, and update the information for the premium content?
- How often should introduction stage premium content be updated?
- Who will prepare the e-mail announcing the premium content and monitor e-mail registrations?
- What types of information are visitors looking for at the comparison stage?
- What criteria do our prospect's use to make purchase or no-purchase decisions for each of our product categories?
- What open content should we offer during the comparison stage?

> Your Web Site Review Team's emphasis should be on identifying the characteristics, information needs, and potential incentives of Web site visitors at each of the five levels of the customer development cycle.

- What premium content information should we provide as an incentive for visitors to tell us more about their information needs and purchase intentions?
- What can you learn as you analyze the information that visitors access during the comparison stage?
- How can we customize the visitor's experience so that the information they provide allows us to personalize their visit to our Web site?
- How can we make our offering as visual as possible?
- Who should have responsibility for updating open and premium content for the comparison stage, as well as preparing e-mail announcing new premium content?
- What are the information needs of our prospects as they approach their purchase decision?
- What kinds of incentives can we provide to encourage visitors to commit to an immediate purchase?
- What types of incentives are the most powerful?
- How can we test our incentives before posting them as premium content?
- How much of the story should we tell in our e-mail announcement of incentives?
- How frequently should our purchase incentives be updated?
- Who should be in charge of developing new premium content merchandising incentives, creating premium content merchandising pages, and creating the e-mail that will drive prospects to the premium content page?
- How can we track the results of our premium content incentives?
- What are the information needs of customers who have just purchased?
- What are the information needs of customers who purchased more than 30 days ago?
- What types of open and premium content can we use to show our appreciation for our customer's purchase?
- What types of information will help our customers maximize the pleasure and benefits they receive from their purchase from us?

> How can we make our offering as visual as possible?

- Is it possible to categorize and deliver customized post-purchase information needs based on what the customers purchased?
- How can we identify potential additional purchases based on the buyer's first purchase, such as accessories, enhancements, or supplies?
- How can we motivate certain categories of buyers to purchase selected items?
- How can we survey our customers to find out how satisfied they are with their purchase?
- Who should be in charge of developing reinforcement stage premium content and promoting it via e-mail?
- What types of information and incentives (selling tools) will encourage customers to recommend us to their friends?
- How can we maintain our visibility in the minds of previous customers so ours will be the first name that comes to mind when our business category is mentioned?
- What are the information needs of our customer's friends?
- Is it possible to categorize their information needs on the basis of what they purchased?
- How can we encourage communication and loyalty among our past customers?
- What concrete tests can we put in place to validate our assumptions?

> Who should be in charge of developing reinforcement stage premium content and promoting it via e-mail?

By the end of month four, your Web Site Review Team should have identified the specific information needs of your customers and prospects at each stage of the customer development cycle. More importantly, they should have also identified a way of satisfying these information needs on premium content pages of your Web site and developed a way of promoting the availability of this premium content to each category of Web site visitors.

It is important to recognize the importance of this accomplishment. Although your Web site may still be fit in the one-size-fits-all category, a great deal of groundwork will have been prepared for creating a true relationship marketing Web site based on the five stages of the customer development cycle.

Month Five

Month five is devoted to technology. While the Web Site Review Team continues to refine information and merchandising issues, during the fifth month a "technology subset," consisting of a few members of the Web Site Review Team—or a new group of individuals—should be grappling with developing the site's underlying database-driven technological framework. Ultimately, the success of your relationship marketing Web site will be based on a sophisticated database technology that tracks individual customers as they move through the five step customer development cycle and provides them with personalized information at each stage.

Questions that your Web Site Review Team's "technology gurus" should be exploring include:

- How can new information be added to the visitor's original record in the e-mail database as it becomes available?
- How can we code the e-mail list so that it will change to accurately reflect the visitor's progress through the customer development cycle?
- How can we simplify our repeat visitors experience by making it possible for repeat visitors to go directly to the premium content they desire?
- How can we eliminate duplicate entries to our registered Web site visitor database?
- Who will be in charge of updating each visitor's database record as he or she advances from one stage to the next?
- How will records of online and offline transactions be added to each Web site visitor's original record?
- Who will be in charge of maintaining the online e-mail database, so what starts out as a simple e-mail list ultimately becomes an intrinsic part of our centralized customer database?
- How can we protect the valuable information stored in our database while making it as accessible to as many people as necessary?
- What is the best centralized database for this information, and will we combine or eliminate other databases?

> The success of your relationship marketing Web site will be based on a sophisticated database technology that tracks individual customers as they move through the five-step customer development cycle.

These issues will not be solved overnight. You will need to consider critical issues like replacing individual computers with networked computers feeding a centralized database, erecting firewalls to protect your valuable customer information from unauthorized access by competitors or malicious hackers who will destroy your information, and setting up on-site and off-site database backups.

By the end of the fifth month, the technical infrastructure should be in place. You are now ready to redesign your Web site, replacing your current Web site with one that allow you to offer personalized premium content for visitors at each stage of the customer development cycle.

Month Six

The sixth month is devoted to redesigning your Web site to accommodate the five stages of customer development. This redesign provides you with an opportunity to analyze which aspects of your Web site worked with your original design and which areas require improvement. This redesign is both aesthetic and technological. The implementation and changeover must be carefully planned. You need to provide continuous access to all visitors when the changeover occurs.

During the Web Site Review Team meetings that take place during the sixth month, now that issues involving information and site architecture have been satisfied, you can concentrate on your site's appearance and navigation. Your Web Site Review Team should focus on the access and page loading speed and make sure the site projects an appropriate image. By the end of the sixth month, your new Web site should be up and running. In place of an inflexible, one-size-fits-all site, your redesigned Web site should contain separate open and premium content pages. It should also offer content tailored to visitors at each of the five levels of the customer development cycle. Your site should also be faster loading, capable of easier updating, and should project an image compatible with your firm's goals and aspirations.

> Your Web Site Review Team should focus on the access and page loading speed and make sure the site projects an appropriate image.

Month Seven

The first 90 days, of your relationship marketing Web site initiative was devoted to analyzing the strengths and weaknesses of your current Web site and setting up an e-mail database that would permit you to use e-mail to keep in touch with Web site visitors.

The second 90 days of your relationship marketing Web site initiative was devoted to determining the information needs of your customers and prospects and developing the administrative and technological infrastructure necessary to use your Web site to satisfy those needs. At the end of the second quarter, your Web site was relaunched, with separate areas of open and premium content appropriate for visitors at each stage of the customer relationship cycle.

Now in the third quarter, the next 90 days will be devoted to getting more traffic on your Web site, but not just any kind of traffic. You want more of the right kind of people to visit your Web site: such as strangers—those you have not dealt with yet—as well as past customers and prospects you may have dealt with but didn't sell the first time around.

The goal of your activities during this quarter is to drive increasing numbers of visitors to your Web site. You want to increase the number of visits and e-mail registrations from prospects who have not yet visited your Web site as well as develop the incentives and procedures necessary to drive past customers to your Web site so they too will register their e-mail addresses.

By the end of this quarter your Web site will have become an intrinsic part of your firm's marketing and communication program, possibly permitting a reduction in traditional media expenses such as conventional direct mail, newspaper, magazine, newsletter, or radio/television advertising.

Plan on devoting this month to examining and improving, if necessary, your Web site's visibility on the various search engines. There are many firms whose business is to look after parts or all of the submission process for you and to help improve your company's positioning in the search engine Web sites. These companies employ a variety of techniques that may or may not be necessary or even appropriate for your business. That said, hiring one of these compa-

> The goal of your activities during this quarter is to drive increasing numbers of visitors to your Web site.

nies may be a good investment, if your budget allows. You'll certainly want to do a little research first to find out whether the cost of these firms justifies the investment. Ask yourself: "What can they do better than I can do?" and "What techniques can they employ I can't?"

Months Eight and Nine

Now that your revised relationship marketing Web site is up and running, you'll want to aggressively promote it to your existing customers and prospects. Because these promotions will involve traditional printing and mailing, the activities necessary during the two months can be grouped together.

The starting point is to make sure that your Web site address appears on every print and broadcast communication associated with your store. Your Web site address should appear on your business cards, letterheads, postcards and newsletters, posters, flyers, as well as all of your firm's advertising.

Equally important, your Web site address should appear on secondary, and often overlooked, print communications like purchase orders, product packaging, employment applications, credit applications, and shipping labels. Your Web site address should appear on all point-of-sale information.

At the end of nine months, your relationship marketing Web site initiative should be in full swing. Let's review the steps you have taken this quarter:

1. *Refined your search engine strategy.* Because you have revitalized your search engine strategies, more and more first-time visitors are showing up at your Web site. Your volume of Web site traffic should be up, but even more importantly, the quality of that traffic will be up as well.
2. *Current customers are getting involved.* Because you are now gathering customer e-mail addresses at the point of sale on your invoices, your e-mail list is growing each day.
3. *Previous customers are getting involved.* By sending postcards or newsletters to previous customers and prospects, offering

The steps you have taken this quarter:
- Refined your search engine strategy.
- Current customers are getting involved.
- Previous customers are getting involved.

them a meaningful incentive for them to visit your Web site and register their e-mail address, you are not only selling more products, you are increasing your ability to quickly, easily, and cost-effectively communicate with customers.

Together, this added visibility should already be paying big dividends for you. This is also creating a powerful foundation from which to increase sales and profits and create an environment that builds success upon success.

The Final Quarter

Rounding out the final quarter in your yearlong Web-based relationship marketing initiative, it is time for you to review what you have accomplished, take stock of the refinements you have made to your business, and see what new opportunities emerge. It is at this stage that you can most likely capitalize on the technologies, databases, and capabilities you have to introduce new relationship and affinity marketing initiatives with little incremental costs and without jeopardizing your existing business.

Changes in Your Business

By the time the first year anniversary of your revitalized relationship marketing Web initiative rolls around, your Web site will be playing an increasingly important role in your firm's day-to-day activities. Several important changes may have taken place in your business plan and your business may be subtly—or not so subtly—undergoing a transformation. Here are some of the changes that you should be noticing.

Increasingly focused merchandising and promotions

In the past, you may have had infrequent, price-oriented promotions. Your merchandising and promotions were of the "same promotion for all" category. Now, however, you are thinking in terms of

> By the time the first year anniversary of your revitalized relationship marketing Web initiative rolls around, your Web site will be playing an increasingly important role in your firm's day-to-day activities.

merchandising promotions aimed at increasingly focused market segments and customers at each of the five stages.

Because data coming out of your online and offline sales is now contained in a single database, you can send e-mail to prospects who have indicated—by the pages of your Web site they have visited—an interest in certain categories of products or services. Likewise, you can now send e-mail promotions that will be welcomed by customers who have purchased specific products or services.

The advantage of e-mail and database marketing is that it costs very little once the infrastructure has been created and the transaction information has been added. Unlike print postcards or newsletters, e-mail is free and, to the extent that it is relevant to the needs of the recipient, welcomed and eagerly anticipated.

Examples

If you are a car dealer, for example, you can invite owners of certain makes or models to come in for test drives when new models appear. You can schedule special new product previews or special incentives for owners of specific models. Equally important, when a prospect indicates an interest in a particular product that you no longer have in stock, you can offer special incentives to owners of that product to take advantage of higher-than normal trade-ins.

You can also re-establish contact with prospects who exhibited an interest in a specific product or service but didn't purchase. For example, when new homes go on the market within a certain price range or in a given neighborhood, using e-mail, Realtors can approach those who previously expressed an interest in similar homes and re-establish contact with the prospect.

The above marketing activities are based on a technique called data mining. This means analyzing your database for prospects or customers who fit certain profiles then preparing and sending e-mail promotions that are customized to appeal to their interests. Out of the entire population in your marketing area, if you are selling specialty products, there is a high likelihood that people who have once purchased a high personal identification product will want to purchase another one in the future.

> The advantage of e-mail and database marketing is that it costs very little once the infrastructure has been created and the transaction information has been added.

Rolling promotions

You may also be utilizing rolling promotions. Rolling promotions occur automatically based on the customer's stage in the customer development cycle and important personal days such as birthdays, the birthdays of family members, or the anniversaries of their purchases.

If you are especially aggressive, and are involved in selling low-margin commodities like supplies for ink jet or toner cartridges, you may be sending out e-mails when the customer's transaction history indicates that they are likely to have run out of supplies. This approach need not be at all intrusive. In fact, if something like this is introduced correctly, your business can be viewed as offering a highly valued service, a convenience that your customers will welcome and become very dependent on.

Surveys are another form of rolling promotion. Automatically, a few days after a transaction takes place, customer satisfaction surveys are sent to buyers asking them to rate your firm's performance and their satisfaction with their purchase. This not only provides you with information not otherwise available—helping you identify your firm's strengths as well as those areas requiring attention—the fact that you care enough to send the survey is enough to communicate a caring and professional image to your customers.

There are powerful survey programs, completely Web based, that can tie into your existing database so the survey responses become part of that particular customer's records. You can then leverage that information to further tailor your promotions for that customer.

Decreased media expenditures

As your begin to focus more and more of your efforts on your core market, those who are most likely to purchase from you, you will feel less pressure to spend a lot of money in "shotgun" media advertising—advertising in newspapers, magazines, and broadcast media characterized by a lot of "waste" circulation to recipients outside of your geographic area or who have no need for your products and services.

Rolling promotions occur automatically based on the customer's stage in the customer development cycle and important personal days such as birthdays, the birthdays of family members, or the anniversaries of their purchases.

A side benefit of focusing more of your merchandising on an intensive e-mail and premium content follow-up of visitors to your Web site and previous customers is that your efforts are relatively hidden from your competitors. When you run an ad in a newspaper, all of your competitors can easily see and compete against your offer by lowering their own prices. But it is much harder for competitors to gain competitive information about your merchandising and pricing when your promotions consist of e-mail sent to Web site visitors and previous customers. Keeping your competitors in the dark and out of the loop prevents them from placing reactive price pressure on you and your growing business.

At the same time that you are cutting back the quantity of your media advertising, you are likely spending increasing amounts of time developing focused merchandising programs aimed at the needs of your customers and prospects. Instead of looking for one or two loss leader products to promote to the general population, you are spending more time fine-tuning your offers so that your e-mail incentives will be welcomed by your previous customers because they are well timed and appropriate to their needs.

Higher margins

The net result of your reduced media expenditures and your increasingly focused e-mail program is that you are no longer exclusively competing on the basis of price. Instead, you are competing on the basis of relevance and timing. You are offering valuable information to visitors that is deflecting your market's interest away from price and towards benefits and assistance making the right choice.

Price competition will never completely disappear. But it is possible to offset destructive price competition by combining fair and reasonable prices with exceptional, personalized service. Fresh roses in a hotel room may not justify a room charge $50 more than equivalent accommodations across the street, but they may go a long way towards offsetting a $25 price premium. Even more effective is remembering a visitor's preference for a nonsmoking room containing a king-sized bed and facing the street when he calls or e-mails to register, or you greet

> It is much harder for competitors to gain competitive information about your merchandising and pricing when your promotions consist of e-mail sent to Web site visitors and previous customers.

him by name at check-in and ask if he'd like to register for a suite now to help celebrate his wife's birthday next month.

Increased accountability and proven results

Your first generation Web site probably did not offer much in the way of accountability. It was difficult to measure the effectiveness of the Web site because there was no way to relate Web site visitors to sales or word-of-mouth recommendations.

As your Web site activities and transaction databases become increasingly joined together, however, it is becoming easier to replace hunches with cold, hard facts. By analyzing and integrating the disparate data points of e-mail you sent, the resulting page visits they made, and, of course, the resulting sales, it is becoming easier and easier to identify those offers that your market best responds to.

Affinity marketing

At the same time that you are becoming more sophisticated in your ability to target your offers to specific market segments using e-mail and premium content pages, you may also be creating alliances with other marketers in your area, working with them to develop packaged purchases such as weekend getaways that not only include lodging but also two-for-one meals at local restaurants; free boat, ski, or snowmobile rentals; or fresh flowers in the room.

As your customer transactions become more and more computerized, you now enjoy the opportunity of better identifying trends—as well as exceptions. You can now easily identify your most valuable customers—those who buy the most and who recommend your firm the most—as well as customers who create their own noticeable trends and blips. Most important, by analyzing your most valuable customers and devoting some time to researching their goals and motivations, you can identify opportunities to partner with other firms, creating incentives for them to again buy from you. This is the core of relationship marketing, and your involvement in these activities puts your business at the pinnacle of modern marketing and serves both you and your customers in countless ways.

> By analyzing your most valuable customers and devoting some time to researching their goals and motivations, you can identify opportunities to partner with other firms, creating incentives for them to again buy from you.

New Business Opportunities

As you monitor your Web site traffic, develop strategic alliances with noncompeting firms, constantly survey your customers, and keep abreast of changing technology, you'll gain a better understanding of precisely what your market desires and how your firm can satisfy these needs. More important, as your Web site begins to play an increasingly vital role in your business, and as you are spending less and less time on routine administrative matters, you may notice the appearance of new opportunities.

For example, if you are the owner of a ski lodge in northern New Hampshire and are co-promoting weekend getaways with other local businesses, you may notice that your activities are responsible for a disproportionately high share of out-of-towners coming to your area. As the implication of this observation sets in, you may come to the conclusion that you are capable of doing a better job of promoting your region than the regional chamber of commerce or their Web site. Perhaps you will become involved with them and through this step become involved with an even broader range of co-marketing opportunities.

A year from now, you may delegate more and more of your daily inn-keeping affairs to loyal employees and devote increasing amounts of time to creating a new business, one that will book visitors to all of the inns and hotels in the area instead of just your own.

If you own a bookstore, you may find yourself not only selling books from traditional publishers, but you may investigate publishing opportunities—helping bring writers and readers together in a new and innovative way. Or you may decide that there are ways of selling other products to your customers via the Web, such as magazine subscriptions tailored to each reader's particular reading tastes.

If you are a Realtor, you may take a more aggressive role in bringing buyer and seller together, perhaps arranging total packages that include financing, home furnishings, and setting up accounts with local businesses.

The model you may want to investigate involves Web firms who are actually more like facilitators or aggregators than traditional businesses. Many Web businesses act as middlemen between customers, factories, warehouses, and overnight shipping companies.

> As your Web site begins to play an increasingly vital role in your business, and as you are spending less and less time on routine administrative matters, you may notice the appearance of new opportunities.

CDNOW, for example, does not own a warehouse full of recordings, does not ship CDs nor does it own the database of information that contains artist biographies or samples of music that visitors can hear on their computer. Instead, CDNOW simply acts as a middleman, tying together the firm that owns the musical database, the firm that warehouses the recordings, and the fulfillment house that ships the orders and takes care of returns.

As time goes by, your business will be transformed in a similar or even more interesting and unpredictable way.

Conclusion

Involvement with the Web can be tremendously liberating. Once you set up a structure that frees you from excessive concentration on day-to-day activities, you will undoubtedly discover numerous creative ways that you can transform your business. It is far more rewarding and profitable to work on your business rather than in your business.

However, you should avoid the temptation to totally abandon your traditional business. Rather, you should look for ways to transform your business by adapting it to new opportunities that the Web offers. If you allow this natural and gradual evolution to take place, you will likely find yourself owning a much more enjoyable business, one that experiences higher margins, less competitive pressures, greater customer loyalty, and is a more important member of the community.

By the end of the first year, your business is now not only enjoying that increased profitability at a time when your personal stress level has been reduced, but you can see the outlines of new business opportunities beginning to emerge. Not only will those opportunities become more evident, but since your business will have successfully integrated the Web into its daily operations, you will find it easy to actually take advantage of those opportunities. The cycle of growth continues.

It's a grand time to own a business.

> Your business is now not only enjoying that increased profitability at a time when your personal stress level has been reduced, but you can see the outlines of new business opportunities beginning to emerge.

For more information on this topic, visit our Web site at www.businesstown.com

Case Studies

Overview of Section IV

Translate theory into practice with case studies for all business types.
Gain ideas you can put into action using worksheet.
Formulate goals for each stage of your Web site.

Appendix: Case Studies

The following case studies will help you translate theory into action and stimulate your thinking about your own Web site. Each case study begins with a description of the challenges the business faces and a worksheet suggesting ideas how the challenges could be met.

By analyzing the backgrounds that introduce each information flow form and the way various small business owners responded to the challenges they were faced with, you'll undoubtedly gain ideas you can put to work as you fill out your own information flow form.

The form encourages you to enter a goal statement for each stage of customer development. You will find it much easier to create content for each stage if you have a specific goal in mind. Be as specific as possible and try to limit your goals to one point. Review the goal statement for each stage of each case study. Do you agree with it? Can you suggest a better alternative? What lessons about goal statements can you apply to your own business?

Notice the last column of the form, headed "Ideas this suggests for your Web site." As you review the case studies, jot down ideas that occur to you as you review each case study. You can always go back later and consolidate the ideas on a single sheet of paper.

Notice how on many of the case studies that information initially posted on premium content pages—like the latest edition of your newsletter—is later posted in the open content areas. This is important because it not only enhances the richness of information available on your Web site, it also "advertises" the richness of information available to registered visitors—thus encouraging casual visitors to provide their e-mail address and register. Notice also how often information gathered at one stage of the customer development cycle shows up in another stage.

CASE STUDIES

The following case studies are included:

Consultants
- Accountant
- Executive recruiter
- Financial planner
- Marketing consultant
- Oral surgeon
- Veterinarian

Retailers
- Art gallery
- Automobile dealer
- Gift shop
- Home theater installation specialist
- Outdoor clothing boutique
- Video rental store
- Wood stove dealer

Hospitality and tourism
- Bakery
- Gourmet restaurant
- Microbrewery
- Motel
- Whale watch

Services
- Beauty shop
- Commercial building contractor
- Photographer
- Day care center
- Electronics distributor
- Graphic designer
- Health club
- Insurance agency
- Realtor
- Secretarial service
- Travel agent

Case Study # 1: Accountant

Independent accountants help small businesses maintain accurate financial records for lenders, prepare and submit local, state, and national tax returns, and help maximize the client's cash flow. Local and regional accountants not only compete with each other but with nationally franchised tax preparation firms.

To attract new business, accountants must project a knowledgeable, professional image. Over time, accountants must also become so knowledgeable about their client's businesses that it becomes difficult for clients to switch.

STAGE OF CUSTOMER DEVELOPMENT CYCLE	OPEN CONTENT	E-MAIL	INCENTIVE OR PREMIUM CONTENT	WHAT IDEAS DOES THIS SUGGEST FOR YOUR WEB SITE?
INTRODUCTION *Goal: Introduce accountant and secure visitor's e-mail address for later follow-up.*	Services offered, areas of expertise and specialization. Education and background. Client list.	Register and identify client needs.	Downloadable Excel template for keeping track of expenses while on the road.	
COMPARISON *Goal: Enhance accountant's credibility relative to competition.*	Case studies of successful relationships. Customer satisfaction survey results. Previous issues of newsletter. Opinions on issues that prospects and customers are likely facing. Appropriate articles for various market segments, i.e., "How to be a successful client" articles to attract new small businesses. Testimonials from previous customers.	Alert prospects to download current monthly or bimonthly newsletter. Teasers to short bulletins whenever important changes occur. Notice of downloadable and forwardable "What to do when your audited" article.	Electronic newsletter discussing implications of changes in economic and political climate. Page describing important changes and how they affect different categories of clients. Downloadable and forwardable "What to do when you're audited" article.	

CASE STUDIES

STAGE OF CUSTOMER DEVELOPMENT CYCLE	OPEN CONTENT	E-MAIL	INCENTIVE OR PREMIUM CONTENT	WHAT IDEAS DOES THIS SUGGEST FOR YOUR WEB SITE?
TRANSACTION *Goal: Expertise*	Description and fee ranges for various categories of service. Explanation of procedures for hiring. Incentives for new books and tapes. Prices for specific categories of work.	Teaser to online "how to score your accountant" survey. Forwardable teaser to coupon page.	Online "How to evaluate your accountant" survey to plant seed of doubt in prospect's mind about service their current accountant is providing. Opportunity to download coupons for free initial meetings or evaluations.	
REINFORCEMENT *Goal: Enhance security that current clients have made the right choice, make it easy for them to recommend accountant to friends and associates.*	Opinions on current issues and challenges. Descriptions of newly added services.	Alert with incentive for yearly customer satisfaction survey. Alerts and advance reminders about upcoming tax deadlines, i.e., quarterly filings, etc. Referral to money-saving coupon page when client pays bills or recommends a new client; notice of downloadable end-of-year gift.	Yearly customer satisfaction survey with coupon incentive. Page with incentive for advance filing and tax preparation. Coupons for special savings on books and supplies relating to financial management. Downloadable planner or software for next year.	
ADVOCACY *Goal: Maintain visibility and become known as "the" authority in the area.*	Question and answer forum. Resources like glossary, list of important books. Links to resources of interest to market.	Teaser to page where visitors can submit confidential questions and receive confidential answers.	Page containing answer to question submitted by prospective clients.	

Case Study # 2: Art Gallery

Although profit margins on individual sales may be very high, art galleries operate in a difficult business environment. Sales often fluctuate with changes in the economy. Trends quickly change. More important, the Internet is changing the business as artists may begin selling their creations direct to buyers.

Independently owned art galleries face many competitive challenges. They compete with other art galleries, museums, and—perhaps most important—indifference. In addition, the Internet also permits galleries in distant cities to compete for a local gallery's customers. Unless the gallery maintains the buyer's enthusiasm for the gallery's unique focus, competence, and personality, the buyer may lose interest in the gallery or buy elsewhere—or be content to simply visit museums.

STAGE OF CUSTOMER DEVELOPMENT CYCLE	OPEN CONTENT	E-MAIL	INCENTIVE OR PREMIUM CONTENT	WHAT IDEAS DOES THIS SUGGEST FOR YOUR WEB SITE?
INTRODUCTION *Goal: Introduce gallery and its philosophy, find out visitor's needs for later follow-up.*	Location, hours, types of art featured. Sample photographs of gallery interior. Gallery philosophy. Description of currently-displayed artists. Profile of owner, key staff.	Acknowledgement of registration. Follow-up with invitation to visit detailed study of currently displayed artist.	Downloadable screen saver of images of samples from previous year's exhibitions. In-depth article describing current exhibits.	
COMPARISON *Goal: Encourage visitors to visit (and revisit) this gallery instead of competing galleries.*	Critics' comments about previous shows. Article about current trends in art and how current exhibition fits in. Comments from previous visitors. Article about the proper ways to display and insure art at home.	Invitation to visit online catalog showing current exhibition.	In-depth information and photographs of currently displayed artist.	

STAGE OF CUSTOMER DEVELOPMENT CYCLE	OPEN CONTENT	E-MAIL	INCENTIVE OR PREMIUM CONTENT	WHAT IDEAS DOES THIS SUGGEST FOR YOUR WEB SITE?
TRANSACTION *Goal: Motivate visitors to action.*	Financing and layaway alternatives. Article describing rental program for corporate art. Article showing trends in pricing for similar artwork. Page describing opportunities to rent gallery for special events.	Link to online survey form offering opportunity for gallery visitors to comment on currently displayed artist's work. Invitation to page with coupons for affinity marketing, i.e., area restaurants, books about current artist, posters. Invitation to page describing posters and catalogs for current exhibition. Alert to online newsletter describing upcoming exhibitions. Alert to special reception/preview of new exhibition. Alert when major pieces on display have been sold or exhibition is about to end.	Online survey form. Coupons for co- marketing, i.e., area restaurants, parking, hotels, etc. Discount page describing posters and/or catalog for current exhibition online ordering information. Online newsletter describing upcoming exhibit. Page describing special pre-opening preview for registered visitors with online RSVP form.	
REINFORCEMENT *Goal: Maintain visibility and generate word of mouth referrals.*	Comments about current exhibition from gallery visitors.	Screen saver of current program for buyers or those who RSVP'ed invitation.	Downloadable screen saver of current exhibit.	
ADVOCACY *Goal: Project a "leadership" position for gallery among art lovers.*	Calendar listing events at other galleries in area (promoting more visits to area). Links to Web sites of other area galleries.	Alert to page describing art scene in general.	Article discussing and interpreting displays at other galleries, recommended restaurants, hotels, etc.	

Case Study # 3: Automobile Dealer

Although many auto manufacturers have taken steps to reduce the number of automobile dealers in an effort to bolster pricing, and the number of large, regional multibrand automobile dealers grows, independent (often family owned) automobile dealers with one or two brands remain a major force in automobile retailing. Until recently, price has been their primary competitive tool.

Independent automobile dealers face pricing challenges from both local dealers selling the same brands as well as distant dealers selling via the Internet. Many automotive manufacturers and importers have reduced dealer profits in an effort to stabilize pricing and are enforcing higher levels of dealer service, making it more difficult for dealers to offer a major competitive advantage. Additional challenges come from the increasing costs of staff acquisition, training and retention.

STAGE OF CUSTOMER DEVELOPMENT CYCLE	OPEN CONTENT	E-MAIL	INCENTIVE OR PREMIUM CONTENT	WHAT IDEAS DOES THIS SUGGEST FOR YOUR WEB SITE?
INTRODUCTION Goal: Encourage visitor registration, mutual introduction.	Brands sold, location, hours. Service and financing options. Brief history. Make/model/color/option search.	Acknowledge visitor registration, introduce personal account representative. Inform visitors when requested cars have been located or have arrived. Invitation to schedule a test drive or appraisal. No obligation lease/finance costs.	Up-to-date product comparison information with other brands. Search feature: invite visitors to describe "dream car."	
COMPARISON Goal: Enhance credibility and personality of dealer versus its competition by engaging visitor in dialog.	Customer testimonials and survey results. Summaries of reviews from major magazines. Financing options.	Motivate visitor to return for more information. Inform visitors when new information has been posted about new models. Driving tips.	Summaries and links of/to latest news, rumors and reviews in automotive press. Seasonal driving tips.	

Stage of Customer Development Cycle	Open Content	E-mail	Incentive or Premium Content	What ideas does this suggest for your Web site?
Transaction *Goal: Provide buyers information of products.*	Current inventory of new and pre-owned models. Confirm appointments.	Inform visitors when new models meeting their criteria have arrived. Schedule delivery. Invite visitors to pages with seasonal savings offers.	Advance notice of incoming new and pre-owned model. Advance offers and price incentives for seasonal accessory and maintenance needs.	
Reinforcement *Goal: Maintain buyer enthusiasm, build word-of-mouth referrals.*	Seasonal driving and maintenance tips (rotated).	Post-sale thank-you, invite buyers to special page with "thank-you gift." Invite buyers to fill out online survey. Invitation to new model introductions. Promote special maintenance offers.	Post-sale online survey. Post-sale "celebration" with affinity marketer, i.e., local restaurant, etc. Event marketing: previews of new models, driving tips. Preferred customer maintenance. Suggested second cars for other family members.	
Advocacy *Goal: Build word-of-mouth recommendation.*	Questions and answers from purchasers.	Posting of "topic of the month" for responses.	Special customer-only previews or presentations. Affinity marketing—special offers for lodging.	

Case Study # 4: Bakery

Independent and regional bakeries are finding a new market niche between nationally franchised fast-food restaurants and more expensive, formal sit-down restaurants. Many serve a variety of healthy sandwiches, soups, and specialty coffees, as well as offer freshly baked breads, bagels, and deserts for home consumption. Daily specials, informal decor, and expanded hours make bakeries a pleasant addition to the culinary scene, whether as a restaurant, a source of sandwiches to take back to the office, or as a source of breads and deserts for home.

Bakeries compete with franchised fast-food outlets, sit-down restaurants, bakery departments located within supermarkets and warehouse outlets, as well as other independent—often well-established and family owned—bakeries. Because of the relatively low cost of the goods sold, pricing incentives are unlikely to provide an effective competitive tool.Introduction

STAGE OF CUSTOMER DEVELOPMENT CYCLE	OPEN CONTENT	E-MAIL	INCENTIVE OR PREMIUM CONTENT	WHAT IDEAS DOES THIS SUGGEST FOR YOUR WEB SITE?
INTRODUCTION *Goal: Establish bakery as source of quality flavors and healthy food.*	Location, hours, parking, atmosphere (i.e., chairs, coffee, music,). Personalize bakery by identifying owner and staff. Describe range of products. Emphasize underlying philosophy of health and flavor.	Acknowledge registration.	Offer downloadable and printable coupon good for a limited time discount.	
COMPARISON *Goal: Position bakery apart from mass-produced baked goods available in supermarkets, emphasize special orders.*	Emphasize role that fresh ingredients and whole or stone ground flour play. Hints for reheating breads at home or baking frozen bread dough available from bakery.	Alert to page containing month's cooking schedule (different breads cooked each day). Alert for seasonal specials.	Monthly page describing seasonal favorites and what breads will be baked each day. Seasonal page describing sandwich recipes based on special breads and deserts.	
TRANSACTION *Goal: Motivate immediate sales and develop new revenue sources.*	Describe catering and large group affairs. Emphasize convenience of preordering breads.	Pre-holiday and visitor-specific alerts. Alert for out-of-state visitors for overnight shipment of special breads.	Encourage pre-orders and prepayments before busy times, i.e., holidays like Thanksgiving, Christmas.	

STAGE OF CUSTOMER DEVELOPMENT CYCLE	OPEN CONTENT	E-MAIL	INCENTIVE OR PREMIUM CONTENT	WHAT IDEAS DOES THIS SUGGEST FOR YOUR WEB SITE?
	Catalog page describing bread baking books, recipes, special knives and toasters, tea pots, etc.	Alert for coupon savings on ancillary products.	Form for ordering cakes for special occasions like cookouts, visitor's birthday, or anniversary. Coupon specials to promote and draw attention to slow moving merchandise like books, toasters, etc. Form for ordering favorite breads not available locally.	
REINFORCEMENT *Goal: Reward frequent buyers and retainer buyers who might live out of the area.*	Describe recipes (i.e., seasonal sandwiches) based on breads the store sells.	Alert to electronic postcard. Alert to coupon specials for frequent buyers.	Electronic postcard visitors can send to their friends offering them an introductory slice of bread and coffee. Page of coupons for visitors who have purchased a certain amount of bread.	
ADVOCACY *Goal: Maintain enthusiasm for bakery as source of an "experience" rather than a "commodity."*	Profile favorite sandwich recipe each month. Links to good health resources and additional sources of recipes.	Alert to question submission page.	Form inviting visitors to submit their favorite sandwich or snack recipe.	

Case Study # 5: Beauty Shop

Every community has numerous independently owned beauty shops. These generally are salons with three or four stations, sometimes rented to independent contractors.

The major competitive challenge that independent beauty shops face are franchises in shopping malls that offer lower prices, night and weekend hours, as well as one-stop parking for multiple purposes (dad and the kids shop while mom has her hair done).

STAGE OF CUSTOMER DEVELOPMENT CYCLE	OPEN CONTENT	E-MAIL	INCENTIVE OR PREMIUM CONTENT	WHAT IDEAS DOES THIS SUGGEST FOR YOUR WEB SITE?
INTRODUCTION *Goal: Mutual introduction making later follow-up possible.*	Store location, hours, credit cards, parking. Background and philosophy of owner/operator. Description of range of services offered. Description of products sold.	Acknowledgement registration (which should include visitor's birthday).	White paper—"Reversing the Effects of Aging." Password access to electronic newsletter.	
COMPARISON *Goal: Show how this beauty shop can do a better job than other area beauty shops.*	Sample "before-and-after" photographs. Customer testimonials. Short biographies and quotes from store staff. Articles describing how to choose and use the various beauty aids sold.	Alert to visit Web site and access newsletter. Alert to new articles and before-and-after features as they are posted.	Electronic newsletter describing new products and their applications.	
TRANSACTION *Goal: Motivate visitor to make immediate purchase.*	Catalog of products and beauty aids sold.	Teaser to coupon page for new customers. Alert when it's time to schedule a follow-up appointment.	Coupon page for first-time visitors. Form for scheduling appointments online. Coupon page for discount on visit one week before visitor's birthday each year.	

STAGE OF CUSTOMER DEVELOPMENT CYCLE	OPEN CONTENT	E-MAIL	INCENTIVE OR PREMIUM CONTENT	WHAT IDEAS DOES THIS SUGGEST FOR YOUR WEB SITE?
TRANSACTION (CONTINUED) *Goal: Motivate visitor to make immediate purchase.*		Alert to coupon page one week before visitor's birthday. Reminders to make appointments ahead of time during busy season. Alert to visit promotional page for limited-time savings. Thank-you and customer satisfaction survey following visit.	Promotional page for limited-time discounts on beauty supplies. Customer satisfaction survey form.	
REINFORCEMENT *Goal: Encourage clients to come back and bring their friends.*	Explanation of "recommend a friend" policy.	Offer for electronic postcard or greeting card registered visitors can send friends. Reference to "thank-you" coupon when visitor recommends a new client who makes an appointment.	Electronic postcard with coupon visitors can send to their best friend on their best friend's birthday.	
ADVOCACY *Goal: Maintain visibility and enhance credibility among both present and potential clients.*	Answers to frequently asked questions. Articles about relationship between physical and mental health and appearance. Links to Web sites offering beauty and fashion advice.	Reference to form for submitting frequently asked questions.	Thank-you coupon page. Form for submitting confidential questions.	

Case Study # 6: Commercial Building Contractor

This large, locally owned family firm has specialized in building commercial facilities such as factories, office parks, and shopping malls for over thirty years. This firm must compete against national firms with lower costs that use "off the shelf" solutions to reduce costs and can buy in bulk.

STAGE OF CUSTOMER DEVELOPMENT CYCLE	OPEN CONTENT	E-MAIL	INCENTIVE OR PREMIUM CONTENT	WHAT IDEAS DOES THIS SUGGEST FOR YOUR WEB SITE?
INTRODUCTION *Goal: Introduce firm as one-stop source for commercial construction.*	Services offered. Areas of expertise and specialization. Education, publication, speaking and work experience. Client list.	Acknowledge registration and provide URL or password.	The 10 most common mistakes businesses make when building new facilities.	
COMPARISON *Goal: Show how firm can be a better job for less cost.*	Case studies. Opinions on issues that prospects and customers are likely facing. Testimonials from previous customers. Resources like glossary, list of important books.	Announce personalized cost saver.	Return on investment calculator, which helps project cost savings.	
TRANSACTION *Goal: Encourage prospect to submit rough project specifications for estimate.*	Contact information. Estimated prices for specific categories of work.	Offer an immediate "ball park" estimate of project cost.	Form making it easy for prospect to submit project details.	

STAGE OF CUSTOMER DEVELOPMENT CYCLE	OPEN CONTENT	E-MAIL	INCENTIVE OR PREMIUM CONTENT	WHAT IDEAS DOES THIS SUGGEST FOR YOUR WEB SITE?
REINFORCEMENT *Goal: Suggest additions and enhancements.*	New case studies as they appear. Quality, credibility building news about current challenges and advancing technology. Links to Web sites or publications reflecting consultant's direct involvement. Opinions on current issues and challenges.	Announce cost-cutting and value enhancing white paper.	Recommended maintenance procedures to reduce costs and enhance value of.	
ADVOCACY *Goal: Encourage previous clients to discuss their design and maintenance lessons learned. Answer maintenance questions.*	Question and answer forum. Links to resources of interest to market.	Announce forum and provide incentive for participation.	Provide Q&A forum and discussion group.	

Case Study # 7: Day Care Center

This family owned business has been in business for over ten years. Many centers start as a means for additional income while allowing mom to stay home with children. A lot of times they start out to help friends and family who can't afford or don't need full-time child care services.

They compete against larger facilities who offer more extensive facilities as well as continuation into preschool and/or nursery school. Larger competitors typically have staff members with teaching certification.

STAGE OF CUSTOMER DEVELOPMENT CYCLE	OPEN CONTENT	E-MAIL	INCENTIVE OR PREMIUM CONTENT	WHAT IDEAS DOES THIS SUGGEST FOR YOUR WEB SITE?
INTRODUCTION Goal: Make it easy to introduce firm to prospective parents.	Location, parking, and drop-off hours, age range of children. Introduce owners and staff. Basic policies, preferences and procedures. Range of fees.	Acknowledge registration.	Electronic newsletter discussing children's health and development issues.	
COMPARISON Goal: Help position this day care center as friendlier and better qualified than competitors.	Pictures of children during the day. Testimonials from satisfied parents. Customer satisfaction survey results. Commentary on issues of the day by owner or staff.	Follow-up email offering a monthly downloadable calendar. Reminder when new issues of electronic newsletter are posted.	Downloadable calendar for next month containing a photograph of one of the children. Electronic newsletter that can be downloaded or printed (or read online).	
TRANSACTION Goal: Encourage early registration and advance payment.	Catalog of child development books and products likely to be of interest to parents.	Alert to page containing discount coupon for first week's care. Alert to visit coupon discount page.	Printable coupon for discount on first week's care. Page containing coupons with discounts on books and child care items.	

STAGE OF CUSTOMER DEVELOPMENT CYCLE	OPEN CONTENT	E-MAIL	INCENTIVE OR PREMIUM CONTENT	WHAT IDEAS DOES THIS SUGGEST FOR YOUR WEB SITE?
		Monthly alert when payment is due and incentive for prompt payment. Request to fill out customer satisfaction form. Link to downloadable screen saver.	Online billing and payment program with discount for prompt payment. Form for filling out survey and submitting comments. New, seasonable, downloadable screen saver of happy children available every quarter.	
REINFORCEMENT *Goal: Make parents feel comfortable and enthusiastic about day care center so they'll refer it to their friends and coworkers.*	Photo gallery of happy children submitted by parents whose children attend.	Invitation to photograph children during a special day and submit photographs for online photo gallery. Alert for upcoming events. Alert to invitation to parents.	Form for reserving digital camera and submitting digital photographs for Web site. Updated page describing upcoming events, like holiday parties or outings, special visits, story hours, etc. Page inviting parents to participate in special events.	
ADVOCACY *Goal: Make day care center the center of a parent's involvement in child's health.*	Parents question and answer discussion forum. Staff reviews of new and classic child care and development books. Links to articles and resources relating to important issues concerning child development.	Link to form for submitting questions and concerns.	Form for submitting questions, comments, or concerns.	

Case Study # 8: Electronics Distributor

Firms typically evolve out of experience as independent manufacturer's representatives who are being phased out as manufacturers develop their own sales structures. A goal is to develop new revenue sources that allow them to sell competing lines of products rather than being restricted to non-competing lines. Another goal is to differentiate themselves from other sources of products and become the preferred choice to buy by becoming a source of information.

STAGE OF CUSTOMER DEVELOPMENT CYCLE	OPEN CONTENT	E-MAIL	INCENTIVE OR PREMIUM CONTENT	WHAT IDEAS DOES THIS SUGGEST FOR YOUR WEB SITE?
INTRODUCTION *Goal: Mutual introduction of distributor and prospective resellers.*	Lines sold. Contact information. Credit requirements. Shipping and delivery options. Special orders. Key personnel and company history.	Acknowledge registration. Alert each time Bimonthly electronic newsletter appears.	Credit application sent and discount information sent in response to registration. Electronic newsletter discusses selling tips and techniques, installation ideas, and ways to cut costs and maximize profits.	
COMPARISON *Goal: Reinforce firm's competitive expertise.*	Summary of makes and models sold. Pricing information.	Alert to page describing visitor's procedures.	Page describing each buyer's unique discount structure and credit limits, payment terms.	
TRANSACTION *Goal: Reduce overhead by making ordering as simple as possible.*	Description of electronic, online buying, order tracking.	Acknowledgement of online orders. Alerts for special offers on slow moving or about to be discontinued merchandise. Alerts for new products.	Forms for online ordering and order tracking. Forms for special merchandise offerings.	

STAGE OF CUSTOMER DEVELOPMENT CYCLE	OPEN CONTENT	E-MAIL	INCENTIVE OR PREMIUM CONTENT	WHAT IDEAS DOES THIS SUGGEST FOR YOUR WEB SITE?
REINFORCEMENT *Goal: Encourage customers to recommend distributor to other firms.*	New products. Special promotions. New services. Industry trends.	Alert for pass-along savings. Alert for information pass-along. Frequent buyer reward alerts.	Page describing pre-introduction special savings. Page describing COD or paid in advance offers on special close-out merchandise. Page describing program that firms can forward to their associates. Page offering special limited-time savings when sales goals have been exceeded and payments have been received on-time.	
ADVOCACY *Goal: Position firm as a source of merchandising information as well as low prices.*	Industry trends Dealer/distributor question and answer forum.	Alert for merchandising tips. Invitation to express questions and concerns.	Page suggesting seasonal merchandising ideas—"what works for others may work for you!" More timely and shorter deadline than bimonthly newsletter.	

Case Study #9: Executive Recruiter

This independently owned, ten-person firm places job candidates in corporate environments. It must compete against other firms offering similar services as well as large professional "headhunter" firms that offer national recognition and visibility and a nationwide database of candidates and job opportunities.

STAGE OF CUSTOMER DEVELOPMENT CYCLE	OPEN CONTENT	E-MAIL	INCENTIVE OR PREMIUM CONTENT	WHAT IDEAS DOES THIS SUGGEST FOR YOUR WEB SITE?
INTRODUCTION *Goal: Establish competence and credibility, qualify visitors*	Areas of expertise and specialization, i.e., industries, etc. Experience; years in business, profile of key members. Description of typical clients.	Acknowledge registration. Follow-up offer to personally answer any specific questions.	White paper describing recent employment and reimbursement trends in areas of expertise.	
COMPARISON *Goal: Gain a competitive lead over other similar firms.*	Emphasize information that sets this firm apart. Case studies (with disguised names) of successful placements. Survey results one month after posting on "registered visitors" area. Report on the changing job market. Dictionary of terms. Customer testimonials.	Invitation to visit service-oriented pages. Announcement of latest issue of electronic newsletter. Bulletin when latest survey results are posted.	Special "How to update your resume" report. Special "What to look for when working with an executive recruiter" report. Special "How to reinvent yourself for the Millennium" report. Electronic newsletter that interprets previous month's news and trends, highlights successful placements, emphasizes areas of need.	

CASE STUDIES

STAGE OF CUSTOMER DEVELOPMENT CYCLE	OPEN CONTENT	E-MAIL	INCENTIVE OR PREMIUM CONTENT	WHAT IDEAS DOES THIS SUGGEST FOR YOUR WEB SITE?
TRANSACTION *Goal: Encourage visitors to register as either client or placement candidate.*	Discussion of registration and fees for successful placements. Warranties. Problem resolution.	Invitation for firms and candidates to formalize relationship. For corporations, bulletin inviting visitor to page describing backgrounds of latest newly registered candidates. For individuals, bulletin inviting visitors to page describing latest opportunities. Request for firms and candidates to fill out post-placement survey.	Page of contracts for clients and placement candidates. Page outlining recent openings. Page outlining newly available candidates. Survey page for firms and candidates.	
REINFORCEMENT *Goal: Maintain firm's visibility and credibility.*	Customer/buyer survey. Applications stories. Hints for using products. Analysis of industry trends and hints of new product to solve problems. New product introductions. Supplies and accessories.	Invitation for individuals to visit "newly hired tips" page. Invitation for firms to visit "assimilation" page.	White paper on hints for newly hired individuals. Tips for assimilating firms into page.	
ADVOCACY *Goal: Maintain visibility and encourage word-of-mouth referrals.*	Industry news forum. Links to industry conferences, publications, and trade shows.	Contact individuals at two-month intervals and find out how they are doing. Invite firms and candidates to confidentially submit salary information. Find out what career moves candidates might be interested in.	Summary of latest trends in areas of specialization. Salary survey for registered visitors only.	

Case Study # 10: Financial Planner

This independent consultant, who comes from a banking background, offers accounting and investment counseling and must compete against banks, stock brokers, and online investment firms offering brokerage services. The firm's goal is to use their Web site to establish and maintain visibility among clients and build credibility by offering personalized investment advice.

STAGE OF CUSTOMER DEVELOPMENT CYCLE	OPEN CONTENT	E-MAIL	INCENTIVE OR PREMIUM CONTENT	WHAT IDEAS DOES THIS SUGGEST FOR YOUR WEB SITE?
INTRODUCTION Goal: Mutual introduction, qualification of income and risk tolerance.	Background, services offered, areas of expertise. Location, phone, fax, hours, fees.	Acknowledge registration. Invite visitors to white paper.	White paper interpreting recent investment trends. Monthly or bimonthly interpretation of recent trends.	
COMPARISON Goal: Enhance capabilities.	Broad article interpreting recent trends. "How to get started" strategy article. Glossary of financial planning terms. Results of ongoing customer satisfaction survey. Case studies of successful relationships.	Invite visitors to take advanced survey of financial goals.	Customized recommendations based on investment goals.	

Stage of Customer Development Cycle	Open Content	E-mail	Incentive or Premium Content	What ideas does this suggest for your Web site?
Transaction *Goal: Motivate prospect to get started.*	Discussion of fees for different services.	Reminders about upcoming office meetings. Reduced fees for limited time periods. Thank-you and invitation to customer satisfaction survey.	Timely investment bulletins. Customer satisfaction survey.	
Reinforcement *Goal: Maintain enthusiasm, resell products, and build closer personal relationship.*	Feature article—"Tips for keeping good financial records and updating goals."	Teaser for latest electronic bulletin/newsletter. Reminders to schedule yearly "financial check-ups."	Bimonthly or monthly interpretation of tips.	
Advocacy *Goal: Build word-of-mouth referrals and recommendations.*	Case studies— investment tips that have paid off for others.	Invitation to take anonymous survey of financials goals and accomplishments. Pointer to visit affinity marketing pages.	Results of anonymous visitor goals and accomplishments. Affinity marketing; discounts for appropriate books and software.	

Case Study # 11: Gourmet Restaurant

This independent restaurant is owned by a chef who enjoys culinary creativity and who has a flare for both cooking as well as entertaining and making strangers feel as welcome as friends and family. He must develop a strong personality and "style" to compete against other specialty restaurants, national restaurant franchise chains. In addition, he must educate and build a strong following and regular clientele.

STAGE OF CUSTOMER DEVELOPMENT CYCLE	OPEN CONTENT	E-MAIL	INCENTIVE OR PREMIUM CONTENT	WHAT IDEAS DOES THIS SUGGEST FOR YOUR WEB SITE?
INTRODUCTION *Goal: Introduction, build e-mail mailing list for low-cost promotional follow-up.*	Food category, price range, years in business. Location, hours, parking, music. Atmosphere, photographs. Sample menu.	Prompt to download French Cooking Tip of the Month.	French Cooking Tip of the Month. Calendar. Free reminders of family special events, birthdays, anniversaries, etc.	
COMPARISON *Goal: Maintain enthusiasm and enhance credibility.*	Reprints of newspaper or magazine reviews, critic's comments. Testimonials from previous patrons. Article describing seasonal specials. Archive of previous "favorite recipes" and cooking tips.	Monthly invitation to download latest "Recipe of the Month" calendar.	Downloadable and printable "Recipe of the Month" club, perhaps combined with a seasonal photograph.	
TRANSACTION *Goal: Provide incentive to make reservations for special events or special promotions.*	Range of prices for various menus and wine lists. Description of catering and takeout service.	Send e-mail reminders one week before birthdays, anniversaries. Teaser to visit frequently updated "promotions" page.	Frequently changed promotional page describing limited-time or limited-availability early-bird or two-for-one specials. Online reservations.	

Stage of Customer Development Cycle	Open Content	E-mail	Incentive or Premium Content	What ideas does this suggest for your Web site?
		Reminders to reserve ahead of time for special occasions, i.e., New Years Eve, Bastille Day, etc. Next day thank-you and request for comment on food and service. Invite visitors to page describing "patrons only" affinity marketing with local theaters, concerts, parking lots.	Event marketing, i.e., wine tasting party, fixed price meals, theme meals, cooking demonstrations. Special tie-ins to local movie theaters or concerts, parking.	
REINFORCEMENT *Goal: Maintain patron's enthusiasm about French cooking so they will want to visit each month.*	Previous examples of chef's favorite recipes. Articles about preparing new seasonal menus.	Announce latest monthly "Recipe of the Month." Teaser to introduce article describing seasonal cooking article. Teaser to page announcing special events.	"Recipe of the Month" page. "Event marketing," i.e., page announcing special events, like wine tasting, theme meals, special events (i.e., New Years Eve).	
ADVOCACY *Goal: Establish restaurant as the fulcrum of French food enthusiasm in the area.*	Reciprocal "travelers links" to similar restaurants in other cities of the country. Favorite French cooking recipes from patrons. Photo gallery of patrons visiting France.	Teaser for page describing latest affinity marketing links. Teaser for "bring a friend" page. Invitation to submit favorite recipes, reviews of French cookbooks. Invite patrons to submit favorite photographs taken in restaurant or while in France on vacation.	Affinity marketing–i.e., offers for travel books or special tours to country of origin. Page describing "bring a friend" offer.	

Case Study # 12: Gift Shop

Independent gift shop specializing in personally chosen imported gifts from Europe. Gifts include high-quality books, bone china, cookware, figurines, linen, and sweaters. Items are considerably more expensive than items available from malls and discount chains.

The goal is to educate the market to the importance of quality as well as maintain the buyer's enthusiasm. By emphasizing stories about the country of origin and the story behind each item's choice, the owner can build a personal bond with customers.

STAGE OF CUSTOMER DEVELOPMENT CYCLE	OPEN CONTENT	E-MAIL	INCENTIVE OR PREMIUM CONTENT	WHAT IDEAS DOES THIS SUGGEST FOR YOUR WEB SITE?
INTRODUCTION Goal: Mutual introduction, identifying visitor's particular area of interest.	Types of gifts sold, store location and hours, credit cards, delivery and shipping information. Sample products and prices.	Acknowledge receipt of registration.	Notification service before birthdays and anniversaries.	
COMPARISON Goal: Find out more about particular products individual visitors are interested in.	Emphasis on benefits that make store different from others , i.e., special "Gift Search" or "Advisor" service. Introduce new products and trends in gift category.	Invite visitors to more detailed survey describing their interests and family and friend's interests.	Advance notification of special promotions in special gift categories.	
TRANSACTION Goal: Motivate immediate sales.	Description of online ordering and shipping.	Reminder about upcoming holiday, or friend or relative's birthday, or anniversary. Teaser to visit page describing specially priced preseason or new products.	Special "early bird" savings before important holidays. Special prices when new, "hot" products are introduced.	

STAGE OF CUSTOMER DEVELOPMENT CYCLE	OPEN CONTENT	E-MAIL	INCENTIVE OR PREMIUM CONTENT	WHAT IDEAS DOES THIS SUGGEST FOR YOUR WEB SITE?
REINFORCEMENT *Goal: Maintain buyer or recipient's enthusiasm for product category.*	Display and shipping tips. Description and comments about new products.	Thank-you for purchase. Special, unexpected coupon offering additional discount after major purchase. Teaser to visit "new product showcase."	Page of coupons containing specially priced items. Short-deadline preview of "what's new" seen at latest trade show.	
ADVOCACY *Goal: Maintain enthusiasm by increasing pleasure from product.*	Photographs showing how gifts are used or displayed in customer's homes. Security, packing and insurance tips, i.e., how to maximize pleasure and minimize disappointment.	Invitation to submit photographs showing gifts at home. Link to affinity marketing page.	Page describing products that would appeal to like minded categories of buyers, i.e., noncompeting gift or bookstores, travel tips, insurance agents.	

Case Study # 13: Graphic Designer

After working for twenty years in a corporate setting, the owner became a victim of corporate downsizing and decides to follow her lifelong dream of being self-employed. Her chosen market ranges from small start-ups to her previous employer. Since opportunities in the immediate area are limited, the goal is to develop a regional reputation for quality and fair pricing.

The Web will be used to establish the designer's credibility, permitting an online portfolio of previous projects. Newsletters and white papers at consistent intervals will keep the designer's name in front of potential clients.

STAGE OF CUSTOMER DEVELOPMENT CYCLE	OPEN CONTENT	E-MAIL	INCENTIVE OR PREMIUM CONTENT	WHAT IDEAS DOES THIS SUGGEST FOR YOUR WEB SITE?
INTRODUCTION *Goal: Mutual introduction of graphic designer and market to each other.*	Describe range of services provided. Introduce designer and staff, profile their backgrounds. Client list. Description of design philosophy.	Respond to visitor registration.	White paper "Ten Ways to Reduce Your Printing Costs." Identify visitor's company size and major concerns (i.e., print, online) and their previous experiences with designers.	
COMPARISON *Goal: Enhance designer's credibility and maintain consistent visibility.*	Post client satisfaction survey results. Display and discuss challenges behind recent print projects, using thumbnail photographs or PDFs. Free downloadable back issue of newsletter. Articles discussing challenges currently facing clients. Testimonials from satisfied customers.	Invite visitors to take online survey. Alert every time a new electronic newsletter appears.	Survey form using free newsletter as premium. Bimonthly electronic newsletter describes latest typefaces, recent design trends, typical design problems, contains URLs to recent online work.	

STAGE OF CUSTOMER DEVELOPMENT CYCLE	OPEN CONTENT	E-MAIL	INCENTIVE OR PREMIUM CONTENT	WHAT IDEAS DOES THIS SUGGEST FOR YOUR WEB SITE?
TRANSACTION *Goal: Encourage a dialog on specific projects by making it easy to communicate with designer.*	Describe basic procedures and policies, problem resolution.	Invite visitors to fill out online Project Estimate Form. Schedule appointments online. Remind clients of upcoming appointments, thank them for their time afterward. Ask clients to fill out online customer satisfaction form after project completion. Alert to page.	Form visitors can submit describing projects they want designer to bid on. Client satisfaction form.	
REINFORCEMENT *Goal: Cultivate repeat business, encourage clients to recommend their friends and coworkers.*	Post recent work. Archive previous "tips of the month." Articles on getting the most out of professional design firms. Hints describing overlooked promotional and marketing ideas. Analysis of industry trends and discussion of new solutions to old problems (less detailed than in newsletter).	Alert to holiday thank-you page. Alert to "tip of the month" page. Alert to page containing electronic postcard or calendar. Alert to Rewards page.	Downloadable screen saver. Page containing a tip of the month. Encourage clients to forward electronic postcards or calendars to friends. Page containing printable coupons for discounts when clients recommendations result in new work.	
ADVOCACY *Goal: Position design firm as well informed in all aspects of print and online marketing.*	Industry news forum. Links to industry conferences, publications, and trade shows.	Alert to updated catalog page.	Annotated catalog or resource page to help clients educate themselves, contains descriptions of discounted new books, magazines (through online affiliate programs).	

Case Study # 14: Health Club

Recently taken over by the local hospital, a small and family owned health club now has to create a much larger client base in order to justify a major investment in expanded facilities.

The Web site will be used to communicate new programs and preventative health tips and techniques to clients. It will also be used to keep area doctors involved, generating referrals.

STAGE OF CUSTOMER DEVELOPMENT CYCLE	OPEN CONTENT	E-MAIL	INCENTIVE OR PREMIUM CONTENT	WHAT IDEAS DOES THIS SUGGEST FOR YOUR WEB SITE?
INTRODUCTION *Goal: Introduce health club to new members.*	Location, hours, facilities, parking. Areas of expertise and specialization	Acknowledge registration, qualify visitor as individual, corporate or health care provider.	Coupon inviting visitor to a sample visit and/or initial consultation. Page describing benefits to firms who provide membership for their employees.	
COMPARISON *Goal: Enhance credibility and find out family's specific health care interests.*	Case studies charting member's health improvements, perhaps before and after pictures. Profiles of staff members. Photographs taken at last event, i.e., family pool party, tennis matches, Christmas party, etc. Articles by staff members on health issues, i.e., exercise, diet. Range of membership options. Description of sample affinity marketing options that members can enjoy.	Invitation to fill out Personal Goal statement. Alert to monthly electronic newsletter.	Survey form for prospective members to establish personal goals. Electronic newsletter announces upcoming special events, i.e., seminars and workshops, schedule of courses for upcoming month, diet and exercise tips.	

CASE STUDIES

STAGE OF CUSTOMER DEVELOPMENT CYCLE	OPEN CONTENT	E-MAIL	INCENTIVE OR PREMIUM CONTENT	WHAT IDEAS DOES THIS SUGGEST FOR YOUR WEB SITE?
TRANSACTION *Goal: Motivate new members to join and existing members to buy more.*	Contact information. Explanation of procedures for hiring. Incentives for new books and tapes. Prices for specific categories of work.	New member coupon alert. Weekly reminder of scheduled physical training sessions. Membership alert to coupon page. Reminder to utilize online scheduling. Alert to "friends helping friends" program.	Coupon specials for new members. Coupon offering members special prices for advance sign up at upcoming programs or workshops. Form for online scheduling of physical training sessions. Electronic postcard that members can send to friends offering free visits or initial consultation.	
REINFORCEMENT *Goal: Build member loyalty and word-of-mouth referrals.*	Tennis, racquetball scores. Anonymous survey summarizing health gains of members.	Alert to rewards page. Alert to online fitness progress form. Alert to affinity marketing coupon page. Alert to birthday coupon page for family members.	Coupon rewards for members who recommend friends who later join. Form allowing members to electronically record their visits, weight loss, etc. Page of coupons offering savings on workout clothing and supplies, restaurants with "healthy choice" entrees and area attractions, i.e., ski lodges, boat rentals, etc. Page with limited time coupons sent one week before member's birthday (movie passes, two-for-one healthy choice meals at area restaurants, etc.).	
ADVOCACY *Goal: Encourage members to share success stories.*	Health care question and answer forum. Resources like glossary, list of important books. Links to resources of interest to market.	Alert to form to submit questions.	Form for submitting questions or comments.	

Case Study # 15: Home Theater Installation Specialist

This two-store chain that formerly sold a broad range of audio video components has to migrate to higher-margin customized sales of elaborate home theater systems because of the growth of online discounting and the arrival in town of several national consumer electronics chains in large stores opposite local malls.

The firm will use their Web site to educate their market to the advantages of customized, professional installations over mass-produced consumer electronics. The Web site will emphasize the firm's expertise in working with architects and contractors to create customized home theater environments.

STAGE OF CUSTOMER DEVELOPMENT CYCLE	OPEN CONTENT	E-MAIL	INCENTIVE OR PREMIUM CONTENT	WHAT IDEAS DOES THIS SUGGEST FOR YOUR WEB SITE?
INTRODUCTION Goal: Mutual introduction of prospect and retailer.	Store location or locations, hours, brands sold, financing alternatives. Store satisfaction policies. Delivery and installation options.	Invite registered visitors to access white paper and/or newsletter describing latest products and installation strategies.	Special report/comparison study on latest products and trends in home theater. Describe and show strategies for integrating home theater components into the home.	
COMPARISON Goal: Build enthusiasm and show how retailer can do a better job of installing home theater system than competitors.	How to buy and use various product categories. In-depth look at featured products. Customer satisfaction stories—results of previous customer satisfaction surveys. How to plan for a home theater. Staff profiles. Event marketing—invite architect or builder to show slides of recent installations done in conjunction with store.	Invite visitors to download planning tools. Invite visitors to learn more options at special "Survey of home theater options and strategies" feature. Offer a free at home consultation in exchange for filling out the survey. Invite visitors to in-store event put on by builder or architect in conjunction with store.	Downloadable layout sheets (i.e., room diagrams) and furniture clipart to help buyers plan their system. "Survey of home theater options and strategies" feature.	

STAGE OF CUSTOMER DEVELOPMENT CYCLE	OPEN CONTENT	E-MAIL	INCENTIVE OR PREMIUM CONTENT	WHAT IDEAS DOES THIS SUGGEST FOR YOUR WEB SITE?
TRANSACTION *Goal: Motivate immediate purchase (or add-on purchase).*	Online ordering and order confirmation. Extended warranty.	Announce first chance at items available at special prices.	Special promotion on discontinued or demonstrator units.	
REINFORCEMENT *Goal: help buyer gain maximum enjoyment from purchase.*	Keep buyers informed by suggested enhancements. Articles about how to use and get most enjoyment from purchase. Descriptions of suggested accessories.	Next day e-mail thank-you and request for comment on service and delivery. Invite buyers to fill out online satisfaction survey.	Satisfaction survey. Newsletter containing in-depth look at latest products, trade show visits, etc. Password-protected page offering savings on suggested accessories.	
ADVOCACY *Goal: Maintain continuing visibility and encourage word-of-mouth recommendations.*	Question and answer forum. Loyalty products, i.e., mousepads, T-shirts, hats, etc. Links to appropriate, but not competing, Web sites.	Invite buyers to participate in question and answer forum. Invite buyers to chat with industry leaders. Invite buyers to Web page describing latest movies and concerts. Co-marketing, i.e., offer special prices on latest software offerings (or even special prices on area concerts or movie previews).	Special page containing transcripts of previous chat sessions. Introduce and describe (or review) latest software offerings, i.e., digital-video-disc movies and concerts, broadcasts. Co-market latest movie and concert releases. Co-market furniture or lighting ideal for home theater applications.	

Case Study # 16: Insurance Agent

This independent, second-generation insurance agency with two full-time and two part-time employees must compete against other insurance agencies as well as online insurance companies selling direct and those that offer twenty-four hour phone service.

The Web site will be used to emphasize the personal care and service the agency provides as well as encourage people to request quotes during off hours and review their insurance coverage by themselves. The agency's Web site will also be used to allow clients to backup their household inventory records online and off premises.

STAGE OF CUSTOMER DEVELOPMENT CYCLE	OPEN CONTENT	E-MAIL	INCENTIVE OR PREMIUM CONTENT	WHAT IDEAS DOES THIS SUGGEST FOR YOUR WEB SITE?
INTRODUCTION *Goal: Describe services offered.*	Services offered. Areas of expertise and specialization. Education, publication, speaking and work experience. Client list.	Offer interactive checklist and evaluate results submitted showing short falls on coverage.	Downloadable home, car, and business coverage checklist (spreadsheet or form)	
COMPARISON *Goal: Show how agent differs from the competition.*	Case studies. Opinions on issues that prospects and customers are likely facing. Testimonials from previous customers. Resources like glossary, list of important books.	Announce online worksheet to compare proposed coverage with existing coverage.	Calculator that compares coverage/cost ratio with competition.	
TRANSACTION *Goal: Encourage already insured to switch coverage.*	Contact information. Prices for specific categories of coverage.	Announce special rates for multiple categories of courage.	Special offer on multiple vehicle discounts, or home, car, and life coverage.	

STAGE OF CUSTOMER DEVELOPMENT CYCLE	OPEN CONTENT	E-MAIL	INCENTIVE OR PREMIUM CONTENT	WHAT IDEAS DOES THIS SUGGEST FOR YOUR WEB SITE?
REINFORCEMENT *Goal: Reward customers.*	New case studies as they appear. Links to Web sites or publications reflecting current opinions on current issues and challenges.	Offer free and easily modified possession inventory worksheet.	Online form for insured to calculate value of their possessions. Online worksheet to plan for changes in retirement or college cost.	
ADVOCACY *Goal: Find out true issues that insured are concerned about.* *Personalize answers to questions.*	Question and answer forum. Links to resources of interest to market.	Invite customers to submit questions and concerns and provide URL of unlinked page for asking questions.	Forms for submitting questions.	

Case Study # 17: Marketing Consultant

In a crowded field, this consultant intends to specialize in helping those in the health care field market themselves more effectively. Previously, the consultant worked as marketing communications director for a large pharmaceutical company.

The Web will be used to communicate the consultant's expertise by providing a monthly newsletter addressing issues doctors, health clubs, and hospitals face.

STAGE OF CUSTOMER DEVELOPMENT CYCLE	OPEN CONTENT	E-MAIL	INCENTIVE OR PREMIUM CONTENT	WHAT IDEAS DOES THIS SUGGEST FOR YOUR WEB SITE?
INTRODUCTION Goal: Describe benefits of specialized services offered.	Services offered. Areas of expertise and specialization. Education, publication, speaking and work experience. Client list.	Provide URL of downloadable document or unlinked page.	"10 Trends Affecting Your Business in the Next 10 Years."	
COMPARISON Goal: Show greater competence and experience than others who don't specialize.	Case studies. Opinions on issues that prospects and customers are likely facing. Testimonials from previous customers. Resources like glossary, list of important books.	Send URL of benchmarking worksheet or URL of newsletter.	Comparison Worksheet: How to evaluate a consultant in your field.	
TRANSACTION Goal: Motivate clients by offering a reduced initial consultation.	Contact information. Explanation of procedures for hiring. Incentives for new books and tapes. Prices for specific categories of work.	Form inviting prospect to describe major challenge and get pointed in the right direction.	Provide a questionnaire form that will encourage prospect to reveal areas of concern.	

STAGE OF CUSTOMER DEVELOPMENT CYCLE	OPEN CONTENT	E-MAIL	INCENTIVE OR PREMIUM CONTENT	WHAT IDEAS DOES THIS SUGGEST FOR YOUR WEB SITE?
REINFORCEMENT *Goal: Sell additional services to client.*	New case studies as they appear. Quality, credibility building news about current challenges and advancing technology. Links to Web sites or publications reflecting consultant's direct involvement. Opinions on current issues and challenges.	Announce article describing a problem other than original problem solved.	Offer a list of other challenges that similar clients have faced.	
ADVOCACY *Goal: Provide tools for clients to sell to their friends.*	Question and answer forum. Links to resources of interest to market.	Announce URL of form "How I solved this problem." Invite clients to forward new articles to their friends.	Form making it easy for clients to describe how consultants solved their problem. Pass along feature for clients to share articles with your colleagues.	

Case Study # 18: Microbrewery

An outgrowth of a successful restaurant open for many years, this microbrewery must compete against national supermarket beers as well as two other regional microbreweries in neighboring states.

The Web will be used to constantly maintain visibility in the market's mind as well as promote special events, recipes, and new brews being developed.

STAGE OF CUSTOMER DEVELOPMENT CYCLE	OPEN CONTENT	E-MAIL	INCENTIVE OR PREMIUM CONTENT	WHAT IDEAS DOES THIS SUGGEST FOR YOUR WEB SITE?
INTRODUCTION Goal: Introduce microbrewery to new markets.	Location, hours, atmosphere, parking. Types of beers brewed, how they differ, what foods go best with each. Sample menu.	Acknowledge registration, password to access downloadable recipe.	Downloadable feature recipe for foods that go especially well with seasonal beer. ●	
COMPARISON Goal: Expand market by describing new reasons to visit brew pub.	Specialty beers, i.e., non-alcoholic. Article describing special steps taken to ensure high-quality product. Testimonials from satisfied customers. Results of customer satisfaction surveys.	Alert inviting visitor to page describing new seasonal brew. Invitation to download recipe appropriate for new seasonal beer.	Information about seasonal beer, i.e., summer ale, winter barley, etc. Downloadable recipe for appropriate food to match seasonal beer.	

STAGE OF CUSTOMER DEVELOPMENT CYCLE	OPEN CONTENT	E-MAIL	INCENTIVE OR PREMIUM CONTENT	WHAT IDEAS DOES THIS SUGGEST FOR YOUR WEB SITE?
TRANSACTION *Goal: Motivate immediate purchase or reservation.*	Describe capabilities for parties and special events. Introduce convention facilities or large group capabilities. Description of beer steins, antique posters, brewing and food recipe books, calendars, coasters. Information about nonalcoholic beers. Brewing secrets stories.	Online reservations for special holiday parties or anniversaries. Invitation for special savings at affinity marketing page, i.e., area attractions, such as movies, concerts, gallery openings, parking.	Page describing price incentives for large groups who commit in advance to holiday parties or annual meetings. Affinity marketing page with money-saving or priority seating coupons for area attractions.	
REINFORCEMENT *Goal: Make past buyers feel special.*	Stories about how new beers are formulated.	Thank-you for visitors who fill out customer survey and include e-mail address and list their birthdays / anniversaries and their friend's birthdays and anniversaries. Invitation for registered visitors to visit page containing coupons for special savings on books, coasters, mugs, etc.	"Great beers of the world" screen saver. Page containing coupons for limited-time, specially priced mugs, coasters, screen savers, etc.	
ADVOCACY *Goal: Maintain visibility and encourage repeat business.*	Photo gallery showing happy people at parties or meetings. Links to home brewing sources of information and supplies. Area news, i.e., upcoming concerts, new movie venues, area drives.	Alert introducing page describing new seasonal beer.	Page describing background of new or seasonal brew.	

Case Study # 19: Motel

Although it has been in business for over 20 years, this motel's primary challenge has been the seasonal nature of its business. Quiet months are too quiet because tourist traffic falls off and there are no businesses attracting corporate travelers to the area.

The Web will be used to promote the region as a destination during quiet times. It will emphasize the many off-season events the area offers and encourage people to take advantage of off-season "get away" promotions and rates.

STAGE OF CUSTOMER DEVELOPMENT CYCLE	OPEN CONTENT	E-MAIL	INCENTIVE OR PREMIUM CONTENT	WHAT IDEAS DOES THIS SUGGEST FOR YOUR WEB SITE?
INTRODUCTION Goal: Include motel on "shopping list" of visitors to an area.	Map showing location, range of room prices, on-site services (i.e., pool, restaurant, etc.). Range of prices throughout the year.	Send password to access premium content. Teaser to visit page with latest seasonally adjusted room rates. Registration should find out reason for visit and potential for future visits to area.	Detailed information about area attractions and restaurants. Downloadable area maps, driving regulations.	
COMPARISON Goal: Help motel gain competitive advantage over other motels in the area.	Comments and survey results from previous guests. Room pictures and sample room service menu. Chart and/or maps showing mileage from major area attractions. Chart showing cost comparisons with other area restaurants.	Teaser to visit updated weather information page. Invitation for registered visitors to visit updated affinity marketing page containing coupons for area attractions, theater, restaurants, airlines, parking, etc.	Up-to-date area weather and clothing information. Page containing coupons for affinity marketing at area attractions and restaurants.	

STAGE OF CUSTOMER DEVELOPMENT CYCLE	OPEN CONTENT	E-MAIL	INCENTIVE OR PREMIUM CONTENT	WHAT IDEAS DOES THIS SUGGEST FOR YOUR WEB SITE?
TRANSACTION *Goal: Encourage immediate reservation.*	Information about especially busy times when advance registrations are recommended. Updated information for special events.	Invitation to visit special "early registration" page. Announcement of special "bring a friend" program. Invitation to use online reservation and registration form.	Page offering special rates for advance reservations and/or registration for special events, i.e., holidays, long weekends, homecoming, etc. Page describing special "bring a friend" program. Online reservation and registration.	
REINFORCEMENT *Goal: Build enthusiasm for future visits and recommendations to friends.*	Summary of recent news from the area, i.e., new restaurants, upcoming conventions or special events. Discussion of changes or renovations.	Thank-you plus opportunity to take online survey in return to download area screen saver. Yearly follow-ups before vacation season or conventions, etc.	Online customer satisfaction survey. Downloadable screen-saver of area attractions.	
ADVOCACY *Goal: Encourage word of mouth recommendations.*	Calendar of upcoming events in area. List of new area attractions.	Notification of page describing current area weather and upcoming events.	Page containing advance notice of periods when it is likely that it will be hard to make reservations. Summary of important area news.	

Case Study # 20: Oral Surgeon

Although located in a town of less than twenty thousand individuals, the area has an overabundance of oral surgeons competing with each other. This oral surgeon must also compete against oral surgeons less than an hour away at a major highly respected, nationally known health care facility.

The solution is to create a Web-based personality for the oral surgeon that will assure potential clients of his compassion and competence and the support of a well-trained staff on premises.

STAGE OF CUSTOMER DEVELOPMENT CYCLE	OPEN CONTENT	E-MAIL	INCENTIVE OR PREMIUM CONTENT	WHAT IDEAS DOES THIS SUGGEST FOR YOUR WEB SITE?
INTRODUCTION *Goal: Build word-of-mouth reputation for compassion by reducing patient's fears before and after procedure.*	Establish surgeon's credibility by reducing anxiety by realistically describing procedure and what to expect. Describe steps surgeon and staff will take to reduce pain. Introduce staff and facilities. Case study to emphasize surgeon's and staff's compassion.	Acknowledge visitor registration.	White paper containing case studies of patients who found procedure less painful than anticipated.	
COMPARISON *Goal: Reinforce surgeon's credibility by communicating meaningful information.*	Comments, letters, or survey results from previous patients. Describe surgeon's track record and accomplishments, i.e., new techniques introduced to area, etc. Describe billing and payment options.	Alert to generic "attitude" article regarding pain management. Alert to page dealing with specific procedure that has to be done.	Empower patient by giving them a positive role to play. Describe steps patient can take to minimize discomfort before and after procedure.	

STAGE OF CUSTOMER DEVELOPMENT CYCLE	OPEN CONTENT	E-MAIL	INCENTIVE OR PREMIUM CONTENT	WHAT IDEAS DOES THIS SUGGEST FOR YOUR WEB SITE?
TRANSACTION *Goal: Continue to smooth out logistics and reduce fear.*	Describe how to prepare for the procedure and what to do after the procedure.	E-mail reminder of appointment. Alert to post-procedure self-help care. E-mail follow-up asking patients about pain. Request for patient to fill out online survey about experience.	Page describing things patient can do to help themselves and determine if pain is excessive. Online survey of patient's experiences—Was the experience better or worse than anticipated? Would you recommend this doctor to your friend?	
REINFORCEMENT *Goal: Reinforce loyalty by continuing communication with patient.*	Article describing Ten Best Dental Self-Maintenance Tips. Introduce new staff as they join the practice.	Reminder of follow-up appointments. Alert describing situation-specific prevention page.	How to prevent this problem from reoccurring.	
ADVOCACY *Goal: Position surgeon as the source of preventative as well as curative medicine.*	Online forum—questions and answers from patients or people with similar problems. Articles and alerts as needed to translate technical articles into patient-friendly language.	Alert to submit question. Alerts as new articles and information are posted.	Form for submitting questions to surgeon.	

Case Study # 21: Outdoor Clothing Boutique

Originally started as the factory outlet store for an outdoor clothing manufacturer, this retail operation has been spun off as a self-supporting entity selling products made by several manufacturers. The focus will be on higher-quality clothing that emphasizes functionality over trendiness and name recognition.

The Web will be used to educate potential buyers to the advantages of its clothing and the necessity of choosing the proper outdoor clothing and gear, not only for comfort but for safety.

STAGE OF CUSTOMER DEVELOPMENT CYCLE	OPEN CONTENT	E-MAIL	INCENTIVE OR PREMIUM CONTENT	WHAT IDEAS DOES THIS SUGGEST FOR YOUR WEB SITE?
INTRODUCTION *Goal: Introduce store as a "four season" source of recreational clothing and keep customers informed.*	Store, location, hours, credit, parking, shipping and layaway policies. Introduce staff by name and background, showing photograph. Personalize store by showing its employees on vacation utilizing the products the store sells.	Acknowledge registration.	Bimonthly electronic newsletter evaluating and introducing new clothing for upcoming season.	
COMPARISON *Goal: Position the store as the most knowledgeable source of information about outdoor clothing.*	Features describing what to look for when purchasing various categories of outdoor clothing. Impressions and profiles of various brands sold.	Alert for each time new electronic newsletter has been posted.	Electronic newsletter discussing products appropriate for next season.	
TRANSACTION *Goal: Motivate buyers and make it easy for customers to order and reorder.*	Full in-store and online ordering information. Describe easily overlooked ancillary products (like books, lamps, backpacks).	Alert to end-of-season coupon savings. Alert to preseason savings. Alert to affinity marketing page.	Page of coupons for special savings on end-of-season merchandise. Page containing limited-time, preseason special coupon offers for newly introduced products. Affinity marketing coupons for ski lodges, photo supplies, maps, tour guides, etc.	

Stage of Customer Development Cycle	Open Content	E-mail	Incentive or Premium Content	What ideas does this suggest for your Web site?
Reinforcement *Goal: Encourage repeat purchases and word-of-mouth referrals.*	Describe reward programs for frequent buyers and those who recommend store to their friends. Event marketing; special visits by high-profile sportsmen, slide shows, lectures, hosting meetings by environmental groups.	Electronic reward for frequent buyers. Alert to electronic postcard page.	Page inviting customers to take pictures of store's products in use in remote locales. Coupons for buyers who frequently purchase. Seasonal electronic page that can be sent to visitor's friends inviting them to site.	
Advocacy *Goal: Position store as portal to outdoor recreational pleasure.*	Portfolio of photographs showing customers using store products. Summary of responses to submitted questions.	Alert announcing request for photographs. Alert for visitors when customer photograph gallery has been updated. Invitation to post specific question and receive confidential response.	Form for submitting confidential question.	

Case Study # 22: Photographer

Originally starting as a photographer for a local in-store portrait studio, this photographer hopes to establish a reputation as the foremost wedding photographer in the area. In order to support himself while establishing his specialty, he must develop a broad client base serving a wide range of needs.

The Web site will emphasize his competence in various areas while developing his emerging specialty.

STAGE OF CUSTOMER DEVELOPMENT CYCLE	OPEN CONTENT	E-MAIL	INCENTIVE OR PREMIUM CONTENT	WHAT IDEAS DOES THIS SUGGEST FOR YOUR WEB SITE?
INTRODUCTION *Goal: Mutual introduction and qualification of visitor's interests.*	Background, areas of expertise. Description of primary service: custom photography for individuals, firms, associations. Client list. Range of services and fees. Description of secondary products and services, i.e., prints, screen savers, calendars, books, hard-to-locate photo supplies, classes, seminars and workshops.	Special "How to be a better client" pages for family, corporate, and wedding photography clients (separate pages for each).	Acknowledge visitor. Send password to access unlinked or protected premium content pages.	
COMPARISON *Goal: Establish photographer's competence by sharing meaningful information.*	Tips and techniques for taking better photographs. Tips of preparing to be photographed. Sample photographs in areas of prospect's interest. Comments and results from online survey.	Tip on how to be a better client. Greater selection of photographs in various client categories with detailed "stories behind the photo." Monthly or seasonal electronic postcard or greeting card visitors can forward to their friends.	Announcement of latest tip or article on photo or lighting technique. Announcement when new photographs are added to client categories. Invitation to send latest electronic card to their friends.	

STAGE OF CUSTOMER DEVELOPMENT CYCLE	OPEN CONTENT	E-MAIL	INCENTIVE OR PREMIUM CONTENT	WHAT IDEAS DOES THIS SUGGEST FOR YOUR WEB SITE?
TRANSACTION **Goal: Provide motivation to purchase.**	Sample fees. Scheduling session. Thumbnails showing photographs available as prints, coffee mugs, T-shirts.	Page allowing prospective client to specify parameters of photo shoot and receive a detailed quote. Ability to schedule photo session. Special preseason savings on books, screen savers, mugs, etc. Page offering discount on photography class or workshop. Online survey for clients following custom shoot.	Announcement of special "quotation" page. Announce pre-season family or corporate photographs. Teaser to visit special savings page. Announce special photography class or workshop. Ask clients to fill out online survey.	
REINFORCEMENT **Goal: Build enthusiasm for photographer leading to repeat primary (i.e., custom photographs) and secondary (i.e., books, calendars, prints) sales.**	New photographs in areas of client interest. Article discussing recent trends in photography and impact.	Downloadable screen saver used as a premium. Downloadable monthly photograph/calendar.	Invitation for previous clients to download thank-you screen saver. Invitation to download monthly photograph/ calendar. Invitation to view latest photographs added to online portfolio.	
ADVOCACY **Goal: Maintain enthusiasm for photography and build word-of-mouth referrals.**	Community question and answer session. Level One links to areas of common interest.	White paper on current hot topic, i.e., impact of digital photography on both amateur and professional markets. Annotated links to more sophisticated Web sites. Page showing electronic postcards and greeting cards that registered visitors can send their friends.	Invite questions about photography. Teaser to download latest white paper on current topic. Invitation to Level Two links. Announcement of new electronic postcards that registered visitors can send to their friends.	

Case Study # 23: Realtor

Tired of dealing with the costs and restrictions imposed when they joined a national franchise, this former independent Realtor, now in its twenty-fifth year, must now establish itself once again as an independent community-oriented Realtor.

The Web site will be used to provide in-depth local information for those looking to move in, up, or out of the area. The goal is to establish the firm as "The firm with the home town advantage!"

STAGE OF CUSTOMER DEVELOPMENT CYCLE	OPEN CONTENT	E-MAIL	INCENTIVE OR PREMIUM CONTENT	WHAT IDEAS DOES THIS SUGGEST FOR YOUR WEB SITE?
INTRODUCTION *Goal: Introduce Realtor and position it apart from competition and identify prospect's needs.*	Introduce firm and individuals backgrounds or philosophies. Location, hours, parking, direct phone, fax and e-mail addresses of associates. Profile of community served. History of firm. Range of houses in area.	Acknowledge registration.	Home buyer information packet in exchange for registration. Home seller information packet in exchange for registration.	
COMPARISON *Goal: Position Realtor as more caring and qualified than competition.*	Sample listings. Describe trends in area Testimonials from previous buyers or sellers. Describe special services available. Information about refinancing. Mortgage rate watch.	Request visitor fill out qualification survey. Inform visitor when new Community Update pages appear. Weather update for out-of-area visitors. Alert to page containing trends.	Request for information about "ideal" dream house or sales situation in return for coupon from area business. Maintain visitor enthusiasm with monthly community updates. Categories of types and price ranges of homes that buyers are looking for.	

STAGE OF CUSTOMER DEVELOPMENT CYCLE	OPEN CONTENT	E-MAIL	INCENTIVE OR PREMIUM CONTENT	WHAT IDEAS DOES THIS SUGGEST FOR YOUR WEB SITE?
	Driving time to area employers and recreational or shopping sites. Weather trends.			
TRANSACTION *Goal: Communicate electronically instead of by phone, fax or mail as much as possible.*	Area resources for out-of-state visitors, i.e., accommodations, restaurants, etc.	Alert when homes meeting criteria appear on market or prospective buyers appear. Schedule appointments online.	Pages describing new listings that meet criteria . Online mortgage calculation. Online mortgage application.	
REINFORCEMENT *Goal: Maintain enthusiasm of buyers and sellers by keeping them informed.*	Positive comparison of area to national or statewide trends. Results of Customer Satisfaction Surveys.	Request to fill out post-sale Customer Satisfaction Survey. Alert when new information becomes available. Alert to rewards page when a referral purchases or sells a home.	Customer Satisfaction Survey with coupons for area businesses as reward. New listings—information about new houses as they become available in area. Rewards page with coupons for those who recommend Realtor to a friend.	
ADVOCACY *Goal: Encourage Web site visitors and previous customers to recommend Realtor to friends.*	Links to community resources.	Alert when new issue of newsletter comes out. Yearly electronic birthday, anniversary, and "move in" cards.	Downloadable and/or printable Real Estate Trends newsletter should continue to be sent.	

Case Study # 24: Secretarial Service

After many years of providing only secretarial services, this firm now wants to offer a broader range of services. They will continue to cater to the small business market and attempt to serve large corporations in the area needing secretarial assistance during busy periods.

The Web site will outline in detail their services and new offerings, capabilities, and price structure. E-mail alerts will be used to constantly remind people of the advantages of outsourcing rather than hiring additional staff or temporary help.

STAGE OF CUSTOMER DEVELOPMENT CYCLE	OPEN CONTENT	E-MAIL	INCENTIVE OR PREMIUM CONTENT	WHAT IDEAS DOES THIS SUGGEST FOR YOUR WEB SITE?
INTRODUCTION *Goal: Introduce secretarial service to market and find out market's needs.*	Describe business and the services it offers, hours, contact information. Description of typical opportunities when the service can often be of service. Who typical customers are. Advantages of working for the firm.	Encourage visitors to take prospective client or employee survey.	Article describing opportunities for employees and employers. Client survey permits clients to identify desirable skills and opportunities when skills are needed. Employee survey permits visitors to register available skills and indicate preferred working hours available. Downloadable premium might be an electronic calendar, scheduling or time-management software program.	
COMPARISON *Goal: Establish service as the best place to work for or hire.*	Profiles of available workers emphasizing skills and past accomplishments. Article discussing the advantages of alternatives to hiring new full-time staff, i.e., outsourcing. Typical client profiles.	Link to comparison chart or employer return on investment calculator page. Link to bimonthly electronic newsletter.	Page permitting clients to compare long-term and short-term costs of staff acquisition versus using secretarial service. Electronic newsletter with articles describing new services and satisfied customers, available job openings.	

STAGE OF CUSTOMER DEVELOPMENT CYCLE	OPEN CONTENT	E-MAIL	INCENTIVE OR PREMIUM CONTENT	WHAT IDEAS DOES THIS SUGGEST FOR YOUR WEB SITE?
	Testimonials from satisfied customers and employees.			
TRANSACTION *Goal: Encourage clients to immediately hire service and potential employees to register.*	Details of hiring firm, procedures, cancellations, etc.	Link to online form for hiring firm or registering as part-time worker. Link to page containing promotional coupons. Link to page containing coupons from area businesses for new part-time employees who register.	Online form for registering availability as part-time worker. Form for online billing and payment options. Page containing discount coupon or partial fee waiver for new clients. Coupon specials for newly registered employees.	
REINFORCEMENT *Goal: Encourage loyalty from both clients and employees.*	Customer/buyer survey. Applications stories. Hints for using products. Analysis of industry trends and hints of new product to solve problems. New product introductions Supplies and accessories.	Link to "reward" coupon for employees. Link to "reward" page for businesses who recommend firm to a new client.	Page containing coupon for loyal employees who complete assignments without lost time, etc. Restaurant meals, tuition reimbursement, etc. Reward coupons for those who recommend firm to new clients. Confidential form for submitting employee and employer evaluations.	
ADVOCACY *Goal: Enhance visibility of firm to human resource departments and potential employees.*	Summary of savings uncovered by return on investment surveys. Survey of issues concerning human resource and employment issues, particularly outsourced services. Links to industry conferences, publications and trade shows.	Invitation to submit questions and suggestions for newsletter articles.		

Case Study # 25: Travel Agent

Established five years ago, this independent travel agent is now faced with aggressive competition from an expanding regional agency as well as "book it yourself" online airline, hotel, and cruise operators.

They must use their Web site to become an invaluable source of information for their clientele.

This information would include independent evaluations of airline and accommodation quality, currency conversion, weather, and alternative travel opportunities not immediately obvious to casual travelers.

STAGE OF CUSTOMER DEVELOPMENT CYCLE	OPEN CONTENT	E-MAIL	INCENTIVE OR PREMIUM CONTENT	WHAT IDEAS DOES THIS SUGGEST FOR YOUR WEB SITE?
INTRODUCTION **Goal: Help independent travel agent survive regional and national price competition.**	Location, hours, payment options, fees, areas of specialization. Emphasis on areas of specialization. Clearly identified target markets: corporate, small business, leisure, home, upscale, geographic area, etc.	Acknowledge registration.	Monthly downloadable and printable travel planning calendar.	
COMPARISON **Goal: Simultaneously build credibility and identify customers' needs to focus on satisfying them.**	Interpret recent changes in economy and politics and how they affect travel planning. Summary of information regarding airline and hotel performance.	Follow-up survey request.	Encourage visitors to provide detailed information regarding travel preferences. Customized alerts and bimonthly electronic newsletter and alerts offering detailed advance information about money-saving opportunities and little-known travel strategies.	
TRANSACTION **Goal: Motivate visitors to make immediate purchase.**	General monthly trends in travel costs and predictions for upcoming months. Catalog pages (affinity marketing) describe hard-to-find books, luggage, and other travel items.	Customized alerts.	Special travel and lodging savings to areas visitor has registered interest in.	

STAGE OF CUSTOMER DEVELOPMENT CYCLE	OPEN CONTENT	E-MAIL	INCENTIVE OR PREMIUM CONTENT	WHAT IDEAS DOES THIS SUGGEST FOR YOUR WEB SITE?
REINFORCEMENT *Goal: Reward customers for loyalty, encourage them to travel more.*	Articles about overlooked travel destinations.	Frequent buyer discount alerts. Customized alerts based on family preferences. Alert to customer satisfaction survey page.	Special coupon discounts for visitors from affinity marketing catalog. Special savings for family members when accompanying business travel. Encourage travelers to complete customer satisfaction survey after trips.	
ADVOCACY *Goal: Make travel agency an information resource rather than just a service.*	Results of customer satisfaction surveys. Links to government, tourism, and other resources, how to complain about airline treatment, etc.	Alert for question form.	Form for submitting question.	

Case Study # 26: Veterinarian

Having completed their residency at a big city hospital, these partners have not been able to buy an established practice in a midsized city. Their goal is to introduce new technology and procedures without losing the small town touch that the previous practice was known for. Their competitors include other area veterinarians, a 24-hour emergency clinic, and two new national "big

box" megastore pet stores that offer grooming and pet supplies at great discounts.

Their Web site will be used to establish their competence and project a feeling of community with area pet owners. Owners will be advised that the practice is always available to help and that pets shouldn't be shuttled off to an impersonal emergency clinic.

STAGE OF CUSTOMER DEVELOPMENT CYCLE	OPEN CONTENT	E-MAIL	INCENTIVE OR PREMIUM CONTENT	WHAT IDEAS DOES THIS SUGGEST FOR YOUR WEB SITE?
INTRODUCTION Goal: Mutual introduction of veterinarian and animal owners.	Location, hours, contact information. Types of animals served, areas of specialization . Additional services provided, i.e., boarding and grooming. Background of partners and staff. Emergency contact information.	Acknowledge visitor registration.	Downloadable "family pet" screen saver sent in exchange for detailed registration.	
COMPARISON Goal: Position veterinarian as friendlier and more competent than the competition, deflect interest away from price.	General health care tips for pets. List local resources for pet lovers, i.e., exercise hours, community leash laws, licensing restrictions, contacts for further information.	Monthly alerts. Seasonal alerts. Political alerts.	Preventative health articles written about care of specific types of animals. Threats to pet health during the current and upcoming season. Informing owners about possible state or local legislation affecting their pets.	
TRANSACTION Goal: Reduce costs and simplify process, develop alternative revenue sources.	Describe advantages of electronic registration.	Invite online registration.	Online registration for routine appointments.	

STAGE OF CUSTOMER DEVELOPMENT CYCLE	OPEN CONTENT	E-MAIL	INCENTIVE OR PREMIUM CONTENT	WHAT IDEAS DOES THIS SUGGEST FOR YOUR WEB SITE?
		Electronic reminders when routine physical exams or shots are due. Alert for preholiday grooming. Alert for new services. Alert for early reservations during busy periods. Affinity market alert. Alerts sent as necessary about unexpected, specific health hazards. Request to fill out customer satisfaction survey.	Catalog page describing ancillary products, i.e., pet foods, health care items, dog beds, books and videos about dogs, products that are stocked or available for shipment after ordering. Announcements of new services, i.e., pet grooming. Encourage pet owners to make early reservations to board pets while on vacation before it's too late and no space is available. Customer satisfaction survey form.	
REINFORCEMENT *Goal: Position veterinarian as the right, friendly choice.*	Summary of latest research in pet health care. References to articles about pet health. Survey results of patients. Reminders about seasonal shots. Announcement of special preseason checkups.	Holiday thank-you. Alert to electronic cards.	Downloadable "lovable pets" screen saver sent at end of year. Electronic postcards or greeting cards that patients can send to their friends.	
ADVOCACY *Goal: Make Web site the center for pet information.*	Posting of winning pet photographs. Nationwide resources for pet information, i.e., magazines, national pet welfare organizations.	Alert for Favorite Pet photo contest. Alert for question and answer. Invitation for pet stories.	Invite pet owners to share their favorite pet pictures. Form for submitting question to community discussion. Collection of heroic or inspiring pet stories by local pet owners.	

Case Study # 27: Video Rental Store

This locally owned video store intends to remain independent, even though two large national franchises have entered the area. Competition is everywhere, including convenience stories, grocery stores, and pharmacies.

The Web site will help clients choose the right movies, check video availability, and permit online reserving of favorite titles. The Web site will also permit renters to comment on rented titles. More important, the Web site will emphasize specialized titles and formats (i.e., DVD) not available in mass market outlets.

STAGE OF CUSTOMER DEVELOPMENT CYCLE	OPEN CONTENT	E-MAIL	INCENTIVE OR PREMIUM CONTENT	WHAT IDEAS DOES THIS SUGGEST FOR YOUR WEB SITE?
INTRODUCTION Goal: Raise market awareness and find out market trends.	Store location, hours, parking, procedures. Areas of specialization.	Acknowledge registration, request to supply family birthdays.	Downloadable screen saver showing front covers of recent releases.	
COMPARISON Goal: Emphasize store's competitive advantage in terms of selection, convenience, and superior information.	Description of store's searchable database and easy online reservations. Back issues of store newsletter containing descriptions of major movies, easily overlooked favorites, and reviews of major movies.	Link to searchable database. Alerts to Electronic newsletter for registered visitors only.	Access to searchable database of major movies with reviewers comments. Downloadable or printable electronic newsletter describing new movies and arrival dates.	
TRANSACTION Goal: Make it as easy as possible for visitors to reserve or rent movies.	Explanation of online reservations and recommendation service.	Reference to latest New Releases page. Recommendations based on previous rentals or submitted form. Alerts to New Releases page and reservation form. Request for visitors to fill out customer satisfaction survey form.	Page introducing new releases and permitting advance reservations in advance of arrival at store. Online checking for movie availability and reservation. Customer satisfaction survey form with reward coupon for completion.	

STAGE OF CUSTOMER DEVELOPMENT CYCLE	OPEN CONTENT	E-MAIL	INCENTIVE OR PREMIUM CONTENT	WHAT IDEAS DOES THIS SUGGEST FOR YOUR WEB SITE?
REINFORCEMENT *Goal: Offer meaningful rewards to frequent customers.*	Description of benefits of frequent renter program.	Automatic notification of reward waiting at appropriate Rewards pages. Forwardable coupon for visitors to send to their friends so they can register.	Frequency-based coupons for free or reduced-priced rentals, waiver of late fees, etc. Downloadable and printable free movie rentals on day of visitor's or family member's birthday. Coupon rewarding visitors who recommend friends who register at site.	
ADVOCACY *Goal: Position the video store as a "portal to the latest Hollywood information."*	URLs of major studios and producers. Bibliography of books about Hollywood and movies available at local library.	Alert when URL links page is updated. Weekly trivia question e-mailed to mailing list (if option is selected).	Frequently updated page containing URLs of new movies. Page containing answer to weekly trivia question and coupon-based reward to those who entered proper answer in form.	

Case Study # 28: Whale Watch

An avid fisherman and outdoorsman, this ex-corporate executive decided to start his own business after retirement. His competition includes several established whale watch and site seeing tour operators.

The Web site will be used to encourage out-of-town tourists to register for cruises before they reach the area. The Web site will maintain the enthusiasm of past visitors by showing pictures of daily sightings as well as promote off-season tours when other operators have gone south for the winter.

STAGE OF CUSTOMER DEVELOPMENT CYCLE	OPEN CONTENT	E-MAIL	INCENTIVE OR PREMIUM CONTENT	WHAT IDEAS DOES THIS SUGGEST FOR YOUR WEB SITE?
INTRODUCTION *Goal: Introduce whale watch to market and permit easy low-cost follow-up with previous clients and prospects.*	Location, city, facilities, parking, costs. Schedule. Experience; years in business. Type of ship(s), safety information. Rain check policy (i.e., if no whales are sighted).	Thank-you for registering. Announcement of special whale sightings.	Downloadable exceptional photograph taken on recent cruise.	
COMPARISON *Goal: Position whale watch as friendlier and more knowledgeable than the competition .*	List and photos of types of whales found in area. Discounts for individuals and groups. Constantly updated gallery of photographs taken on recent cruises along with list of recent whale sightings. Article describing things to bring, i.e., clothing. List of area accommodations and restaurants. Illustrated article with photo tips for taking better whale pictures.	Invitation to download next year's Whale Watch calendar. E-mail summarizing recent sightings and guiding visitors to updated photo gallery.	PDF calendar for upcoming month featuring recent photograph taken from onboard ship.	

STAGE OF CUSTOMER DEVELOPMENT CYCLE	OPEN CONTENT	E-MAIL	INCENTIVE OR PREMIUM CONTENT	WHAT IDEAS DOES THIS SUGGEST FOR YOUR WEB SITE?
	List of local camera stores that rent pro-quality photo equipment. Information for teachers interested in chartering boat for school groups. Testimonials and survey results from previous attendees.			
TRANSACTION *Goal: Make reservations easy to obtain and encourage repeat business.*	Online reservations and bookings. Discounts for repeat visits. Incentive for advance, i.e., preseason, bookings ahead of time. Announcement of upcoming special cruises.	Alerts for coupon pages for undersold cruises or last-minute availability. Alerts for page describing early payment advantages. Thank-you/acknowledgement for booking. Reminder three days before cruise. Thank-you following cruise, attachment showing "official" cruise photo.	Discount coupon for early morning, late afternoon, or evening cruises. Discount coupon for undersold cruises. Coupon incentive for early booking and payment. "Official" cruise group photo of passengers or best whale photo.	
REINFORCEMENT *Goal: Enhance visitors pleasure and pleasant memories.*	Online survey. Best "Official" photograph of each cruise posted (i.e., photo by crew-member). Summary of recent sightings.	Post-cruise request for visitors to visit fill in survey located on unlinked Web page. Announcement to visit or download PDF containing end-of-season wrap-up article and "best of season" photos.	End-of-season "wrap-up" article and "best of season" photographs.	
ADVOCACY *Goal: Make whale watch the focus of following year's vacation plans.*	Opportunity for visitors to submit and share photos taken on whale watches. Letters from school children. Constantly updated list of current sightings, water temperature, weather, etc. Links to resources, like Discovery Channel, containing information about whales.	E-mail reminder to submit photos taken on each cruise to photo contest. Invitation to print out discount coupons for area restaurants, galleries, etc.	Coupon for submissions and photo contest. Discount coupons for local restaurants and parking.	

Case Study # 29: Wood Stove Dealer

Coming in to take over the family business, the owner was disappointed at the seasonal nature of the business. Most business was done in the fall and early winter, while relatively little business was done the rest of the year. Competition included two other independent wood stove dealers in the area who did little to promote themselves.

The Web site will be used to emphasize his "one stop" shopping for both wood stoves and gas fireplaces and inserts. The business base will be expanded to include installation, repairs, and firewood sales. In order to develop a year-round business, he will promote outdoor barbecue supplies and high-quality gas grills not available elsewhere.

STAGE OF CUSTOMER DEVELOPMENT CYCLE	OPEN CONTENT	E-MAIL	INCENTIVE OR PREMIUM CONTENT	WHAT IDEAS DOES THIS SUGGEST FOR YOUR WEB SITE?
INTRODUCTION Goal: Mutual introduction, encourage visitors to register their e-mail address.	Store location or locations, hours, brands sold, financing alternatives. Store satisfaction policies. Delivery and installation options. Market expansion—emphasize economic and reliability benefits of supplementing oil or electric heating with wood heating.	Acknowledge registration.	White paper describing experiences of customers during previous winter, i.e., typical savings, days power was out in area, etc.	
COMPARISON Goal: Emphasize store's competitive advantages relative to competition.	How to buy and use various product categories. In-depth look at featured products. Customer satisfaction stories. Staff profiles. Event marketing—local architect or builder describes how to integrate wood stoves into different rooms of home.	Follow-up inviting customers to visit page containing in-depth information. Offer a free home visit to analyze specific heating requirements. Invitation to special event (architect or builder's talk or slide show).	Special report comparing top brands and models sold in detail.	

STAGE OF CUSTOMER DEVELOPMENT CYCLE	OPEN CONTENT	E-MAIL	INCENTIVE OR PREMIUM CONTENT	WHAT IDEAS DOES THIS SUGGEST FOR YOUR WEB SITE?
TRANSACTION *Goal: Provide incentive to buy right now.*	Special preseason promotion, i.e., wood stoves in June, outdoor barbecue grills in March. Yearly preseason maintenance (i.e., August chimney cleaning and stove safety checkup or spring barbecue stove checkup.) Opportunity to purchase extended warranty/service contract.	Invite visitors to visit Web page describing preseason promotion. Invitation to schedule chimney cleaning and stove check-up or gas barbecue checkup. Offer buyers special article about the efficient use of wood stoves (or barbecues). Thank-you for purchase.	Special article describing proper techniques for starting wood stoves, keeping them running during the day, safety tips for ash removal, list of areas sources for properly seasoned wood.	
REINFORCEMENT *Goal: Encourage repeat business by enhancing buyer satisfaction and providing incentives to buy again (and recommend store to friends).*	Suggested enhancements, i.e., accessories, fans, etc. Description of accessories and supplies, no discounts. News about new products (i.e., wood stove models, barbecues) as they become available).	Thank-you for purchase (or service) and request for comment on service and delivery. Invitation to read special article about sources of quality wood stove. Preseason savings on gas for barbecues. Announcement of special savings on supplies. Invitation to special page on selecting woods. Announcements of savings on about-to-be-discontinued models.	Articles about how to use and get most enjoyment from purchase. Special savings on supplies and accessories for past customers.	
ADVOCACY *Goal: Build loyalty by maintaining visibility and encouraging word-of-mouth recommendations.*	Moderated "Questions and answers about wood heating" forum. Offer branded "loyalty products, i.e., gloves with store logo, etc. Links to appropriate, but not competing, Web sites, i.e., EPA. Archive of previous gas barbecue recipes.	Invite buyers to share their previous season's experiences. Invite visitors to special "advisories" about anticipated winter conditions. Invitation to visit latest "recipe" page.	News about anticipated winter weather. Summary of previous winter's experiences. Affinity marketing, i.e., discounts on sources of seasoned firewood. Discounts for gas for barbecues Latest Barbecue Recipe of the Month.	

Glossary

Adobe Acrobat. Adobe is a software publisher whose Acrobat program permits you to format documents that can be read on another computer, even if the software program that originally created the document or the typeface designs used in the document are not available on the recipient's computer. You can download the Adobe Acrobat Reader for free from Adobe's Web site: *http://www.adobe.com.*

alert. A short, unexpected, e-mail focused on a single topic, typically encouraging the recipient to pick up an incentive located on an unlinked page of your Web site.

attached files. A file accompanying an e-mail message. Most e-mail programs permit you to send and receive attached files.

autoresponder. Feature of certain e-mail programs located on servers that automatically responds to e-mail requests for information or passwords. Autoresponse software can be used to send an e-mail confirmation that the visitor has been added to the firm's database and will receive future mailings.

banners. Small advertisements on a Web page used as a revenue builder. Clicking on a banner takes you to the advertiser's Web site.

BCC. Acronym for blind carbon copy. The blind carbon copy feature of most e-mail programs permits you to send the same e-mail message to numerous individuals without revealing the recipients' e-mail addresses to each other.

bulletin. An announcement of a special promotion, typically located on an unlinked page of your Web site.

churn. Negative term referring to constantly searching out new customers to replace lost customers. A costly and inefficient way to run a business.

click-through. A measure of the effectiveness of a banner or link by measuring how many visitors clicked on the banner and visited the Web site. An imprecise measurement because it doesn't measure how long the visitor stayed at the Web site or whether they made a purchase.

community. Creating a feeling of loyalty among customers and prospects by permitting them to share information with each other through chat rooms or moderated discussion groups.

cookies. Small files that are automatically downloaded from a Web site to a visitor's computer. Cookies can be used to identify the visitor (by their computer's built-in address, not their name or any other address) and keep track of the pages visited and their stage in the customer development cycle. Not entirely trouble-free, since users can set their browsers to decline cookies. Another source of problem occurs if an individual visits from a business, home, and laptop computer (in which case they would count as three visitors).

CRM (customer relationship management). A generic term that means to build long-term customer relationships by offering incentives for customers to remain loyal instead of taking their business elsewhere.

cross-marketing. Creating marketing incentives in partnership with other noncompeting businesses. An example would be a bed-and-breakfast offering two-for-one meals at a local restaurant in exchange for advance reservations over a normally slow weekend.

customer development cycle. Refers to the five stages that define the relationship between a business and its customers and prospects.

customer lifetime value. A measure of customer loyalty based on customer revenue or profits a customer generated over the length of the customer relationship rather than a single time period.

customer retention. The philosophy of treating customers so well that they lack any reason to go anywhere else. The philosophy of building your business on the basis of repeat sales, past customers, and word-of-mouth recommendations.

download time. A measure of the time it takes for Web pages to appear on a visitor's computer. Large graphic files can significantly slow down your Web site's performance, discouraging visitors from remaining.

e-zine. Short for an electronic newsletter that is sent to visitors to your Web site at consistent and predictable intervals. In contrast to alerts and bulletins, e-zines typically contain more in-depth information and may contain short descriptions and links to new articles recently added to your Web site.

form. Part of a Web page containing one or more fields for visitors to enter their e-mail address (and/or additional information) accompanied by a Submit button that visitors click on to transfer their e-mail address and other information to you as e-mail or that automatically adds the information to your e-mail database.

FTP. Acronym for File Transfer Protocol, a reference to the software used to upload your Web site from your computer to the server or to transfer a file from your Web site to a visitor's computer.

hits. An outmoded and inaccurate way of measuring Web site performance by measuring the number of files that were transferred from the server to a visitor's Web site. Generally unreliable because each text file and each graphic counts as a hit, when what you're generally interested in is "How many different visitors visited my site today?"

home page. The first page of your Web site. The contents and design of your home page are crucial because if it does not offer significant benefits or load quickly

enough, visitors will quickly move on to another Web site.

incentive. A marketing term referring to information that is used to encourage visitors to your Web site to register their e-mail address or provide more information about the product or service they're interested in purchasing.

information architecture. Emerging field concerned with creating user friendly Web sites that load quickly and make it easy for visitors to locate desired information.

Internet service provider (ISP). Firm that owns the servers or high-speed computers and fast Internet connections used to host your Web site and connect it to the World Wide Web.

learning corporations. Relationship marketing term that describes firms that customize their products or services on the basis of their customers' preferences and previous purchases.

list server. E-mail database that keeps track of list additions and deletions and sends out e-zines, alerts, and bulletins to large mailing lists.

navigation. The underlying structure of your Web site, referring to the way pages are linked to each other either through a graphic navigation bar or text links (generally underlined and in blue). Your Web site succeeds to the extent it is easy for visitors to intuitively locate desired information.

open content. Information on pages accessible to any visitor to your Web site.

opt in. Giving visitors the option of subscribing to your e-mail newsletter, alerts, and bulletins

opt out. Automatically adding your visitor's e-mail address to your newsletter, alert, and bulletin database and only removing their e-mail address if the visitor specifically asks to be removed.

password protected. Pages that can only be accessed after first entering a password identifying the visitor as someone authorized to view the page. Used to deliver incentives and premium content to visitors as they proceed through the customer development cycle.

PDF (Portable Document Format). The format that Adobe Acrobat uses to create files that can be read by any computer, regardless of whether it's running the Apple Macintosh or Microsoft Windows operating system or has the fonts or software programs used to create the initial document.

premium content. Incentives, such as in-depth information, comparisons, interpretations, or discounts that appear on pages that are either password protected or unlinked.

privacy statement. A written commitment on your Web site that outlines your firm's commitment to protecting your customers' and prospects' privacy by not selling, sharing, or loaning any information submitted by Web site visitors with any other firm or organization.

screen saver. A small file that automatically activates on a user's computer after a certain amount of time has elapsed since the keyboard or mouse have been touched. Screen savers serve a practical purpose in that they avoid a single image burning itself into a computer monitor. Screen savers are also ideal incentives as they can consist of photographs or illustrations that create pleasant associations with your business.

server. High-capacity computer, or computers, that connect via high-speed lines to the World Wide Web. Visitors to your Web site do not access your personal or desktop computer, they access your files after they have been stored on a server, which may be owned by your firm or located at an Internet service provider's offices.

signature. Information automatically added to the bottom of the e-mails you send, which may include your firm's name, phone, fax, Web-site, and e-mail contact.

spam. Derogatory term used to identify unsolicited e-mail. In general, you should never send e-mail to someone unless the recipient has indicated an interest in receiving news or information from you.

subject header. The "headline" of your e-mail, the first words that catch the recipient's eyes. The more benefit-oriented your subject headers, the more likely your e-mail will be read.

tracking software. Software residing on a server that measures the number of unique visitors who visited your Web site, how long they spent, and what Web sites they came from.

traffic log. Summary of visitors to your Web site, maintained on your server, identifying visitors by computer number, the time of day they visited, the pages they visited, the length of time they spent at each page, and the previous and next Web pages they visited.

unlinked page. The title of an unlinked page does not show up on your Web site's navigation bar. Instead, the page's specific URL, or page location, must be copied or typed in. Unlinked pages are used to provide premium content used as an incentive to encourage visitors along the five-stage customer development cycle.

upload. The process of transferring files from your computer to the server, a computer connected to the World Wide Web, typically through special high-speed lines. After creating your Web site on your personal computer, you must transfer the files to the server.

URL (Universal Resource Locator). A Web site's address; the location on the World Wide Web where a particular Web site can be located.

Web site. A Web site consists of the home page—the first page visitors reach when they type in your URL—as well as all the pages associated with it.

zipped files. Files that have been compressed to reduce their size so they take less time to transmit from one computer to another.

Bibliography

Cross, Richard and Janet Smith. *Customer Bonding: 5 Steps to Lasting Customer Loyalty.* Chicago: NTC Books, 1996. An economic overview of the trends that emphasize the importance of reselling past customers instead of constantly searching for new customers.

Godin, Seth. *Permission Marketing: Turning strangers into friends, and friends into customers.* New York: Simon & Schuster, 1999. An excellent and entertaining discussion of the failure of traditional "broadcast" advertising marketing in today's media-saturated economy.

McKenna, Regis. *Real Time: Preparing for the Age of the Never Satisfied Customer.* Boston: Harvard Business School Press, 1997.

——. *Relationship Marketing: Successful Strategies for the Age of the Customer.* Boston: Addison Wesley, 1991. A watershed book that marked the transition from mass marketing to personalized marketing.

Peppers, Don and Martha Rogers. *The One to One Future: Building Relationships One Customer at a Time.* New York: Doubleday and Company, 1993.

——. *Enterprise One to One: Tools for Computing in the Interactive Age.* New York: Doubleday, 1997.

Peppers, Don, Martha Rogers and Bob Dorf. *The One to One Fieldbook: The Complete Toolkit for Implementing a 1to1 Marketing Program.* New York: Doubleday, 1999.

Pirillo, Chris. *Poor Richard's E-Mail Publishing: Creating Newsletters, Bulletins, Discussion Groups, and Other Powerful Communication Tools.* Lakewood, Colo.: Top Floor Publishing, 1999. An extremely detailed look at exactly what's involved in establishing an e-mail program, written for business owners and managers as contrasted to large corporations.

Reichheld, Frederick F. *The Loyalty Effect: The Hidden Force Behind Growth, Profits and Lasting Value.* Boston: Harvard Business School Press, 1996. The first book to put a price tag on the advantages of maintaining loyal customers and employees.

INDEX

speed considerations
   frames, 233
   text links, 232
   text vs. visuals, 231-232
   thumbnails, 232-233
typographic restraint, 229
visual restraint, 231
Dialog, 42, 46, 50, 54, 70
Direct mail. see also Promotion
   promotion with, 205-206
Discussion groups, 34-35

E

e-commerce, development of, 28-29
e-mail. see also database; e-mail message
   attached files with, 180-181
   capturing, 40, 65, 92, 239-240
   coordinating with transactions, 191
   database for, 188-191
   as incentive, 132
   incoming and outgoing, 187-188
   options for, 181-182
   reinforcement with, 116, 119, 179-182
   relation to Web initiative, xi-xii, 140
   summary approach with, 180
   unsolicited, 187
   using effectively, 63, 161, 178-179
   wireless, 26-27
e-mail alerts, 179
e-mail message
   address, 183
   housekeeping and privacy statement, 186
   message body, 184-185
   personalization of, 183
   signature, 185-186
   subject line, 182-183
e-mail teasers, discussed, 179-180, 181-182
Education, conducting at Web page, 18
Evaluations, by visitors, 154-155
Existing business
   characteristics of, ix
   entry into Web culture, xii
   opportunities for, 13
Extranets, 35-36

F

Failure. see also Success
   factors affecting, x-xii
Financial resources, determining, 143-144
Financing methods, for new ventures, xii-xiii
Follow-up, 42, 46, 50, 55, 70-71
Forms. see also Qualification; Registration
   for qualification, 72, 240
   for registration, 84
Frames, options for, 233

G

Gift certificates, 130, 200. see also Incentives
Goals. see also Marketing goals
   defining, 142-143
   for qualification stage, 87-88
   for reinforcement stage, 115-116
   for site design, 152
Graphics. see Visuals

H

Hardware, relation to Web site performance, 215-216
Human resources, 144

I

Image. see also Visuals
   projecting on Web site, 82-84
Incentives. see also Content; Promotion; Registration
   coupon specials, 131
   for customer reinforcement, 17, 18, 117-119
   e-mail, 132, 200-203
   gift certificates, 130
   informational, 201-203
   newsgroups and forums, 131-132
   newsletters, 131
   privacy, 203-204
   testing, 210
Information. see also Database; Technology and information
   collecting, 16-17
   compared to design, 157
   distributing, 17-19
   identifying and developing, 139, 156
   in information-oriented site, 49-50
   in inner-directed site, 45-46
   processing and handling costs, 5, 30
   in relationship marketing site, 69-70, 87
   in transaction-oriented site, 52-54
   in Web site
     in general, vii-viii, 42, 148-149, 150
     "me first" approaches, 150-153
Information resources, 144-145
Information stages, discussed, 157-158
Information-oriented site. see also Web site
   in general, 41, 48-49
   limitations of, 51-52
Inner-directed site. see also Web site
   discussed, 44-47
   in general, 41
   limitations of, 47-48
Interactivity
   with prospect, 94
   of Web page, 9-10, 17
Internet service providers (ISPs), affect on Web

site performance, 215-216
Intranets, 35-36
ISPs. see Internet service providers

L

Layout. see also Design
   restraint with, 230
   of Web pages, 83, 227
Links, for text, 232
Logic, in design, 226-227
Logos, 87, 231-232
The Loyalty Effect (Reichheld), 64

M

Mailing list. see also Promotion
   "rolling" mailings, 209
   updates for, 208-209
Market segmentation. see Qualification
Marketing goals. see also Affinity marketing; Goals
   analytical, 153-154
   determining, viii
   partnership, 154-156
"Me first" approaches, for Web initiative, 150-153
Media
   advanced, 27-28
   cost reductions for, 258-259
Meta text, 196

N

Navigation. see also Web site performance optimization
   in general, 39-40, 87, 238
   relation to performance, 221
Newsgroups and forums, 131-132
Newsletters, 131, 180

O

Ogilvy, David, 17
Opportunity
   for existing business, 13
   for new business, 261-262
Options, presenting on Web site, 82

P

Parker, Roger, vii-viii
Partners
   affinity partners, 207
   customers as, 207-210
   for promotion, 206-207
Passwords. see also Incentives
   in cookies, 220
   as premium, 202-203
Performance. see Web site performance optimization

Adams Streetwise® books for growing your business

Complete Business Plan
$17.95
ISBN 1-55850-845-7

24 Hour MBA
$17.95
ISBN 1-58062-256-9

Customer-Focused Selling
$17.95
ISBN 1-55850-725-6

Finance & Accounting
$17.95
ISBN 1-58062-196-1

Hiring Top Performers
$17.95
ISBN 1-58062-684-5

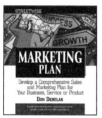

Marketing Plan
$17.95
ISBN 1-58062-268-2

Managing People
$17.95
ISBN 1-55850-726-4

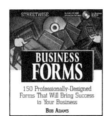

Business Forms w/CD-ROM
$24.95
ISBN 1-58062-132-5

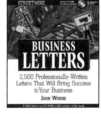

Business Letters w/CD-ROM
$24.95
ISBN 1-58062-133-3

Motivating & Rewarding Employees
$17.95
ISBN 1-58062-130-9

Small Business Start-Up
$17.95
ISBN 1-55850-581-4

Time Management
$17.95
ISBN 1-58062-131-7

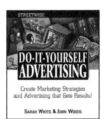

Do-It-Yourself Advertising
$17.95
ISBN 1-55850-727-2

Small Business Turnaround
$17.95
ISBN 1-58062-195-3

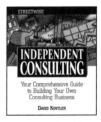

Independent Consulting
$17.95
ISBN 1-55850-728-0

Available wherever books are sold.

How to order: If you cannot find this book at your favorite retail outlet, you may order it directly from the publisher. BY PHONE: Call 1-800-872-5627. We accept Visa, Mastercard, and American Express. $4.95 will be added to your total order for shipping and handling. BY MAIL: Write out the full title of the book you d like to order and send payment, including $4.95 for shipping and handling to: Adams Media Corporation, 260 Center Street, Holbrook, MA 02343. 30-day money-back guarantee.

Visit our exciting small business Website: www.businesstown.com

FIND MORE ON THIS TOPIC BY VISITING
BusinessTown.com
The Web's big site for growing businesses!

- ☑ **Separate channels on all aspects of starting and running a business**
- ☑ **Lots of info of how to do business online**
- ☑ **1,000+ pages of savvy business advice**
- ☑ **Complete web guide to thousands of useful business sites**
- ☑ **Free e-mail newsletter**
- ☑ **Question and answer forums, and more!**

http://www.businesstown.com